04500

Women, Power, and Dissent
in the Hills of Carolina

Women, Power, and Dissent in the Hills of Carolina

MARY K. ANGLIN

University of Illinois Press

URBANA AND CHICAGO

♾ This book is printed on acid-free paper.

Library of Congress Cataloging-in-Publication Data
Anglin, Mary K., 1952–
Women, power, and dissent in the hills of Carolina / Mary K. Anglin.
p.   cm.
Includes bibliographical references and index.
ISBN 0-252-02739-6 (cloth : alk. paper)
ISBN 0-252-07052-6 (paper : alk. paper)
1. Women—Appalachian Region, Southern—Social conditions.
2. Women—Employment—Appalachian Region, Southern.
3. Mica industry—Appalachian Region, Southern.
4. Moth Hill Mica Company.
5. Appalachian Region, Southern—Social conditions.
6. Appalachian Region, Southern—Economic conditions.
I. Title.
HQ1438.A14A64   2002
305.42'0975—dc21   2001005640

In memory of Hazel Roberts and Julie Cale Morgan,
whose lives have been an inspiration

Yes, sir, what you see is the weeds, but you don't see what we don't see.

—Ernest J. Gaines, *A Gathering of Old Men*

Contents

Acknowledgments

THIS BOOK REPRESENTS the culmination of a long-term project on women's factory labor but not the end of my commitment to Southern Appalachia. In conducting the original field research in the 1980s, and in subsequent research on western North Carolina, I relied heavily on the kindness of strangers, friends, and family. Without their support and considerable contributions, I would never have written this book.

First and foremost, my heartfelt thanks go to the women and men who worked in mica "houses" as part of federal stockpiling programs and for the company I refer to here as "Moth Hill." I greatly appreciate their generosity and willingness to speak with me despite a well-justified distrust of writers and, for some of those still employed in the places about which they spoke, apprehension about the effect of their critical remarks. I have tried to honor their concerns by delaying the publication of this book until most of the women whom I interviewed were no longer working at the mica factory and by staying mindful of the politics of my representations. While the interpretation offered here is most assuredly mine, I have tried to do justice to what I learned of their experiences and wisdom about making a living in these mountains. I am especially grateful to Zona Watson, Frances Stokes, Hazel Roberts, and their families for their patience, immense kindness, and willingness to become my teachers and friends. These are pseudonyms, but they know who they are.

I want to thank other people connected with the mica industry—in particular, the owners of Moth Hill Mica Company—for the information and access they offered me. Royce Payne (his and the names that follow also are pseudonyms) allowed me to interview him on six occasions and permitted me to do the field research at Moth Hill. John Walter Payne gave me a tour of the factory, answered questions throughout my stay, and generally made it possible for me to pursue my research project. Muriel Payne graciously consented to be interviewed twice. Local experts on the mica industry of western Carolina, including supervisors for the federal stockpiling program and owners of other factories, also gave generously of their time.

John M. Parker III and Frank G. Lesure, geologists with the U.S. Geological Survey, provided me with materials and their own commentaries on the research of the USGS in the 1940s and 1950s. Dr. Joyce M. Thisse provided me with texts on occupationally induced lung disease and helped me make sense of that literature. In answering my queries about an incident from the 1950s, the National Labor Relations Board turned a vague citation into valuable information on labor relations and union organizing.

Many people assisted in the library research by finding secondary sources on the history of mica; locating a wealth of archival materials on nineteenth-century western North Carolina; unearthing data on labor patterns, local industries, and income distribution in mid- to late twentieth-century Southern Appalachia; and helping me find my way through the publications of the U.S. Census, from the handwritten manuscripts of the nineteenth century to information made available through the Internet. Kate Black and other staff members from the Special Collections and Archives of the M. I. King Library at the University of Kentucky; Zoe Rhyne and the staff at the North Carolina Collection of the Asheville Public Library; Chester Pankowski at the Center for Improving Mountain Living, Western Carolina University; and Burl McCuiston, reference librarian at Lenoir-Rhyne College, were enormously important to this undertaking. The staffs of the Library of Congress, the Wilson Library at the University of North Carolina, the North Carolina Museum of Archives and History, and especially the various libraries of the University of Kentucky—the Agricultural Information Center, Geological Sciences, and the W. T. Young Library—provided resources from their collections and helped me in invaluable ways. Diana Haleman, Robin Heath, Christiana Miewald, and Hunter Purdy, fine scholars in their own right, provided able assistance in this research. In this regard I am grateful to such independent bookstores as Malaprops Bookstore, Blue Moon Books, and Joseph Beth Booksellers for helping one more writer to do her work.

Generous financial support for this project was provided through an Appalachian Studies Fellowship, Berea College; the James Still Fellowship, University of Kentucky; the National Women's Studies Association/Pergamon Press Scholarship; Grants for Research Assistance, College of Arts and Sciences, University of Kentucky; and the Summer Faculty Research Fellowship, Division of Research and Graduate Studies, University of Kentucky.

The list of teachers, friends, and colleagues to whom I am grateful, for their advice, support, and helpful criticism, is too long to enumerate here. A partial listing would include Dobree Adams, Jane Adams, Dwight Billings, Karen Brodkin, Richard Couto, Deborah Crooks, Maria Patricia Fernandez-Kelly, Stephen Fisher, Christine Gailey, Archie Green, Jonathan Greene, John Inscoe, Shirley Lindenbaum, Sally Maggard, Gordon McKinney, Ruth Milkman, Sandra Morgen, Donald Nonini, Rayna Rapp, the late William Roseberry, Linda Sharpless, Barbara Ellen Smith, Carol Stack, Ida Susser, and Karen Tice. I am enormously grateful for all that you have done—some intervened at specific moments during this project, and some (you know who you are) helped over the long haul. Thank you, Judy McCulloh of the University of Illinois Press, for shepherding this book through to completion.

Finally, I want to express my appreciation to Jane Hatcher for the sage advice and encouragement she has provided for many years. Without her support neither this book nor I would have made it.

* * *

Portions of this book derive from the following previously published material:

"Looking Beyond the Factory: Regional Culture and Practices of Dissent," *It Takes More Than Class: Approaches to the Study of Power in U.S. Workplaces* (Albany: State University of New York Press, 1998), 53–72.

"Engendering the Struggle: Women's Labor and Traditions of Resistance in Rural Southern Appalachia," *Fighting Back in Appalachia: Traditions of Resistance and Change* (Philadelphia: Temple University Press, 1993), 263–81.

"Strategic Differences: Gendered Labor in Southern Appalachia," *Frontiers: A Journal in Women Studies* 14:1 (1993): 68–86.

"A Question of Loyalty: National and Regional Identity in Narratives of Appalachia," *Anthropological Quarterly* 65:3 (1992): 105–16.

Introduction

"As OLD AS THE HILLS, we say, and it's probably the Blue Ridge Mountains we're thinking of." So begins a special publication of the National Geographic Society devoted to the Blue Ridge, the eastern range of the Appalachian Mountains that stretches from West Virginia to Georgia. Not only the landscape of Southern Appalachia captures the interest of the National Geographic Society, for the people dwelling there appear almost timeless, like the mountains themselves. "This battered and misty rumple in the skin of North America seems to have been always old, to have been there from our beginnings, to have fostered the aged artifacts of our eastern mountain folklore and folk life: old quilts and old storytellers, old legends and myths and folk remedies, old fiddlers and old songs, old dances, old byways, churches, skills, and crafts, old battles, old cabins" (R. Fisher 1998:12). If this language sounds familiar, there are good reasons for that. Appalachia occupies a special position within American popular culture. It is the wilderness, the counterbalance to the intensely urbanized East Coast. These mountains are a place of incredible beauty and compelling "folk life."

While the National Geographic Society's "park profile" depicts "a unity of people and place, past and present," other renderings are not so beneficent (R. Fisher 1998:8). Southern Appalachia has also been home to Eric Robert Rudolph, infamous as one of the FBI's "Ten Most Wanted Fugitives" (since May 1998), sought in connection with the bombing of two abortion clinics, an urban gay bar, and "Olympic Park" in Atlanta and the deaths and devastation that ensued. Media accounts of Rudolph have invariably led to the shadowy side of this strange wilderness. As a writer for *The New Yorker* put it, "This part of North Carolina, like much of southern Appalachia, has always been jealous of its privacy. The Scotch-Irish who settled here in the early nineteenth century brought with them a talent for making whiskey and a distrust of outside authority. Until the middle of this century, government rarely touched this remote society except when state agents called 'revenuers' came to bust up stills" (Horwitz 1999:47). Bootlegging, hostility toward outsiders and especially the law, isolation—these too are popular images of Appalachia. It hardly matters whether the images are factual; they *seem* like the truth. The *New Yorker* writer depicted Rudolph as both outlaw and "folk hero" to the people of western Carolina, inasmuch as he hated the federal government, his local knowledge allowed him to camp in the forest without detection, and he evaded FBI operatives and others who searched for him (Horwitz 1999:46; Associated Press 2001). Thus, although Rudolph was not actually *from* Southern Appalachia, he appeared enough like a native son to count as one—at least from the perspective of the *New Yorker*. And the hundreds of "potential boltholes—mostly abandoned shafts where men once mined mica, talc, and gemstones"—reflect a conspiracy of mountains and fugitive (Horwitz 1999:48).

The paradox of Appalachia articulated by such accounts is that it is at once beautiful and desolate, suspect and quaint, abundant in natural resources but impoverished, and unchanging. The photographer Shelby Lee Adams took these ironies to even greater extremes for a "fashion shoot" in eastern Kentucky on behalf of the *New York Times Magazine.* Dressing the residents of two Appalachian communities with clothes furnished by Brooks Brothers, Philosophy di Alberta Firretti, Guess, and others, Adams posed his "models" to look like churchgoers wearing their Sunday best in the style of the Works Progress Administration photographs by Walker Evans, Dorothea Lange, and Russell Lee (Adams 1999; Sischy 1999:39, 48). "Appalachia will never be Paris," read the accompanying text, "but its inhabitants may have a tighter hook on what's happening in fashion these days than the ladies who fork up six figures for couture" (Sischy 1999:48). Although one seventy-nine-year-old man, a "retired janitor and coal miner," wore his *own* clothes for the shoot, the discerning shopper would be able to find "almost identical" ones at Banana Republic and Dickies (Sischy 1999:48). "Here the tables are turned" in "the fun of fashion" and through the machinations of Shelby Lee Adams and his collaborator from the *Times* (Sischy 1999:48). Poverty was transformed into "haute couture," while fiction became fact.

Talking Back

Whether grandiose or simply belittling, these portraits of Appalachia have not gone unnoticed and unchallenged by their subjects.[1] Commenting on the more usual association of Appalachian poverty with lowbrow culture—exemplified here by Jeff Foxworthy's "redneck jokes"—Anne Shelby raises an important question: "Redneck jokes define poverty as a matter of inferior taste. If these people are poor, they probably deserve it, and it's probably their own fault. If they live in trailers, have bad teeth, and only go to the fifth grade, it's because they choose it, because they are ignorant and stupid, ridiculous somehow. They are, in any case, not to be taken seriously. If we had to take them seriously, what might we have to do?" (Shelby 1999:158). What, indeed, would it mean to give careful consideration to history, politics, economics, and culture in Appalachia, and to take poor people seriously, on their own terms? What would happen to Adams's poses, explanations for the phenomenon of Eric Rudolph, *National Geographic*'s approach to Southern Appalachia? More important, what would the residents tell us about this region or more generally about political economies, the making of wealth and poverty in the United States, that we might otherwise never know?

Such questions lie at the heart of this book. I use the approaches of ethnography and ethnohistory to explore the experiences of women earning the minimum wage (and before there was such a thing) for their work in processing mica, a nonmetallic mineral found in the western Carolina mountains and used in everything from the gas lanterns and wood stoves of the nineteenth century to electrical appliances, automobiles, electronics and communications technologies, warfare, CAT scans, radiotherapy, and space exploration in the twentieth and twenty-first centuries.[2] This is the story of women's contributions to household and regional economies for the past century or more and how industries such as mica came to be organized around women's labor. Based on eight months of field research in one rural factory, I examine how, without the formal recourse to power afforded by union membership or definition as "skilled labor," women used the power of memory, their own readings of gender relations, and local cultural forms to challenge the paternalistic rhetoric of company owners.[3] The declining economic status of the mica industry and the downsizing of the local company—and women's jobs in particular—meant that female employees experienced the very real limits of their informal strategies. Even so, they carved out a space within the productive spheres of mica work and, as one worker put it, "bossed themselves."[4] This is, in short, a book about poor people in Southern Appalachia talking about resistance, collusion, and their negotiation of local and national political economies.[5]

Yet, its subject matter concerns more than that. What I learned from daily conversations with factory workers, and by going home with several of the women from the plant, was their refusal to be seen only in terms of what they did to earn a living. Just as the old stereotypes that rendered Appalachian women simply as wives, mothers, or daughters—essentialized family members who occupied the realm of the private—failed to measure the complexities of their lives, neither could they be reduced to the gendered dynamics of waged labor (see Smith 1998; Anglin 1999). Theirs was not a disavowal of class identity but rather the staking of claims as important members of working-class mountain communities beyond the limits of the factory. In addition, the employees of what I will refer to by the pseudonym "Moth Hill Mica Company" taught me about the value of regional traditions, including evangelical Protestantism, that informed their daily activities and were far more than techniques (however effective) for opposing factory management.[6]

On the most fundamental level this is equally an inquiry into the construction of historical accounts and what gets taken as fact. If scholars such as Nicholas Dirks (1990:28–29) and Michel-Rolph Trouillot (1995:28) are correct in arguing that relations of power constitute the very basis of historical records, exploring these records for silences and erasures becomes important, as does examining the narratives that are regarded as authoritative. How might our understanding of regional commerce change if the voices of laboring women and men carried the same weight as those of elite citizens and government officials? What happens when we examine census records and other official documents for the ways that they reflect dominant interpretations and the social hierarchies in which they are embedded? Should an "engaged anthropology" have a role in reconstructing narratives of Appalachia's past, as well as reconsidering the heterogeneity of experiences and social locations that characterize its present? These questions inform my use of oral histories, interviews, historical documents, and government records to explore the early years of the mica industry in western North Carolina and to examine the implications of that contested history for analyses of contemporary political economic conditions. Here I emphasize the importance of locating rural working-class women as active participants in that history— not onlookers, as previously supposed—just as I scrutinize census records for what they might reveal about the relations of gender, race, and class in nineteenth- and twentieth-century western North Carolina.[7]

Appalachian Histories

In approaching Appalachia as I am, I am following precedents set in the late twentieth century by social historians, historical sociologists, historical geographers, and anthropologists. They argue for a view of Appalachia as a geographic area cross-cut by internal divisions, complicated connections with other parts of the United States, and the particularities of local history.[8] Alan Batteau (1982), for example, calls attention to the activities of local elites who, in seizing control of the resources of the mountains, impoverished their neighbors. Others, like Mary Beth Pudup (1989, 1991), analyze early Euro-American settlement of Appalachia, with special attention to indicators of social stratification. These include the ability of elites to influence the drawing of county boundaries, as well as the establishment of land deeds and county seats, in order to increase their own wealth and influence.

John C. Inscoe (1989), Martin Crawford (1989), and Gordon B. McKinney (1988, 1995) look at the southern mountains in the period before the Civil War. In particular, they investigate the web of connections—political, economic, and familial—that tied wealthy citizens in the southern mountains to their peers in eastern North Carolina. Rather than a "region set apart," the Appalachia of these texts is integrally linked to the centers of power and markets of the lowland South. Similarly, Durwood Dunn (1988) depicts eastern Tennessee as an area with a well-developed cash economy, as well as a slave-owning elite that sided with the Confederacy and against its neighbors, many of whom backed the Union, in the desperate times of the Civil War (see also McKenzie 1994). Altina Waller (1988) finds that the quarrel between the Hatfields and McCoys was a dispute about economic development and the future of the Tug Valley, not the blood feud that has been so well popularized (see also Billings and Blee 2000). Furthermore, lawyers representing outside interests in the newly discovered coalfields of the Tug Valley greatly inflamed this dispute. Taken as a whole, these analyses replace a portrait of self-sufficient and egalitarian yeoman communities with intimations of the range of class fractions and racial identities that marked Appalachia, wherein individual households assumed different relationships to petty commodity production, agriculture, and merchant capital.

John Finger (1984, 1995), Theda Perdue (1979, 1985, 1990, 1998), Thomas Hatley (1991), and Sarah Hill (1997) have written about the Eastern Band of the Cherokee and their struggles against white encroachment (much of it illegal according to the treaties of the day) on tribal lands in the Southern Appalachians. Although the Cherokee women "could not stem . . . the strong undertow engendered by the depopulation, recurrent warfare, and demands of economic involvement in colonial trade," Hatley argues, they should be recognized for their place in Native American and U.S. histories as the maintainers of traditional indigenous practices in the face of overwhelming odds (1991:50, 51). Equally noteworthy were the complex relations between black slaves and the Cherokee—both with respect to the use of slaves in establishing white colonies in Indian territories and, later, the presence of wealthy

Cherokee as plantation owners and slaveholders themselves (Finger 1984; Lucas 1997).

Western North Carolina and other areas of Southern Appalachia were not amenable to the intensive agriculture of lowland plantations, for the terrain was too steep and the soil insufficiently fertile for this kind of farming. Nonetheless, some of the wealthiest landowners owned slaves and relied on their labor to make their agricultural operations profitable. More important than farm labor, however, was the value of slave labor to mercantile enterprises. Slaves worked as store clerks and produced commodities ranging from wagon wheels to plugs of tobacco to men's clothing (Inscoe 1989). Female slaves performed domestic service, worked in agricultural production and homemade manufactures, and were forced to bear and relinquish children as valuable commodities in the slave trade (Anglin 1995; Inscoe 1989).

At the same time, elite practices of slaveholding did not necessarily translate into support of the Confederacy by all the residents of Southern Appalachia (Inscoe 1995). Counties literally divided; families split over the issue of slavery and divided their loyalties between the Union and Confederate causes; and the Underground Railroad used the complex geography of the Blue Ridge Mountains to its advantage (Mann 1993; McKinney 1995). Moreover, freed as well as enslaved African Americans lived in nineteenth-century Appalachia. According to Dwight Billings and Kathleen Blee (2000; see also Sprague 1993; Tedesco 1993), freed African Americans owned land and farmed in eastern Kentucky in the mid- to late nineteenth century when they were forcibly dispossessed of their holdings as the result of litigation, the denial of credit, and other economic practices. In the hostile climate of the late nineteenth century, African Americans with economic resources left agrarian eastern Kentucky (and western Carolina), and those who remained often fell deeper into poverty. The coalfields of Central Appalachia provided one destination for migrating African Americans, who found employment in the mines and later fought for unionization in battles as violent and devastating as those of the mid-nineteenth century (R. Lewis 1987; Trotter 1990; Turner 1985).

What distinguishes these intellectual projects has been their unwillingness to "reduce complex and intricate historical and social diversities to a few prominent cultural images" (Bond and Gilliam 1994:16). The new social histories collectively challenge stereotypes of Appalachia that still find their way into American popular culture (D. Billings, Norman, and Ledford 1999). It is no coincidence, in other words, that Adams, Horwitz, R. Fisher, and Sischy would select the images they have to represent Appalachia in the 1990s. Their rhetoric echoes that of the local color school of the mid-nineteenth and early twentieth centuries and its subsequent manifestation in culture of poverty theories, media representations, and popular arguments.

Poverty and "Local Color"

Indeed, the notion of an "Appalachia" was invented by the local color movement, postbellum travel writers penning accounts of "a strange land and a peculiar people" in *Scribner's Monthly, Appleton's Journal, Lippincott's Magazine,* and other magazines with a national readership (Harney 1870; Shapiro 1978; C. Williams 1961). Titles like "The Despot of Broomsedge Cove," "'Blockaders' and the 'Revenue,'" and "Our Contemporary Ancestors in the Southern Mountains" played up the imputed eccentricities of an "Appalachian people" far removed from modernity and the readership of those publications. In the writings of the local color school, "Scotch-Irish mountaineers," descended from "pure Anglo-Saxon stock," engaged in dialects and cultural practices reminiscent of the Elizabethan era (Batteau 1990:62–74). These writers conveyed the Appalachian mountain chain, isolated from forces of war or industry, as a place of innocence and incredible beauty.

However, these writers did not portray Appalachia only as Nature in its most pristine form. In addition to the travel writers who spoke of native beauty and quaint custom, representatives of northern churches and the medical profession wrote about the needs of mountaineers for resources available only through outside aid. The two accounts were complementary rather than contradictory. Travelogues, as Shapiro (1978) notes, justified and later gave way to the documentation of poverty in the southern mountains. Both invited representatives of the moneyed sophisticated North to come to Appalachia or at least to offer their resources. Writing on behalf of the Presbyterian Church, for example, Florence Stephenson described those to whom the Home Mission Board ministered:

> I wish I could show you some of the most thrifty and industrious families where the children and grown people wear homespun of good quality and bright colors. These colors make the people as they walk about bright and pleasing spots on the landscape and cause them to be more cheerful than they could be if dressed in brown and gray among the dense woods and dark green of the surrounding mountains. The people are unconsciously doing the natural and becoming thing, just as the holly-tree in their midst brightens itself with red berries and the dark, austere rhododendron bush puts on its glory of blossoms. Usually, there is but little light and brightness inside the home walls, the native schoolhouses and churches. (1912:13–14)

Presented as something akin to natural resources and a population in desperate need, western North Carolinians could be transformed by mission schools into "beautiful, happy, useful Christian[s]." Their alternative fate, according to Stephenson (1912:16), was depicted by a colloquialism: "[They] done had no raisin', but were jist jerked up."

More explicit renditions of a "culture of poverty" appear in the work of Thomas Dawley, who undertook an investigation of child (and women's) labor in the mountains of North Carolina and Tennessee at the behest of the U.S. Congress and the federal Bureau of Labor. The following passage reflects Dawley's findings: "There were cabins, shacks and houses almost everywhere it seemed, that one could be placed. Even old tobacco-barns rotting away with neglect, were inhabited. Slattern-looking, idle women were sitting in doorways with children, dirty and ragged like themselves, moping around. They were the women and children that toiled not, neither did they spin" (1912:182). Such children also did not play but resorted to eating clay and chewing the snuff their mothers fed them to "stop their yellin'" (Dawley 1912:182). Under these dire circumstances "their bodies are actually starved by the food that fails to supply the nourishment for growth and development of the human body and mind, and then comes the whiskey that makes them mad, and sometimes drives them to killing one another" (Dawley 1912:183). The synergistic combination of poverty, stunted development, madness, and violence in Dawley's account describe an Appalachia no longer viewed as innocent but rather as lawless and beyond the civilizing influences of the twentieth century.[9] Does this, somehow, sound familiar?

From the standpoint of the new social histories, the representations of the local color movement and the well-orchestrated reply to its call for outside intervention merit further examination in light of subsequent economic development in this resource-rich region. "Benevolent workers" brought "uplift" to the mountains in the form of mission schools, churches, settlement schools, and crafts revivals, while medical missionaries and government agents likewise came during the early decades of the twentieth century to help out in the mountains (Becker 1998; Shapiro 1978; Tice 1998; Whisnant 1980, 1983). Regarded either as the allies of capitalist entrepreneurs or champions of a way of life that was to be preferred to "the horrors of an inevitable industrialized future" (Shapiro 1978:184–85), the benevolents brought their gendered and class-based logics of reform to Appalachia—with lasting effect on mountain communities.[10] Moreover, the War on Poverty during the 1960s and the antipoverty programs of the late twentieth century gave new life to the benevolents' hegemonic interpretations of Appalachian culture (see

Couto 1975, 1994; Glen 1995; Isserman 1997; Kiffmeyer 1998; Tickamyer and Tickamyer 1987; Weiler 1997; Whisnant 1980).[11]

Put another way, the benevolence movement itself yielded twin progeny. The first was the traditions of folklorism, which documented the unique folk culture of the mountains, the fantasy that benevolent workers attempted to create/preserve. The second, of course, was an early version of the culture of poverty theme that would be more fully developed in social science as well as popular discourses of the late twentieth century.[12] While participants in the folk movement collected artifacts of Appalachian folkways, followers of the culture of poverty approach focused their attentions on the aberrant, if rustic, traditions of the southern mountaineers.[13] The net effect, in both instances, was the use of static notions of culture in the study of Appalachia and its exposition as a geographic or cultural region that was destitute, anachronistic, and of little consequence for the rest of the United States.

Politicized Cultures and Counternarratives

I offer this book as one response, an argument for richly textured ethnographic analyses reflective of the diverse historical processes, political-economic structures, and cultural contexts comprising the area we know as "Appalachia." Far from irrelevant, as this account will illustrate, residents in places like western North Carolina have a lot to teach us about the resilience of local cultures in the face of global economies and about contending with informalized labor practices and other problems associated with economic restructuring or disinvestment. Such issues are central to the region's history.

I begin this inquiry in chapter 1 by using census records from 1880 and 1990 to present a long view of the social and material contexts for two western North Carolina counties. I use findings from the federal censuses to justify an analytic framework that, counter to the local color schema, highlights relations of gender, race, and class in this part of Southern Appalachia. Important to this undertaking too is the examination of biases conveyed through government documents about how households are organized, what kinds of economic contributions are recognized, and who is considered to be a full citizen.

In chapter 2, I take up questions about anthropological field research and my activities as an ethnographer. There I discuss my interests in participating in an engaged anthropology and the biases of a middle-class academic examining labor relations in Appalachia. My encounters with local residents and factory workers regarding issues of accountability and the problematic representations of the past form an important dimension of this chapter and this ethnographic project.

Chapter 3 presents an overview of the mica industry as it developed in western North Carolina and the linkages between regional, national, and international markets in this commodity. Using interviews with workers and local elites, in conjunction with materials from the U.S. Geological Survey and other records of the early history of mica, I examine the web of gender, class, and racial and ethnic relations around which the domestic mica industry was organized.

Chapters 4, 5, and 6 are ethnographic accounts centered around my field research at Moth Hill Mica Company and surrounding communities. In chapter 4, I discuss the importance of kinship, gender, and class relations within the factory. Focusing on one factory department in particular, I describe women's work routines and explore issues of production, layoffs, and shop-floor politics. Chapter 5 takes up the narratives of two women of different generations—their reflections on family, involvement in local churches, and experiences of waged labor—to place greater emphasis on the experiences and relationships that workers bring into the factory. I offer this chapter as a way of disrupting simplistic assumptions about worker loyalties, the potency of the productive sphere, and the sense that women make of their lives. Chapter 6 examines relationships of power and dissent from the perspective of prior analyses of class relations in Appalachia, the work of Antonio Gramsci (1971) and others on hegemony, and feminist perspectives on gendered labor. Within the paternalistic setting of the mica factory, women engaged in social and kin-based networks, religious discourse, and their memories of the past in order to disrupt, and sometimes to collude with, the authority of the factory owners.

The conclusion endeavors to pull together this sequence of narratives as part of an anthropology of gender, labor, and place. A critical dimension of this project concerns the question of how historical and ethnographic knowledge is produced—and challenged—regarding the hinterlands of Southern Appalachia. In a final sense, however, this and other discussions articulate a single theme: the ways in which women from western North Carolina have waged a "routine struggle for bread and roses," for the continuance of their productive lives, for dignity, and for remembrance (Shapiro-Perl 1984).

Mountain people
can't read,
can't write,
don't wear shoes,
don't have teeth,
don't use soap,
and don't talk plain.
They beat their kids,
beat their friends,
beat their neighbors,
and beat their dogs.
They live on cow peas,
fatback and twenty acres
straight up and down.
They don't have money.
They do have fleas,
overalls,
tobacco patches,
shacks,
shotguns,
and liquor stills,
and at least six junk cars
in the front yard. Right?
Well, let me tell you:
I'm from here,
I'm not like that
and I am damn tired of
being told I am.

—Jo Carson, *Stories I Ain't Told Nobody Yet*, 28–29

1. Relocating Appalachia: The Social Landscape of Nineteenth- and Twentieth-Century Carolina

THIS CHAPTER TAKES its inspiration from the work of Jo Carson and others who are creating literature *of* and *from* Appalachia. However, the point of departure is more in keeping with the new social histories of Appalachia than literary works, for here I explore census and other records in order to rearrange conventional wisdom about Southern Appalachia and to place this study in the social and material contexts of western North Carolina as best we understand them. Such an undertaking has many liabilities, not the least of which are the biases of government officials writ large in public documents, the scantiness of those accounts, and the awkward, at times counterintuitive, language of statistics in which they are embedded. Mindful of these limitations, I will examine the public record for what it *can* tell us about two western Carolina counties in the late nineteenth and twentieth centuries and what inferences we might draw in subsequent discussions of correspondence, oral histories, and interviews concerning those periods. Despite the appealing notion of a bucolic and timeless setting located somewhere in America, I will show that economic disparities and shifting social relations have proved a significant force in the history of the southern mountains.

As Carson's poem attests, Southern Appalachia in the late twentieth and early twenty-first centuries defies easy categorization and so did this part of the United States at the close of the nineteenth century. Then and now women as much as men were integral to the functioning of households, farmsteads, settlements, and business enterprises of various descriptions. The Cherokee, aboriginal inhabitants of the southern mountains, constituted an important segment of the population and Appalachian history. Slaves and their descendants, native-born whites, people of multiple ethnicities, and immigrants from various parts of the world—not simply the British Isles—likewise have made up part of the region's population. While some residents were or quickly became prosperous, others were impoverished and made to contribute to the profitability of elites, if not the well-being of local communities, under conditions that often proved coercive.[1]

Thus, the difficulties imposed by geography notwithstanding, neither was Southern Appalachia isolated and homogeneous in character nor was it unaffected by the forces that shaped the United States as a whole during the the nineteenth and twentieth centuries. This region's resources have been used to fight wars and to create immense wealth. By the late nineteenth century the mountain South was connected to international markets and changing technologies, as well as the political concerns of the nation, and such connections remained important in the political economies and social relations at the close of the twentieth century.

That is the unexotic setting, one that is perhaps less easily recognized, in which my study of the North Carolina mountains begins. My aim has been to develop an ethnographic account that draws upon women's experiences in a regional industry, with emphasis on one factory in particular, and their lives apart from the workplace, in order to reorient understandings of gender, the social relations of labor, and regional culture in rural Southern Appalachia. The focus of this inquiry is ultimately the narratives of the people whom I encountered as workers employed in the plant where I did my field research and those long since retired from factory work. Their conversations depicted working-class residents of the mountains neither as militant heroes nor as the pawns of oppressive bosses—two prevailing images of the region—but rather as people laboring with dignity and determination amid difficult circumstances. Furthermore, as interviews with factory owners and my observations of the plant show, the endeavors of factory workers in Appalachia, both men and women, speak to local contexts of international economic processes, variously described as the "globalization of production," "flexible accumulation," or "international capitalism."[2] Equally important, this ethnographic material presents an opportunity for reconsidering issues of power and contestation (see, e.g., Black 1990; S. Fisher 1993; Gaventa 1980; H. Lewis, Johnson, and Askins 1978; S. L. Scott 1995; Seitz 1995).

Examining the present contexts of waged labor in the southern mountains has required engagement with historical material. By looking at a broader expanse of time, it is not only possible but necessary to replace one-dimensional notions of tradition and modernity with an increasing awareness of the complexities of previous eras and the fluidity of current conditions. No longer can Appalachia be simply regarded as a land of poverty or a problem to be solved with the right combination of wisdom and progress but must instead be understood as the locus of interventionist discourses with ulterior motives: missionary, entrepreneurial, literary, academic, and otherwise. What emerges foremost from these investigations of the past, however, is greater appreciation for the complexity of cultural identities and social locations in a region often summed up as Anglo-Saxon, egalitarian, and, of course, poor.

Information collected through the expanded population census of 1880 provides the basis for a schematic account of late nineteenth-century western North Carolina and, reviewed in conjunction with other resources, allows us to compare this period with socioeconomic conditions found in the 1990s.[3] With respect to the two-county area that is the focus of this study, for example, this comparison permits consideration of questions about racial and ethnic diversity, changes in population size and composition, levels of wealth and poverty (the latter measured crudely in the 1880 census), kin ties and the organization of households, the range of occupations, the significance of farming, and other concerns across the expanse of a century or more.[4] What emerges are the many ways in which to be a farmer in an area once dominated by agriculture—as well as other forms of livelihood, and the lack thereof, for the residents of these mountains. As Mary Beth Pudup has observed of eastern Kentucky (1991:236, 240–41), rather than a "retarded frontier," with all its pejorative connotations, the mountains of Carolina provide another example of capitalist development.

In what I refer to as "Pike" and "Clark" counties, more than three-quarters of household heads listed agriculture as their primary occupation in the population schedule of the 1880 census (U.S. Census Bureau 1883a).[5] That figure would undoubtedly have been larger had census takers allowed female heads of household to declare farming their occupation or, indeed, to be counted as productive members of farm families (U.S. Census Bureau 1883a; see also Jensen 1980; Abel and Folbre 1990; Eagan 1990; and Folbre 1991).[6] A small proportion of heads of household, fewer than 2 percent of those enumerated by the 1880 census, listed their occupation as that of farm *laborer* or "hireling" and, in some instances, observed that they had "no regular abode." All told, at least 80 percent of the households in this two-county area derived their income primarily from farming.[7]

What is most striking about the farmsteads, on further examination, are their differences—differences in terms of magnitude of operations; access to crucial resources, including land and labor; and the social relations around which they were organized. One in 14 households (7 percent) included female and male servants who lived and worked on the premises. Doubtless, some of these farms also called upon the services of the casual day laborers mentioned earlier. Then, too, nearly a fourth of all farms (24 percent) housed extended families, defined by multiple generations of a family and/or collateral kin (adult siblings, cousins, brothers- and sisters-in-law, etc.). In many instances this arrangement reflected the reliance of heads of household on younger generations for farm labor and, equally, their obligation to support dependent family members. Farmsteads headed by younger men often incorporated older relatives, as well as collateral kin, who resided there as productive members, kinspeople in need, or a combination of the two.[8] Along with servants and those classified as "kin" (who were sometimes one and the same), a few households recruited additional members through the conventions of adoption, apprenticeship, and "binding," or indentured, servitude. While fewer than 2 percent of households engaged in the latter practices, their existence nonetheless suggests the importance of having sufficient sources of labor to meet the demands of agricultural production and the decidedly nonegalitarian work settings that were part of farm life in the late nineteenth century.

Farms in Pike and Clark counties varied considerably in size. The vast majority (65 percent) consisted of fewer than 100 acres, enough to secure subsistence needs but little more, and 8.5 percent of the farms had fewer than 10 acres.[9] On the other hand, 32 percent of the farms in this area were moderate in size, holding 100 to 500 acres, and a wealthy minority (2.8 percent) exceeded 500 acres. While most farms were cultivated by landowners themselves, nearly a third (29 percent) were rented through share-cropping agreements whose terms were highly favorable to landlords (U.S. Census Bureau 1883b). If we consider together those who worked and lived in other households, those who lived independently but referred to themselves as "hirelings" or "farm labor," and tenant farmers, many households had limited access to farmland in the late nineteenth century and thereby the means to ensure their own survival.[10]

What might be considered "middling" households maintained their ownership of farms through economic strategies that included releasing family members into waged work (2 percent), keeping boarders (2 percent), and agricultural practices tied to cash cropping, in addition to subsistence production. Artisanal households, and those headed by professional men, likely combined farming activities with the occupations recorded by the census takers.[11] As was true for their peers in eastern Kentucky and other parts of Appalachia (Pudup 1991), merchants, lawyers, and other elites that appeared in the 1880 census of these western Carolina counties might have engaged in still other endeavors tied to landownership: renting land for "shares" or money, speculating in mineral resources, and developing commercial enterprises. Leaving aside such conjectures, it is noteworthy that residents in Clark and Pike coun-

ties held occupations ranging from ornamental painter, editor, teacher, physician, hotel keeper, merchant, and dentist to midwife, nurse, bookkeeper, U.S.
marshal, shoemaker, keeper of poorhouse, millwright, wheelwright, brick
mason, saddler, weaver, tayloress, blacksmith, tinsmith, house painter, hotel
cook, laborer, servant, washerwoman, carpenter, minister, soap maker, clerk
of court, druggist, engineer, store clerk, foreman, mine hand, and mica miner.[12] Clearly, not all were farmers and certainly not full time.

If the 1880 census identified girls and women mainly by virtue of their
relationship to heads of household, information about gendered economic
relations still can be gleaned from this problematic source. As I have noted,
the population schedule did record women's involvement in gender-
stratified occupations such as midwife, washerwoman, or tayloress and also
the work of teaching and servanthood (domestic/field labor) where both
women and men found employment, if in different capacities.[13] Women
appeared to be primary sources of income in a number of households, either because they were identified as having work while male heads of household were "without occupation" (less than 0.5 percent), or because they
themselves were heads of household (7.5 percent).[14] Yet identification as
"female head of household" cannot be taken as evidence of equivalent socioeconomic status, for women occupying that role came from vastly different circumstances that encompassed paupers, artisans, elites, laborers, and
farm families with modest resources.[15]

Equally important to this brief inquiry into the social landscape of nineteenth-century western Carolina are the differences in race and ethnicity
registered by the 1880 census. The use of "Black," and the more ambiguous
"Mulatto," by census enumerators reflected national constructions of race
in the aftermath of the Civil War and the specific histories of slavery and white
settlement of Cherokee territory in western Carolina (Inscoe 1989; Finger
1984, 1995). Combined, those persons designated as "Black" or "Mulatto" in
the census made up 5 percent of the population at large—blacks alone constituting 3.2 percent of the general population—and more than 15 percent
of the residents of Jonesboro, the largest town within this two-county area.
Within these populations were represented both households of color (4.6
percent of all households), as well as persons of color working and residing
in white households (11 percent of the households with servants). Doubtless,
the interactions between these forms of residence were complex, including
the movement of people from one arrangement to the other in response to
changing economic circumstances, but the population manuscript provides
no information about this. However, the composition of households of color was testament to the variation present and to the complexities of race

relations in that era, for residential groups in many instances incorporated multiracial marriages, kinspeople of different racial backgrounds, and/or unrelated people of color.[16] In regard to occupation, most households were organized around farming (62 percent), with smaller numbers involved in artisanal work, farm work, and other forms of waged labor, not to mention mica mining.[17] Households of color were not uniformly poorer than their white counterparts; the census counted 6.5 percent of black and mulatto households as having resources sufficient to maintain servants, in comparison to 8.3 percent of white households.[18]

To cast this discussion of nineteenth-century Pike and Clark counties in slightly different terms, just over half (54 percent) of the households in the 1880 census corresponded to the image of self-reliant nuclear families farming the land. And, considering that some of the households were landless farmers renting fields on "shares," or the promise of future crops, 54 percent clearly is an overestimate of the significance of one variation on farming. Likewise, that calculation does not consider the possibility of *female*-headed farmsteads, nor does it distinguish farmsteads managed by African Americans and people of multiple racial or ethnic ancestries from Euro-American farms. In sum, far fewer white yeoman families—those reputedly "distinct relic[s] of an Anglo-Saxon past" (Fox 1901:5)—farmed the Carolina mountains than popular accounts of Appalachia would have us imagine.[19]

More than a century later the agrarian base of Pike and Clark counties had eroded almost to the vanishing point. By 1992 the number of farms had declined by more than half (57 percent), and the amount of land in farms was less than a third (28 percent) of the number recorded in the 1880 census.[20] Only 3 percent of the 1990 labor force was employed full time in agriculture, although many residents continued to grow cash crops—burley tobacco and Christmas trees, in particular—to supplement their earnings from other sources (Center for Improving Mountain Living 1992).[21] Yet the phenomenon of "factory-working farmers," for whom the exigencies of working the land have yielded to the dictates of waged labor, was not so much a reversal of previous times as the culmination of long-standing processes of capital accumulation and economic dependency (Kingsolver 1992; see also Salstrom 1991 and Dunaway 1996).[22] What has persisted, despite economic dislocations, are historical memories and the cultural significance of farming for many residents of these counties.

The efforts of regional elites, corporations both large and small, politicians, outside investors, and government officials to harness the wealth of the mountains to their respective ends had a decisive influence on the economies of western Carolina counties. In the late nineteenth century this meant the development of extractive industries centered around forest products and mineral resources, as well as commercial agriculture. Successive strategies of economic development added still other forms of manufacturing that capitalized on the abundance of cheap labor to be found in rural Appalachia. Textile factories, hosiery mills, furniture plants, and electronics manufacturers and other high-tech firms found their way into western Carolina during the first half of the twentieth century and left toward its close, when the creation of export-processing zones and international treaties such as the North American Free Trade Agreement (NAFTA) made it more profitable for manufacturers to move their operations outside the United States (see Moody 1995).[23] In the aftermath of capital flight the economies of western Carolina have increasingly looked to service-sector industries to compensate for the loss of manufacturing jobs.

Twice as many of the jobs available in 1990 to the residents of Pike and Clark counties were in service-producing industries than in those that produced goods.[24] Given the current emphasis on developing resort areas and second homes for the wealthy residents of other areas, it is not surprising that the number of service jobs continued to increase (+21 percent), while employment in manufacturing declined (–5 percent) from 1990 to 1995 (Mountain Resource Center 1998).[25] Thus, even though unemployment might be characterized as moderately low—with an official rate of 6.4 percent in 1990—the jobs most readily available in Pike and Clark counties were those with lower wages and few or no benefits, and they were often part time and/or seasonal in nature (U.S. Census Bureau 1992b; see also Center for Mountain Living 1992 and Mountain Resource Center 1998).[26] In these respects western Carolina counties have followed economic trends comparable to those experienced elsewhere in the United States but, as Couto has observed, the western Carolina counties fared better than other parts of Appalachia (Harvey 1989:157; Couto 1994:82–100).[27]

A liability of statistics is that they can blur, rather than reveal, differences. To argue that "decent jobs" are becoming scarcer in western North Carolina is not to ignore important distinctions within the occupational structures of the 1980s and 1990s. The differences between, for example, county jobs with wages tied to the state pay scale, jobs in unionized factories, waged labor in fast-food restaurants, clerical jobs, work in chain grocery stores or locally operated vegetable stands, health professions, maintenance work at area resorts, and employment in small manufacturing operations have meant that some residents had middle-class salaries, while others' earnings fell considerably below the average income in North Carolina (and far below that reported for the nation as a whole).[28] And if more people were living in poverty in western Carolina than elsewhere in the state,[29] Pike and Clark counties nonetheless had their share of elites with large land holdings, businesses, and/ or development schemes.[30] This much had *not* changed, although the specific configurations of class reflected economic conditions, social contexts, and political sensibilities—counterhegemonic as well as dominant—at the end of the twentieth century.[31] I will turn to these latter issues shortly.

Exploring questions about heterogeneity through the lens of race and ethnicity reveals another limitation of statistics, namely, that they allow a partial glimpse of dynamic social relations and all too easily create a sense of continuity where none existed. So it is that we learn that 98 percent of the population of Pike and Clark counties was white in the 1990s (U.S. Census Bureau 1990b; Mountain Resource Center 1998; North Carolina Office of State Planning 1998)—surely a carryover from their Anglo Saxon origins? Yet to engage in this kind of logic, as has happened all too frequently in studies of Appalachia, requires discounting the findings of the 1880 census, forgetting that the southern mountains once held enslaved people of African descent, erasing the history of native peoples in the region before white colonization (and the illegality of white settlement on Cherokee lands), ignoring historical events and other factors that forced many African Americans and Native Americans to leave the North Carolina mountains, and, finally, minimizing the significance of contemporary populations of color.[32] That Jonesboro had a sizeable African American population during the latter half of the nineteenth century and throughout the early decades of the twentieth, but no longer, should prompt us to ask what happened. The persistence of small, racially mixed communities (e.g., Redding in Clark County) should likewise command our notice, despite or perhaps *because* the population census shows that in 1990 less than 1 percent (0.7 percent) of the population in these counties was African American.

Census takers in the early twentieth century were unable to account for the migration of Italian workers who were building railroads through the North Carolina mountains. In recent times the Census Bureau has acknowledged that it has significantly underestimated the presence of Latinos/as, both as migrant workers and year-round residents. According to the 1990 census, they comprised 0.6 percent of the general population of Pike and Clark counties. More recent estimates put the figure at 1 percent, with the caveat that this still might not be accurate, to reflect the increasing significance of (underwaged) Latino/a labor to the economies of North Carolina and the Southeast.[33] Then again, the exclusionary logic of the bureaus of the Census and Indian Affairs with respect to systems of racial and ethnic classification might help to explain why the census identified only 0.2 percent of the county residents as American Indian.[34] While the populations of Pike and Clark counties were predominantly Euro-American in 1990, as in 1880, what this has meant in terms of social forces, past and present, is a matter for further consideration. At the very least, given what these censuses show, the tripling of the population during this period entailed selective patterns of in- and out-migration and not simply processes of "natural increase."

Finally, efforts to reconstruct the socioeconomic contexts of gender and women's lives in late twentieth-century western Carolina entail comparable dilemmas. While females in Pike and Clark counties constituted 50.5 percent of the population and headed 7.5 percent of all households in 1880, 51.2 percent of the population in 1990 was female, and women headed 23.2 percent of all households (U.S. Census Bureau 1880, 1883a, 1990a, 1990b).[35] However, there are different conclusions to be drawn from these statistics, depending upon whether we emphasize the presence (and presumably also the viability) of female-headed households or their economic vulnerabilities.[36] The population manuscript of the 1880 census, viewed in conjunction with findings from the 1990 population census, provides a caution against assuming commonalities of experience and/or social status for women living apart from men.

Indeed, although female-headed households were skewed toward the lower end of the economic spectrum in 1990, nearly a quarter of the households had annual incomes of more than $25,000, and a small proportion of these could be considered elite.[37] Such suggestions of difference point to the importance of women's labor, in addition to other sources of income and strategies for survival.[38] And we might make similar arguments about the centrality of women's work to the livelihoods of other kinds of households, including those centered around a married couple (64.4 percent of all households in Pike and Clark counties; see U.S. Census Bureau 1990b), those formed around siblings (not listed in the 1990 census), and those in which women did not actually reside but were connected by bonds of kinship or community (not discernible through the census, but see Stack 1974; Schmink 1984; Halperin 1990; and Beaver 1986). What the 1990 census does show is that nearly half (49 percent) of all females aged sixteen and older—and 54 percent of women with children younger than six—participated in the (formal) labor force in these two western counties, while 58.5 percent of the general population was so engaged (U.S. Census Bureau 1990c). Countless others, women and men, were involved in informal economic activities: producing commodities as self-employed workers, buying and selling goods at flea markets and other venues, exchanging labor for other goods and services, and working in the production of cash crops claimed by household heads (Becker

1998; Greene 1990; Eagan 1990; Oberhauser 1996; S. L. Scott 1996). However difficult to trace through public documents, the value of "home" (as contrasted with "public") work for household and regional economies provides another way to consider articulations of gender, ethnicity, and labor.[39]

For all the shortcomings of census records and statistics, this tour of western Carolina counties in the late nineteenth and twentieth centuries opens up several possibilities. First and foremost, it shifts our understanding of the North Carolina mountains from that of a backward or extraordinary region —the "Other America" publicized by Michael Harrington in the 1960s[40]— to a part of the rural United States with its own intricate history. Second, paying attention to historical constructions of race/ethnicity and gender, and their more contemporary representations, forces a rethinking about just who lives in the southern mountains and how the resulting interpretations account for complex social relations (or perhaps fail to do so). Finally, if synthetic and anachronistic cultural definitions do not match the reality of one section of Southern Appalachia, we must reexamine what the term *culture* means. Can notions of regional identity or local tradition be usefully employed without reessentializing or "whiting out" Appalachia—and, if so, how? To concretize these possibilities, I turn to ethnography and, to a much lesser extent, oral histories of women and men laboring in mica, an extractive industry organized around the abundance of this nonmetallic mineral in the North Carolina mountains. Where statistics leave off—lived experiences in all their unevenness—is precisely where ethnography begins.

2. Questions of Authority: Practices and Politics in the Field

But lurking in the background of American culture is a movie set. The scene is a lawless, backward wasteland populated by the Dukes of Hazzard, the Beverly Hillbillies, L'il Abner, the feuding Hatfield and McCoy clans, the feral dimwits in "Deliverance"—the ignorant and the violent wild men of urban America's nightmares. Kentuckians and others throughout the Appalachian Mountains and the rural South have long been oppressed by these images.

Like many Kentuckians who leave the South, I have experienced the shame these images impose upon us. They make you deny your language and your story and accept as authority others' view of you.
—Bobbie Ann Mason, "Recycling Kentucky"

Legacies and Misconceptions

LONG BEFORE I found my way to the Moth Hill Mica Company, I learned about problems of representation in the Blue Ridge Mountains. Neighbors and informants posed questions, framed in terms of the troublesome methods of writers and photographers who had preceded me. Was I going to write a book like "that Sheppard woman, and tell a bunch of lies, tell how mountain women are low class?"[1] Was I going to "make fun of people in the mountains?" Catch them off-guard as they went to church or worked on their farms, photograph them in their oldest tattered work clothes? These were not questions to be taken lightly, no matter how much I might want to distinguish my intentions from the more egregious of my predecessors.

I could have added to this list of misrepresentations the work of government bureaucrats who "documented" the North Carolina mountains as the land "where poverty, ignorance, and immorality prevail" and argued that child labor was the answer for a people "not only lawless but lazy" (Dawley 1912:265, 242). I might also have mentioned the missionaries who wrote church home boards and the public at large about "little mountaineers" in need of "moral training" and "educational advantages" otherwise unavailable to them (F.

Stephenson 1912:3; Whisnant 1980, 1983; but see also Tice 1998). More relevant still would be the work of academic researchers, health professionals, journalists, and others writing since the 1960s about how to solve the *problem* of Appalachia, defined as an enervating combination of geographic isolation, inadequate material resources, and cultural backwardness.

Yet much as the aforementioned stereotypes motivated me to engage in a different kind of ethnography—a narrative of the mountains antithetical to "cultures of poverty"[2]—my neighbors' questions hung in the air. Who was I, really, and on what basis would I write about the mountains? What would be the effect of my writings? At root, as Talal Asad, as well as Roger Sanjek (1990), has observed, these were concerns about power and the responsibility of the ethnographer:

> My point is only that the process of "cultural translation" is inevitably enmeshed in conditions of power—professional, national, international. And among these conditions is the authority of ethnographers to uncover the implicit meanings of [politically] subordinate societies. Given that is so, the interesting question for enquiry is not whether, and if so to what extent, anthropologists should be relativists or rationalists, critical or charitable, toward other cultures, but how power enters into the process of "cultural translation" seen both as a discursive and a nondiscursive practice. (Asad 1986:163)

I offer this chapter as a reflection on the well-placed concerns of residents in the mountains of North Carolina and an accounting of my experiences in the field.

When I first started this research, I was a graduate student newly returned to the South after completing my studies at a university located intellectually, as well as geographically, in the heart of New York City. I left New York determined to address significant gaps in understanding about the American South, an area only recently (and provisionally) recognized as legitimate material for anthropological inquiry, and to do so in a way that would not reproduce the nostalgia, romanticism, or enmity that the region so often has inspired. My task, instead, was to examine constructions of gender and family in Southern Appalachia through the lens of political economies, cultural traditions, and history. Moreover, I felt it important to study the southern mountains not as an outsider, entering and exiting some months later for the purposes of objectivity and productivity, but as a resident. I would become enmeshed in the daily fabric of life because it was where I had chosen to live rather than simply a place to study. This meant becoming involved in local issues, not for their educational value so much as for the expression of obligation and connection to the community in which I had relocated. Years later, looking back on these decisions, I am painfully aware of the naïveté that they reflect—in addition to the determination to take part in an "engaged" anthropology. I am not sure what I would change, however, inasmuch as my mistakes and misguided idealism brought me a greater appreciation for the complexities of this region.

I stumbled on the topic of mica after exhausting other potential fields of inquiry. I had taught continuing education classes at the local college, worked as a volunteer in county mental health centers and health departments, grown and harvested burley tobacco alongside other residents, and sought access to Appalachian families through whatever means I could fashion. What I learned was that Appalachian families did not want to be found, at least not by the likes of me. I did have contact with families in crisis through my volunteer work, but that was privileged information, not the stuff of field notes, and told me little about the population as a whole. As a young unmarried woman living separately from her own relatives, I was something of an anomaly to the people I hoped might become my informants, and my research endeavors were limited by local understandings of gender, class, and kin relations.

Oral Histories and Factory Lives

Over time, as I became increasingly aware of these complexities, I decided to follow the advice of Carol Stack: to study what was accessible, what was common knowledge in the mountains. That meant talking with women of older generations—neighbors, friends, and frequenters of the local senior citizens' center—and finding out what *they* considered important. From them I learned about mica.

Mica formed part of almost everyone's family history in the settlement where I was living and in the counties nearby. Older women proudly told me of how they had "built their houses from mica." What they meant was that as young unmarried daughters—and later as married women with children of their own—they worked in small manufacturing operations known as "mica houses," where they split blocks, or "books," of pure mica into thin sheets, used large scissors to cut the sheets into various shapes and sizes, or worked on punch presses that fashioned parts from the mineral. In some instances women performed these activities as part of a family endeavor that included prospecting for and mining mica, then selling the finished product to factory owners or local merchants.

Revenues from mica work helped subsidize family farms and support households no longer tied to the land. A neighbor in her eighties told me about going to school through the seventh grade, when she "took a notion" to make some money by going to work in a mica house. While her father raised livestock and farmed thirty acres of oats, wheat, and corn with the help of his workhorses, and cut acid wood or sometimes mined 'spar (i.e., feldspar) on the side, she earned $1 for ten hours of punching mica into parts. That money came in handy, especially after her father was crippled in a mining accident and could barely tend to his farm.

I learned that people spoke of mica in the past tense, as a mineral and industry whose heyday belonged to a bygone era. "Something's took the place of mica" was a phrase I heard often in these conversations. Not only had mica given way to other industries and sources of employment within western North Carolina but few public records of its history survived. What remained, instead, were the memories of those who had labored in that industry for many decades, and so I began to conduct oral history interviews with factory workers and owners.

In all, I interviewed seven women associated with mica houses other than the one that is the focus of this ethnography and spoke with one skilled male worker who was employed by another mica company; the owners of three additional mica companies (three men, as well as two women married to factory owners); a former supervisor for the "mica depot" established by the federal government in the 1950s; and two geologists, one of whom had retired from the U.S. Geological Survey. Those interviews provided narratives about mica mining and work activities within mica houses that extended about seventy years into the past and were invaluable guides through the early days of mica. I heard about girls of twelve being recruited to work in mica and married women returning to work once their children had reached school age; about working conditions in the small, informally organized factories; about "rich men's mines" and the complications of prospecting for mica; and about the "government mica programs" of the 1940s and 1950s.

At the same time, piecing together the divergent experiences and perspectives of these informants into an overarching account of the mica industry was difficult. I kept looking for more sources, more insight into how this industry meshed with lives and political economies in western Carolina for the first half of the twentieth century. Someone recommended Royce Payne as an expert on mica and the history of western North Carolina.[3] Then in his eighties, he was also the son of an entrepreneur who had started a mica business in the early 1900s. His Moth Hill Mica Company continued to operate despite the declining market for mica.

I spoke with Royce Payne, who was accompanied by his wife and grandson, on a rainy Friday night and then not again for several years. By the time I returned, Royce Payne was no longer actively involved in the daily affairs of the mica company, whose management had transferred to a younger generation of Paynes. In short, Royce Payne was prepared to talk at length about the history of mica and the company his father had started. I interviewed him six times for several hours at a time during the course of six weeks. We talked about his family, his father's start in mica, the mica industry's contributions to the regional economy, the Civil War, the building of railroad systems over the treacherous landscape of the western counties, and much more. Finally, Royce suggested that I tour the factory with his son, who managed the major operation. It was the opening for which I had long waited.

Royce Payne's son, John Walter, was many things, but by all accounts, including his father's, an entrepreneur was not one of them. He had left his own work in emergency medical services behind and had come into the mica business out of a sense of obligation to his father and the Payne legacy. Consequently, John Walter Payne managed his father's "plate mica division" in a manner variously described as lackadaisical and flexible. It was in this context that he gave me an initial tour of all the facilities at Moth Hill: the central offices where the secretary and the bookkeeper worked and where John Walter and his cousin Ed Payne were located; the department known as the "Lower End," which housed the punch presses and equipment to fabricate "rings" and segments; "Upstairs," which was the department where women engaged in hand labor, assembling pieces of mica onto sticky sheets of plastic or paper; the "Upper End," which housed machinery to produce "micanite," or laminated mica plate, drums of shellac and other laminants, and huge presses to squeeze excess liquid from the sheets of laminated mica. Across the road was another building where the "pure mica" operations, which had been the hallmark of the past, continued on a considerably smaller scale. It was the only time I was permitted complete access to the factory, but shortly thereafter I received permission to conduct field research in the division that John Walter Payne managed.

Sanctioned as it was by Royce Payne and mediated by his son, my entry into Moth Hill thus immediately established a gulf between the undertakings of factory employees and my interests as an observer. As a result of my tour and conversations with John Walter, I was identified with the elite that ran the factory. Doubtless, factory workers had also watched my visits to Royce Payne's house, across the river from Moth Hill, and had speculated about my purposes there. There was, indeed, little possibility for anonymity in a factory with fifty employees, many of whom had worked there for thirty years or more (and many of those of lesser tenure had been preceded by family members). One came to work for Moth Hill as a neighbor or a kinsperson but never as a stranger.

Fieldwork in the Plant

It was no surprise, then, that factory workers viewed me with some skepticism. Who were my people, they asked, and where did they live? What church did I belong to? I answered their questions forthrightly, in the process revealing the distance between my origins in urban Virginia and their lives in the North Carolina mountains. I also tried to explain my presence by identifying myself as a schoolteacher who had to complete a project for an advanced degree and thereby keep her job. My research, however, was subject to just as many questions. Factory workers wondered, as had Royce Payne, why I would choose such a topic. More to the point, why would I willingly enter a factory building in such poor shape, and with so many health hazards associated with the work that took place there, for the sake of a research project?

Only after I was befriended by two women, who worked in different departments within the factory, did I begin to have any real sense of the ways that Moth Hill employees interpreted my identity. Hazel Roberts, who had worked at the factory for thirteen years and was highly regarded by her peers, took it upon herself to establish connections with this peculiar visitor. As she later told me and the managers who were standing nearby: "It didn't take me all that long to figure out you wasn't that interested in mica. I figured you was lonely." Through my affiliation with Hazel Roberts and her co-workers on "the Upper End"—Zona Watson, Frances Stokes, Gertie Russell, and Annie Burleson—I found a place within Moth Hill. Hazel Roberts told me that Moth Hill employees distrusted me because I had "no people here." In effect, she became my family by "taking [me] home" to meet her parents and brother, thereby initiating a pattern of regular visits for meals and conversations.[4] Hazel also brought me to her church, Long Hill Baptist, and introduced me to other members of her congregation. We talked regularly on the telephone about the politics of Moth Hill, as well as topics further removed from the daily grind, and she interceded on my behalf at the factory.

Put another way, my entree came through management, but the employees determined whether, and how, I would be able to do field research within the plant. I learned this lesson in very concrete terms when, one month into my research, members of the Upper End kidded me about being an "industrial spy." Although the charge seemed ludicrous insofar as the technologies used by the company were neither sophisticated nor recent inventions, and the comments on the Upper End were lighthearted, the joke rebounded through the factory and demonstrated the fragility of my ties there.

The crisis was resolved when June Robbins, a friend and member of another factory department, suggested that I pay a visit to Royce Payne. What

I learned during my visit was that factory workers had come to John Walter and Muriel Payne, another factory owner, with questions about my presence at Moth Hill. They raised this concern with Royce: to a portion of the workforce I was someone who had gone into the plant with approval of the Paynes but with no real reason for being there.

I learned from Royce Payne that three decades earlier, at the height of the government efforts to promote mica, such a "spy" had visited the factory, waiting until the second shift to spend time with the workers and find out about Moth Hill's productive processes for another manufacturer. If little had changed by way of technology in the intervening decades—Moth Hill's hold on the declining market of the 1980s lay in its ability to harness the energies of its workforce in labor-intensive processes—what lingered from that earlier experience was a sense of precariousness. The viability of the mica business, the status of production orders, and the stability of employment were closely tied in the rhetoric of managers and employees alike, as I came to understand more and more during my fieldwork. The joking accusation about industrial spies was a way of warning me early on that these were very real considerations. "You know how rumors get started," Royce Payne observed. We parted on amicable terms—Royce having regaled me with stories of his prowess with a rifle and other tales of his youth—but I knew I had come close to being denied reentry to the factory. On my return to the factory the next day June Robbins and her co-workers on the "Lower End" told me how they'd seen my car in Royce's driveway "almost to quitting time." That episode provided a lot of valuable lessons about negotiations within the factory and presaged my dependence on the women who had extended kindness and aid when I needed them most.

And it wasn't just my background and the "spy" suspicions about me that made me so conspicuous at Moth Hill. If you wanted a job at there, you went through kin and neighbors, and that's how you kept it as well. You could not make it without finding out from older, experienced hands how things went, and you had to demonstrate a willingness to operate through established channels of authority. Furthermore, declaring yourself trustworthy was hardly enough: young hands had to display their loyalties in the daily routines of the factory. The latter principle presented problems for the fieldworker or the factory worker who wanted to get along with everyone, because the departments had established exclusionary networks. Enveloped by a complex system of alliances and antagonisms, *not* as a lone individual, a Moth Hill employee then negotiated the politics of job assignments, production decisions, and interactions with co-workers. What had saved me from being ousted, I am sure, was June Robbins's willingness to give me advice (and, in this way, serve as a mediator within the factory) and my responsiveness to her suggestion.

I cannot claim to have understood all this at the time; however, I did realize that to continue at the factory meant associating myself with a specific departmental network and conferring regularly with senior women. Although I continued to visit different parts of the factory, I did not move about freely. Following the practice of friends and kin of Moth Hill employees, rather than attempt to punch in or out of the factory with the first (and, at that point, only) shift, I came in informally and hung out with the people I knew. I visited first with June Robbins on the Lower End and then went off to see Hazel Roberts and her colleague, Frances Stokes, during the second half of the shift. Hazel, Frances, and I took dinner together, sharing food and eating on top of the plate-making machines where they worked or heading outdoors if the weather permitted. When Frances or Hazel was "sent Upstairs" because not enough orders had come in to keep her occupied on the Upper End, I would follow her there—at least for a while.

My interactions with male factory workers were likewise circumscribed. According to local conventions about gender, casual conversation between unrelated men and women, even in a public space, carried the suggestion of sexual interest. Women did not initiate contact with men who were not their kin, nor did they venture into male domains, within the plant or beyond. Thus, when Hazel Roberts told me that she wanted to check on the health of a male co-worker but couldn't because "it just ain't right," she also warned me not to contact her sometimes-boyfriend. In a tone that was only half-joking, she said, "You [call him] and I'll beat your brains all over the road 'till you don't have any left. Then I'll pick you up off the road." It was slightly less complicated to talk with male supervisors, who had regular dealings with the women and men employed in their departments, as well as management, and could be engaged in discussions about productive processes or the status of work orders. To the extent that I made contact with male laborers, I accomplished this by going through women who were kin or co-workers and by holding conversations in their presence. I listened to what Hazel had to say.

I made alliances through my readiness to work. When I assisted Gertie Russell and Hazel Roberts in a particularly frustrating round with one mica plate machine (and "bad mica"), and wound up with my hands in a vat of varnish, Gertie was impressed. She later told Hazel, out of my hearing, that I wasn't "afraid to get [my] hands dirty." I also helped when the women worked on the "flexible," a custom-made mica plate (mica laminated with varnish or resins to make it adhere as a sheet) that required additional hand labor to pull out "trash"—bad mica, or pieces of broom, or even Indian coins and paper that spoke to the origins of this mica—and patch the holes with "good mica." That was one of my favorite jobs because many hands were required, including those of Zona Watson, who was in her seventies and semi-retired, and the conversation flowed. In the department Upstairs I was encouraged to try "laying mica by hand," no easy feat because the mica was slippery and of inconsistent size and quality, while the plastic backing on which the pieces were to be spread out, like a deck of cards, was sticky with varnish and unforgiving of human error. And although I sometimes laid the mica pieces at odds with my partner, who was sitting across from me and working the other side of that three-foot square of plastic, I received (indirectly) the praise of one of the more experienced hands and made greater inroads in establishing friendships there.

On the Lower End I would sometimes assist June Robbins as she sorted bad "washers" (parts punched out from the "plate" made in the other departments) from the good. Quality control at Moth Hill involved sifting out trash in the form of oddly shaped pieces of mica plate, occasionally "mashing" or putting pressure on washers to see if they would hold together, and visually comparing the lot to a template of the part in question. Because the latter activity required an acuity for which I was ill prepared, I simply sat and watched. June Robbins told John Walter Payne that I wasn't afraid of "rough work" and should be given a part-time job on the Lower End. June told John Walter that I knew a lot about the plant because I had even studied the books that Arval Gardner, supervisor on the Lower End, used. She argued persuasively, and then the subject was changed to something less serious. When Arval later asked me if I wanted a job, I said I might be interested—but I really hoped that the opportunity would never materialize. "'Mites' is for chickens," he told me, meaning that I was to commit myself to the Lower End or pass it by. Arval and June undoubtedly perceived my declining of their offer as a slight, as much as I tried to downplay that aspect. At the same time, this event may have created inroads for me Upstairs and on the Upper End, where workers were more welcoming of my presence and expressed antipathy toward the Lower End.

On Friday afternoons, when women performed janitorial duties in preparation for the weekend, I helped sweep the floors. Clearly, participation in work efforts did not transform my awkward status as observer in the factory, but it did offset some of the distance that separated me from Moth Hill employees. During these activities the women I worked with in various departments, upstairs and down, were more than willing to answer my questions and to volunteer information. Discussions turned to issues of occupational safety and health, health problems of workers within the plant, pro-

duction orders, management directives, the possibility of layoffs, gender relations on the shop floor, work histories, families, community life, and the
Paynes themselves. Workers were forthcoming with questions of their own
as, for example, when several women who were members of local Baptist
churches inquired about the odd traditions of the Episcopal Church—from
the baptism of infants to the rites of confirmation and "holy communion"—
in which I had been raised. I asked the women at Moth Hill about mica work
and social networks and growing up in the mountains; they in turn were
interested in my life story.

There were also questions that I was not allowed to ask, events and issues
about which I knew only fragments. For example, I never understood why
Hazel, Frances, and I boycotted a birthday celebration for one of the workers Upstairs. Birthdays were occasions for ice cream and cake and were generally something that workers enjoyed. I realized that a political statement
was being made, but I never knew just what it was we were saying or to whom
or whether this had specifically to do with me. Similarly, when the son of the
supervisor from the Upper End got married and had a wedding shower, Hazel
and I were the only people from the department to attend. Both Carl Fisher
and his son, Jack, who also worked in the factory, appeared to be well liked
by their co-workers. Why did no one show? Would it have been any different if a "household shower" had been held in the plant, as was done for Belle
Stokes from Upstairs when she moved into a new trailer? Had Gertie Russell and Annie Burleson, senior women on the Upper End, quietly denied that
possibility to their boss? Life on the shop floor, and away from it, was seemingly characterized by tensions and ambiguities.

My field research at Moth Hill suddenly came to an end on April 18, 1988,
when I received a phone call. "Why are you going to Moth Hill so much?" a
low voice demanded of me. "Who is asking me?" I replied. The caller identified herself as Muriel Payne and reminded me that she was part owner of
the company. She continued, "Now, why are you still going to Moth Hill? I
never heard of such a thing. You have been going there for a year now. What
do you want?" We talked about my research, the interviews that I had conducted with her and the dissertation that I planned to write for my advisers
back in New York, but the message was, "Don't go back in there."

In a subsequent conversation Hazel Roberts explained the situation by
saying, "It's tax time, honey, and they're at it." Word had spread around the
Upper End the previous day that something was up between the Paynes and
me. Once Muriel Payne notified the front office "to call the law" should I show
up there again, *that* news made its way through the plant. I was not the only
one affected, as at least one employee had been fired from the pure mica di-

vision at the same time, but these developments left me at a loss as to how to complete my research.[5]

My status as persona non grata at Moth Hill notwithstanding, I continued to interview factory workers in their homes, attend Long Hill Baptist Church on a regular basis, and visit Hazel and her family as well as Zona and Frances in their homes. I was allowed to finish all but two of the interviews that I had planned, and this I attribute to Hazel's interventions with her co-workers. At her suggestion I also wrote letters on college stationery (with "all the initials after [my] name") to Royce Payne, Muriel Payne, and the Moth Hill employees, thanking them for their participation in my research. My letter to the factory workers was posted near the time clock where workers punched in and out.

I left the field altogether in June 1988 but returned in the fall to present my research at the local community college. I invited people from the factory to attend and found Hazel Roberts and her mother; Frances Stokes; and Zona Watson, as well as several members of the Payne family, in the audience. Without identifying herself as a participant in my field research, Hazel Roberts engaged in the discussion that followed my talk and offered her perspective on the concerns of working-class women. Afterward, I asked Hazel, Frances, and Zona as well as the Paynes if they thought I had fairly represented mica work and the factory and was greatly relieved to receive their approval. Only then could I envision writing this ethnography.

In sum, I conducted field research at Moth Hill Mica Company from August 1987 through mid-April 1988. Three to five days a week, for six to seven hours at a time, I visited the factory, entering into conversations with groups of workers and conducting informal interviews with individual employees.[6] In this manner I was able to interview twelve of the sixteen men who worked in the main section of the factory: three unskilled workers, five skilled workers, two supervisors, and the two owner-managers.[7] I interviewed each supervisor and owner-manager at least three times during my fieldwork but conducted only one interview with the other male workers because conventions about gender segregation made further contact problematic.

I also interviewed women on an informal basis within the factory. This proved to be an important alternative for women reluctant to have me visit them at home and a counterbalance to the artificiality imposed by the tape recorder.[8] The limitation, however, was that I could not take notes in the factory and so had to depend on my memory until I could write up field notes for that day. Interviews at home were taped or, in two instances, transcribed at the time, and these are distinguished by being numbered. With respect to the twenty-five women who worked in the main building, I conducted semi-structured interviews with nine women in their homes, as well as at Moth Hill, and with eight women workers only in the factory. All told, I spoke with six workers from the Upstairs (including the only female supervisor in the factory), four women from the Lower End, the five women who worked on the Upper End, and the secretary and the bookkeeper in the main office. In addition, I interviewed one woman who had retired from her unskilled job at Moth Hill and one of the Payne women involved in managing the company but rarely present at the plant.

I asked general questions and allowed my informants to determine the direction of the interview. They were assertive about asking me questions of their own, as they had throughout the course of my research. Several women interviewed in their homes voiced concerns about how I might use the information that I had been gathering through my fieldwork. Anonymity was not the only important issue; they also were concerned about how I might represent factory workers in my writings and what bearing this would have on their employment at Moth Hill. Their comments, along with the observations of anthropologists about the "micropolitics of interviewing" and fieldwork practices, have been a significant influence on my approach to this material (Zavella 1987:26–28; see also Sanjek 1990 and M. Fine 1994).

In addition to June Robbins from the Lower End and Mae Webb, who worked Upstairs and was a close friend/mentor for Hazel Roberts, I relied most heavily on the women of the Upper End—Hazel Roberts, Frances Stokes, Zona Watson, Gertie Russell, and Annie Burleson—for their insights into factory relations and kin and community ties. Many of these women were in their fifties and sixties and still working full time at the factory. Zona Watson provided me with an oral history that extended and often countered Royce Payne's views on Clark County. She spoke of out-migration to the coalfields of West Virginia and the canning factories in Washington, D.C., circuit preachers, schooling in the early twentieth century, farming practices, intricacies of local kin networks, and the dignity of working-class life in the western Carolina mountains.

Looking to the Past

I came to Moth Hill with a keen interest in the history of women's labor in the mountains, and I left there all the more determined to put those eight months of conversation with factory workers into broader perspective. I can still hear Hazel declaring to everyone gathered in that community college auditorium: "Mountain women are strong! We could scratch a living off a rock if we had to." I think about how her early death stilled that remarkable life, only a small dimension of which could be described by the work that she did for the state minimum wage (and unemployment checks when orders were down). I am aware of the arduous circumstances that propelled Zona and Zeyland Watson across the country in search of work, then back to Moth Hill when the Paynes were hiring, and that brought Annie Burleson off her truck farm and into the factory. I remember Frances Stokes telling me how she prayed for a job so she could afford the "good Christian education" she wanted for her son, then asked her father to put a word in for her at Moth Hill.

I ponder Mae Webb's working for forty cents an hour fifty years ago—which, she said, went further than the $202 she earned for a week's labor in the late 1980s—while her husband tended the farm and took care of the kids. I recall the stories that Terri Watkins, June Robbins, Bonnie Lou Watkins, Frances Stokes, and others told of aunts and mothers who used to work at Moth Hill, as well as Royce Payne's tales about recruiting new employees by visiting with their kin down at the Oxford general store. And then I go back to the first reports about mica, related by those who worked as young girls and older women in the mica houses of the early 1900s.

My concern has been to place these narratives into perspective, first by acknowledging the basis for my own interpretations and the questions asked of me throughout the course of this field research. Describing those influences does not make this collaborative research, for the authority to write this account, and the mistakes, ultimately rest with me. That is something I learned from my informants and my encounter with shop-floor politics at Moth Hill.

Since completing the ethnographic research, I have focused on the history of mica and community relations in this part of Southern Appalachia. I have looked at county records and newspaper accounts pertaining to local industry, economic conditions, churches, histories of prominent families and settlements, race relations, and other dimensions of social and political life in the twentieth century. I have gone back to census records of the late nineteenth and early twentieth centuries to find out more about the intersections of domestic labors and "public work" in women's and men's occupations. Field notes recorded by geologists working for the U.S. Geological Survey, in combination with the professional papers produced by the USGS, constitute a set of archives on mica—including information on mine owners and laborers, as well as the yield of specific mineral deposits—that extend back to the 1860s. Those sources provide the foundation for the interpretations advanced here, in combination with recent writings that supplant ideas about "Appalachian exceptionalism" (D. Billings, Pudup, and Waller 1995:9, 14) with three-dimensional accounts about a vast and diverse region. Certainly, no one story can be told about the Blue Ridge Mountains, no simple truths about women's lives in or outside factory walls. Even mica, while a significant aspect of the economy and labor practices of nineteenth- and twentieth-century western Carolina, remains but one facet of an enigmatic past and an equally complicated future.

3. Carolina Mica

Now we've seen the mica business get *awfully* low. Mica business
got low in the '20s and right after World War I. Mica business got
low in the early '50s till the Korean War. It was low in the 1950s
'cause we'd caught up from that backlog in '45. And it got low in
'60 and '61, just before the Vietnam War—I'm telling you, it really
boomed then. It may come back again; some use may come for it.
But I can't see it. I'm no prophet; *I* can't see it.
—Interview 17

THROUGHOUT THE mica industry's 130-year history, some people have become millionaires, others have lost money, and still more simply made a living in the Blue Ridge.[1] In the latter half of the nineteenth century, elite residents of the area, merchants connected to regional markets, and northern
speculators alike recognized the abundance of mica deposits in the North
Carolina mountains and the profit to be made in extracting this resource.
During the century that followed, they developed mines, built roads and railroads to transport their yield, and established mica houses to convert the raw
materials into valuable commodities. For residents of more modest means,
mica was a source of "public work" that provided the wages they needed to
help maintain family farms or to support themselves if they had no land. Beyond sending unmarried daughters (and later wives) to labor in mica houses,
and sons or husbands to the mines, many households engaged in their own
small-scale operations that produced mica for barter at local stores as well as
for sale to the mica establishments. Some families endeavored to make their
fortunes by prospecting for those comparatively rare mineral deposits that
they could work into mines of great productivity *and* high-quality mica, and
they were aided, at various points, by government programs that loaned
money and equipment to exploratory efforts in mica mining.

However, the value of mica fluctuated dramatically in national and international markets and, as the opening epigraph suggests, boom periods were

invariably followed by times of steep recession. Working in mica was itself an unpredictable endeavor. Mica mines were not easy to locate; more often discovered by accident than shrewdness or logic, they could just as easily disappear when large deposits of mica suddenly "played out." Productive mines could also provide disappointing results if the mica they yielded was determined, after processing and further inspection, to have stains, cracks, or rifts and therefore minimal utility. To draw on the words of one informant, from the standpoint of individual prospectors and would-be entrepreneurs, mining mica was a lot like gambling: "You want to know if the next card you turn up . . . you're anxious to see the next card, to see if it will play somewhere. You're anxious to see it. Well, when you split that piece of mica, you're anxious to see what's down there. You may run into where it's pretty and solid, and you may run into where there's a grain or two . . . a piece of rock in it that ruins it, or you may run into a wave in it, or something or other. You're always anxious to see" (interview 19).

Competition from nations in Africa, South America, and Asia—particularly India, whose mica was considered by some buyers to be superior to domestic versions in both quality and cost—raised the stakes even higher. Whether a fascination, a gamble, a disease, or simply a business—as mica has been variously described—neither the benefits nor the risks of mining were shared equally. Throughout the turbulent history of mica local entrepreneurs and venture capitalists made considerable profits from their involvement in this industry, while they have, in literal and metaphorical terms, rearranged the mountains of North Carolina.

This chapter follows three threads in the history of western Carolina mica: the place of the mineral in international, national, and regional markets and politics; the activities of speculators and entrepreneurs to establish mica commerce in the mountains; and the experiences of women and men who labored in the early days of mica. The myriad activities generated by processes of obtaining, selling, and working in mica were for many decades a crucial, if unstable, component of local economies in western Carolina. Yet their effect on people and communities in the mountains, more than political economic conditions per se, is the focus of this discussion. Indeed, the starting point for my ethnographic research was not so much a fascination with mica as attention to the comments of older women who proudly told of how they had contributed to their parents' farms or helped build their own houses from money that they earned in mica factories. The story of mica thus illustrates the long-standing significance of women's labor, and the intricacies of gender and class relations in Southern Appalachia, not a break with traditions of the past.

Nineteenth-Century Commerce in the Mountains

To trace the origins of the mica industry requires us to move our historical inquiries even further into the past, to the middle of the nineteenth century when merchants and entrepreneurs first developed an interest in this mineral. At that time western Carolina was connected to the national economy through extensive trade networks organized around the export of various commodities produced in the mountains, as well as the importing of goods like coffee vital to the consumption patterns of residents (McKinney 1988; Anglin ethnographic interviews; see also Dunaway 1996). Such endeavors as farming, driving stock, manufacturing durable goods, timbering, land speculation, mining, collecting plants for sale to floral and pharmaceutical companies, artisanal work, domestic labor, tourism, peddling, and establishing mercantile enterprises comprised the foundation for regional and local economies and helped shape social relations in western North Carolina.

While many mountain households farmed primarily for purposes of meeting their own subsistence needs, they were neither self-sufficient nor removed from the marketplace (see Crawford 1991; Deyton 1947; Inscoe 1989; Mann 1992; and McKinney 1988, 1995).[2] Tenant farmers and sharecroppers, who made up nearly a quarter of farming households in mid-nineteenth-century western North Carolina, produced agricultural commodities for the profit of their landlords and only secondarily for their own purposes (Dunaway 1996:92; see also J. D. Reid 1976). Within the local economy poor and "middling" households bartered agricultural goods for the coffee, sugar, salt, and cloth that they did not produce. Poor and middling, as well as wealthier, farmers grew cash crops for sale to merchants in nearby towns such as Knoxville or Asheville and to markets farther away in Charleston and Savannah. Those with lesser means pooled their resources to pay the wagoners to haul their goods to market (Deyton 1947:453; Dykeman 1955; Inscoe 1989). Farmers in western North Carolina also sold feed corn and other grains to drovers who herded livestock through the mountains, on their way to the markets of the lowland South (Deyton 1947; Wellman 1973). And, indeed, western Carolina livestock made up a considerable part of that traffic (Clingman 1877; Deyton 1947; Inscoe 1989; McDonald and McWhiney 1975).

Households contributed to the economy of nineteenth-century western North Carolina through yet other means. In addition to providing laborers for area farms and business enterprises that might require them, often on a temporary or seasonal basis, households engaged in small-scale production of goods for sale as well as for barter with merchants. Such "homemade manufactures" encompassed a broad range of commodities that included

textiles, wearing apparel, household implements, and "necessities and comforts," in addition to furniture, farm tools, and building supplies.[3] Like the
"market garden produce" listed in census records of the mid-nineteenth century (U.S. Census Bureau 1860), and arguably agricultural production taken
as a whole, these were economic activities in which women's—as well as
men's—labor figured significantly.[4]

Moreover, not all labor was freely given. In addition to indentured servitude and the practice of "apprenticing" young children to court-appointed
masters who claimed their labor in return for board and the promise of an
education, slavery was an integral part of the economies of antebellum Southern Appalachia.[5] While elites in western North Carolina held smaller numbers of slaves and traded in slaves to a lesser degree than their peers elsewhere
in the South, they nonetheless relied on slave labor to support agricultural
production on their farmlands.[6] Given the relatively small scale of mountain
farms, however, more important to elites was the use of slave labor in non-
agricultural activities such as manufacturing and mercantile enterprises.
Slaves were made to produce goods (from bricks and iron to wagon wheels
to plugs of tobacco to men's clothing, hats, and shoes), assist shop owners,
and engage in maintenance work of various kinds (Inscoe 1989:68–91). The
domestic labor of female slaves likewise sustained the small number of ho-
tels in the region and the many households that kept boarders (Anglin 1995).
In these diverse capacities slaves helped their masters establish and/or sus-
tain profitable businesses and, along with the practices of apprenticeship and
indentured servitude, served as precedents for the coercive labor practices
that followed (see, for example, Dawley 1912).

It was in the context of this mixture of productive activities, labor strategies, and economic resources that the mica industry commenced in western
North Carolina soon after the end of the Civil War. Farmers and would-be
entrepreneurs looked to the mountains as the source of raw materials—animal, vegetable, and mineral—that they could process and ship with agricultural produce to regional markets or trade with local merchants for other
commodities. Local elites, for their part, sought to open up the western half
of the state to extractive industries and other forms of commerce, thereby
increasing their own revenues. This they achieved by promoting the region's
assets to out-of-state investors, directing their energies to the construction
of a railroad system that would transport commodities in and out of the
mountains, and forming political alliances with members of the elite in the
eastern half of North Carolina (Inscoe 1989:117–20, 1984:149, 152, 166–67;
McKinney 1988:14–15; Bannister, Cowan, and Co. 1869; Clingman 1877; Wray
1931; Anglin ethnographic interviews).

Perhaps the most powerful booster was Thomas Lanier Clingman, who drew upon his experience in the U.S. Congress and his ties across the State of North Carolina in locating an audience for his advertisements about the western counties.[7] In a letter written to the North Carolina Land Company, for example, Clingman (1877:122) described the high mountains as an area where "a horse will often sink to his fetlocks in a thick, black, vegetable mould and the growth, whether timber, grass or weeds, appears to be as luxuriant as in the swamps of the low country." Clingman concluded his letter of April 7, 1869, with the following observations:

> The prices of land throughout this entire region are very moderate compared with those of similar lands in the Northern states, while the population, though sparse, is quiet, orderly, and moral. The negroes [*sic*], not constituting one-tenth of the entire population, are scarcely an appreciable element. Emigrants with little capital can easily obtain the necessities of life, and may at once commence the business of stock raising, and cheese, butter and wool, and such agricultural productions as will best bear transportation. Manufacturing and mining operations will soon follow these branches of industry. I have no doubt that if the people of the Northern States knew this region as I do they would move down in large bodies immediately to take possession of it. (124)

Not only the fertility of the soil and plentiful supplies of timber, minerals, and flora were noteworthy. Part of the "natural wealth" (Bannister, Cowan, and Co. 1869:79) that the mountains offered were its residents, cast as being in need of employment; capable of hard work; "quiet, orderly, and moral"; and—significant to supporters of the Confederacy, as Clingman had been— of predominantly Euro-American origins and ethnic identities.[8] Given abundant natural resources, a tractable population, and the prospects for agriculture and manufacturing, the North Carolina mountains thus provided the setting for the wealthy citizen "to place there his charming villa" and the industrious to make money (Clingman 1877:124).

Clingman was interested in the geology of the mountains, particularly the prospect of locating silver deposits of sufficient scope to warrant further investigation, if not full-scale mining. To this end he embarked upon various expeditions to investigate the mineral resources of western North Carolina and consulted with other miners and experts in geology on his findings.[9] Clingman failed to unearth evidence of workable silver ore, but he did discover substantial mica deposits and a number of mines, some of which were abandoned and others actively worked at the time of his visits in 1867 and 1868: "There seems no doubt but that there is a tract of country of more than one hundred and fifty miles in extent capable of producing good mica, in quantities sufficient to supply a very large demand. Should that demand continue, these mines might be worked profitably to the depth of a thousand feet or more, and for centuries to come" (132–33).

While Clingman and L. E. Persons of Philadelphia are credited with opening up the North Carolina mountains to intensive efforts in mica prospecting (Stuckey 1965:416–17; Sterrett 1923:167–68), others were involved in inaugurating "modern" mica mining.[10] Benjamin Franklin Butler, a member of the U.S. House of Representatives and a colleague of Clingman's from the State of North Carolina, organized the Mountain Mining Company in 1868 to explore the western counties for gems and precious metals. Like Clingman, Butler soon became involved in mica as an offshoot of these endeavors (Padgett 1943:158, 173–74). Then too, Union sympathizers traveling through western North Carolina had learned of the wealth of minerals that the mountains held, and they returned after the Civil War to capitalize on their knowledge:

> I guess you heard that story about Robert Murfree's grandfather, Mr. Stewart, Mr. Rodger Stewart . . . running [an] underground railroad during the Civil War. . . . He would keep these Yankee prisoners that had gotten loose, gotten away, or Yankee sympathizers or somebody who had got cut off from their unit. He would hide them of a day and then tell them to travel a certain way at night and tell them who would hide them the next day, you see. Underground railroad. Well, some of those men, then, came back later on after the war was over with and started mining. That is true. (interview 17)

Just how many Yankee speculators came back to seek their fortunes in mica is not evident, nor are the results of these early efforts well known. Stewart was successful in establishing a mica mine with the help of northern capital.

However, it was two Knoxville, Tennessee, merchants who turned mica mining in the Blue Ridge into a substantial enterprise. They became aware of Clingman's finds in 1868 when he engaged a drover to haul the best of the mica blocks, along with his livestock, to the markets of Knoxville. John R. Heap and his partner, Elisha Clapp, were dealers in tinware and stoves (which used isinglass, or mica, for oven windows) and could appreciate the quality of the mica crystals that Clingman had sent to market. Shortly thereafter, they dispensed with the Knoxville business and set to prospecting in the North Carolina mountains (Stuckey 1965:417). Others followed their example or— like Stewart and the local elites that had come to Clingman's attention—simply continued their own activities. Clingman, however, had little interest in the mica trade and continued his search for silver and emeralds.[11]

The Wealth of the Mountains

The burgeoning mica industry had significance for nonelite residents of Southern Appalachia, especially during Reconstruction when mountain communities—as elsewhere in the South—contended with the disruptions in commerce and livelihood that were the legacy of the Civil War. Day laborers found mica work in 1870 to be slightly better paid than the iron mines nearby, where "wages are low and the miners are not able to sufficiently clothe their children to send them to school." Like the iron mines, however, employment in mica was unsteady: "In the mica mines in this country, good hands get from 80 cents to $1.00 per day, but they are not working full time now" ("Laborers' Views" 1989). For those with access to mica-rich land and the means to work it, small-scale, informal mining endeavors of their own, otherwise known as "groundhogging" operations, were more profitable (Sterrett 1923:20–21).[12] Operators of small mines could sell their mica directly to mica dealers or to local merchants. Certainly, by 1874 the merchandise offered by Asheville's general stores featured mica, as an Englishwoman made evident in her travel narrative for the *London Daily News* of August 8, 1874: "All the shops are general shops. I have gone to buy a bit of ribbon, and have seen horrible raw hides, barrels of nails, meat, groceries, and every imagineable [*sic*] thing for sale, including, perhaps, masses of mica, which is found in the neighborhood and the roads sparkle with it everywhere" (quoted in Dykeman 1955:59).

Nonetheless, in the early days of the mica industry the market for the nonmetallic mineral was limited. As glazing for gas lamps and stove windows, mica was quite effective, for it was a pliant and translucent material that transmitted light without radiating heat. Gas lamps in Paris, as well as in U.S. cities, cast their light through North Carolina mica (Anglin ethnographic interviews). The problem was that this application could use only large pieces of the mineral—split into very fine sheets—and mica crystals of this size were comparatively rare. In other words, beyond the difficulties inherent in finding mica deposits was the problem of finding deposits that produced crystals suitable for commercial use. Mining often meant creating large quantities of what was then considered worthless mica (Stuckey 1965:413).

Thomas Edison's invention of the electric motor in 1878 changed all that (Skow 1962:30). His invention required high-quality insulating material that could withstand extreme heat and repeated bombardment by high voltages. Mica easily met these specifications, and so a new market was created for the industry (Jahns and Lancaster 1952:2, 4–5, 16–17; Stuckey 1965:410–13). Most important, smaller pieces of mica proved nearly as usable as larger ones in this new application, diminishing, if not eliminating, the problem of "waste" mica. Mica mining became more profitable as a result of these developments, and as the 1880 census revealed, growing numbers of Pike and Clark countians were taking up this occupation.[13] They explored new mines and redeveloped old ones in the decades that followed.

Some mines worked during this period were quite prolific. One mine is said to have produced $10,000 worth of mica by 1886, while the yield of another mica mine up to 1893 was estimated at $75,000, and still another mine produced $175,000 worth of mica between 1870 and 1896 (van Noppen and van Noppen 1973:352; Sterrett 1923:245). And although mica deposits typically yielded small crystals—the average commercial "book" was "about 5 inches across and one-fifth to one-half as thick as it is wide"—some crystals were of legendary proportions (Lesure 1968:16). One mica block is said to have weighed a ton and was so large that "six men were able to dance on this crystal at one time" (Sterrett 1923:260). According to W. C. Kerr, the state geologist for North Carolina, "I have known a single block of mica to make two full two-horse wagonloads, and sheets of mica are sometimes obtained that measure three and four feet in diameter" (1880:459). Between 1867 and 1882 about 400,000 pounds of mica, valued at $800,000, were mined and processed in North Carolina. Most of that mica came from properties owned by Heap and Clapp, whose mica ventures proved quite profitable (Sterrett 1923:168; Stuckey 1965:417).

At the same time, production figures for the 1880s and 1890s suggest problematic trends for the mica industry. In 1880, 40 tons of rough-cut and trimmed mica—valued at $127,825—were extracted from mines throughout the United States, chiefly in North Carolina.[14] In 1884 U.S. production yielded 74 tons worth $368,525; however, in 1886 mica production plummeted to 20 tons valued at only $70,000 (Stuckey 1965:412–13).[15] Mica production continued to fluctuate, increasing to 38 tons worth $100,000 in 1892, only to decline by more than half in the next two years (Chowdhury 1941:144–45).

These boom-and-bust cycles reflected problems in mining; technical limitations, particularly with respect to the size and "grade," or purity, of domestic mica; and, last but hardly least, the limited market for this commodity.[16] Then too, the emergence of India in 1885 as a source of relatively inexpensive high-quality mica had immediate ramifications for the mica industry of the United States.[17] So significant was India as a source of mica that the United States imposed a tariff on foreign mica in 1890, and it has remained in place ever since (Chowdhury 1941:146–48; Sterrett 1923:19–20; U.S. Tariff Commission 1938, 1947).

India's importance as a supplier of mica was not simply due to the abundance of good mica to be found in the mines of Bihar and Orissa, Andhra Pradesh, or Rajasthan (Chowdhury 1941; Murthy 1964; Rajgarhia 1951; Spence 1912). To the contrary, research conducted by the U.S. Geological Survey shows that North Carolina mica and Indian mica were comparable in both quality and quantity (interview 28; see also U.S. Bureau of Mines, *Minerals Yearbook* 1942:1522). The advantage that India enjoyed was based primarily on the costs of production, particularly the price of labor, which rendered Indian mica vastly less expensive than Appalachian mica.[18]

Production costs proved a vital factor in the mica industry, chiefly because of the peculiar nature of the mineral. Because mica ran in deposits of irregular sizes and shapes, and was brought out in blocks that then had to be cleaned, trimmed, split, and graded according to size and quality of the sheet, mica mining and processing were not operations that could be easily mechanized: "You can't build machinery to work mica. There's not anything made like hosiery machines or textiles" (interview 19; see also interviews 17 and 22). Rather, this was a labor-intensive industry, with wages figuring heavily in the costs associated with mica fabrication.[19] What profits could be made in mica consequently derived from the use of underpaid skilled and semiskilled labor, as well as minimal investment in production facilities (Labour Bureau 1972).

That the U.S. mica industry did not die out entirely with the importation of mica from India was the result of several factors: the successful imposition of tariffs on mica from international sources, political factors that rendered foreign sources of mica not completely dependable, and the machinations of domestic mica companies.[20] Since the turn of the century, certainly, India had become a major supplier of mica used in the United States (Murdock 1942:1; Spence 1912:21–23, 45–46; U.S. Tariff Commission 1938:100–105). Nonetheless, domestic mica production reached new heights in the twentieth century, because of the factors noted earlier and developments in electrical technology that created further applications for mica. The invention of the radio, for example, led to the use of mica in the tubes and condensers that formed the basis for this device.[21] Similarly, mica became an important component in instrument panels for airplanes and electric trains and in Alexander Graham Bell's telephone—technologies that, together with the radio, transformed the political economy and cultural practices of the United States.[22] Entrepreneurs in North Carolina responded to these opportunities by establishing mica houses, early variants of processing factories, to produce for the emerging market.

Mica Houses and Factories

Like many mica companies in western North Carolina, Moth Hill Mica Company began in the early decades of the new century and was based on a combination of northern capital and local knowledge. One of that company's founders, Daniel Payne, had been born amid the wreckage of the Civil War. In the words of Payne's son (and successor in the mica factory), "He was a remarkable man in a way. Without bragging, I don't want to do that, but he was born right after the Civil War here, and this was a poverty-stricken country then. . . . There was no money, no schools, no nothing. . . . He was of a family of twelve children. And all the boys, when they'd get eighteen years old, they'd leave home" (interview 16). Daniel Payne received an eighth-grade education, as had his brothers, and made his start as a merchant "buying galax and different roots and herbs from local people, and shipping them to Philadelphia and New York" (interview 17).

During his travels north Payne learned of the ready market for mica and began mining mica on land acquired through purchase or lease. In the narrow storage space of a springhouse "not near as big as this room," he employed an "elderly" white man and, in a move emblematic of the legacies of slavery, a "big, fat, strong black girl" to cut the mica into marketable shapes (interview 17).[23] This young woman is the only person of color known to have worked in a mica house and only at its inception, when working conditions were the most rudimentary.[24] Daniel Payne and other entrepreneurs hired African American men to work in mica mines, however, and the ironworks nearby was reported to have a section of company houses known as "Little Africa" where laborers of color resided.

Payne prevailed upon one of his contacts in New York to find customers for fabricated mica parts and shortly thereafter established a business partnership and a corporation by the name of Moth Hill Mica: "[Jackson, the New York contact] was interested in mica, and my father was shipping him some mica. He was shipping it on overseas or wherever he could sell it. [Jackson] got interested in forming a company, so they formed Moth Hill Mica Company" (interview 16). Moth Hill "imported" a family of experienced mica cutters from a county nearby and intensified its production of fabricated mica. In place of the small log "mica house" that had replaced the earlier springhouse operations, "they had built a big wooden building down here for the Moth Hill Mica Company" (interview 17).

Trimming and sheeting mica, sorting it into commercial grades, and cutting it into pieces as large as possible and still free of defects required considerable skill. Moth Hill employed both men and women to perform those tasks, but only men ran the big kick presses that punched out washers to be used as insulation in electric motors and telephones, among other things. When Moth Hill expanded its punching operations and changed to more efficient equipment, it hired women as competent, reliable, and, above all, inexpensive labor:

> Women would run the power shears, all they had to do is stick a piece of mica under it now and mash the pedal. A woman could do any job over there as good as a man.
> [Interviewer]: Were there more women hired, or were there more men?
> Oh yeah, more women. Many more women.
> [Interviewer]: And why did you hire women for those—
> You could hire them cheaper. You still can, but it's not right. Isn't that what you folks were fussing about? (interview 18; see also interviews 22 and 35)

Women outnumbered their male co-workers by as much as 10 to 1 in mica houses of the early twentieth century (interview 35). This redefined labor relations, according to the older women who provided oral histories of mica work in the 1920s, 1930s, and 1940s.[25] While men were still called upon to grade and sheet mica as skilled processes, they were hired primarily to "wait on the machines"—bringing mica to be punched out on the presses, carrying away the waste mica, and making repairs when the equipment broke down (interview 33). Older women too trimmed and sheeted mica, while unmarried women and girls as young as twelve ran punch presses, operated by a foot pedal, to cut mica into various kinds of parts. As Nolda Stokes explained it:

> Now when you cut disks, they'd come down. You'd have a box under there somewhere. It'd fall into the box. Now washers and things like that, we'd have the barrel settin' under the machine.

> Yeah, and I cut—now mica'd be fixed for you when you cut that up—the shape of a fish. I cut that, and the shape of an orange, and different things, you know. . . . I cut them little bitty washers. That's the one that I'd hold the pedal down and let it run. Just keep it moving, hold the pedal. (interview 2)

Although the women were supposed to work as quickly as they could, the irregularities of the mica meant a good deal of hand labor. If the piece of mica was too thick, they had to split it further into sheets thin enough to put in the machine to punch. When they had to make certain disks of clear mica, according to Stokes, women would have to inspect the mica carefully and work around any stains in the pieces they were punching: "Well, there's a certain lot you was a-cuttin', some you cut. When you cut this, it had to be clear, with nothing on it, it *had* to be clear" (interview 2). Nor could the mica contain cracks or rifts that might compromise its function as insulating material. As Ruby Johnson emphasized, this added another dimension to the work performed by women on the punch presses: "You couldn't have no cracks in it, nowhere, for the round disks, I think. Or in the [parts used in electric] irons. . . . We had to sort it. Yeah, we checked each one before we'd cut it on the machine" (interview 3). Further, workers had to put the mica into the presses "the right way," or they would "spoil it" by creating nicks and cracks in the pieces they cut (interview 33). Above all, women were to be economical, taking two to three pounds of mica on their lapboards at a time and working it up into as many disks or washers or ornaments as possible: "You got, you had to have so many pounds. And they even checked to see if you was wasteful with what you cut, and let hauled through that machine, if you let any go through that could have been another washer or two" (interview 3). A young boy was paid to sort through the waste mica and retrieve pieces that might be amenable to further punching. These were handed back to the women operating the presses, and doubtless the supervisor was made aware of such omissions.

Work days were long in the early decades of mica industry, before the reforms of the National Recovery Administration (NRA) in 1934: ten hours, excluding a half hour for dinner at noon and the long walks home over the mountains. "I know we'd start before daylight, and it'd be getting about dark when we'd quit of an evening in the wintertime. We'd work ten hours a day. . . . When I wasn't married, I was living up there with my daddy and mama. Well, we'd start walking, and sometimes maybe we'd get a ride. When we didn't, we walked" (interview 2). The buildings could be drafty and cold in the wintertime, particularly in the most rudimentary of mica houses. There, I was told, women workers had to pull their frozen skirts away from the floor when they got up from their work tables and punch presses.[26] However, the primary hazard that women described was losing fingers when the punch presses jammed, as routinely happened. From the vantage point of Nolda Stokes, it took ingenuity and defiance by workers to avoid injuries of this kind because the mica companies did little to prevent them:

> But they, they's bad to double trip, though. Georgie said she was workin' on one [press] that, she was cuttin' something, anyway, she'd have to put her hand in there. . . . And she said it was double trippin'. She said she wasn't going to work on that machine. There was another girl, I forget who they put on that machine. Georgie said she wasn't on there ten minutes 'til she cut her finger off and it fell into the box!
> [Interviewer]: Oh! Did they fix the machine then?
> Well, they worked on them, but they'd still double trip. The one [I worked on],

I had to put my fingers through there and place my mica. I'd always stick my
foot under my pedal to keep it locked so it wouldn't trip. (interview 2)

This hazard persisted throughout most of the twentieth century, until the
Occupational Safety and Health Administration required mica companies to
install guards on punch presses and shears. Even then the guards could do
little to protect hands that had to move fast and often *into* the equipment.

Long hours, hazards, and handwork notwithstanding, women made very
little money in the 1920s and early 1930s.[27] Women made ten cents an hour
in the 1920s, when Ruby Johnson went to work:

It started at a dollar a day!
[Interviewer]: I think they were trying to make you rich!
Yes, and when we got a dollar and a quarter [a day], oh, we thought that was
   fine. Finally we got a dollar and a half, and that was the limit [in 1929].
   (interview 3)

By the late 1930s women were earning forty-five cents an hour and men for-
ty-six cents at Doubleback Mountain Mica. Perhaps the difference in hour-
ly rates represented a raise, as Jess McRae conjectured about the company he
later came to own, or the assumption that men were called upon to perform
more complicated tasks in the factory (interview 35). In either case it was
testament both to the fact that men's labor was more highly valued than
women's and that neither received high wages for mica work—even with the
establishment of the NRA. Yet this was "public work," when little was to be
found. Patience Waldrup, Julia Monroe, Liza Roberts, and Nolda Stokes all
spoke with regret about having to leave their jobs due to layoffs or obligations to kin and households:

I'd just as soon split mica as eat. (interview 28)

It just about killed me to stop working. I loved it so. (interview 29)

[I had] a lot of kinfolk there [in the mica house]. I hated to leave it.
(interview 30)

But, well, I didn't quit, you see. They got where they weren't getting no orders,
and I was laid off. And I never did go back to work after that. Orders would get
scarce, you know, and they'd have to lay the hands off. (interview 2)

Despite words suggesting that she had left mica work permanently—due
to layoffs at the mica house and her husband's preference that she start a
family rather than find work elsewhere—Nolda Stokes added the following
commentary by way of clarification: "No, I worked more *after* I was married,
after James died, than I did before. Because social security back then, I think

it was $12 and a half, with children growing. I don't remember. It seems like mine was a little. It wasn't much. It wasn't enough to live on" (interview 2). The unexpected death of her husband in a (feldspar) mining accident not ten years after Stokes had left mica processing, ostensibly for good, propelled her back into the workforce to provide for her three children as well as herself. Although kinspeople pressured her otherwise, she declined the prospect of remarriage: "I told them I didn't have time to marry; I had to work too hard! I never did want to marry again" (interview 2). Laboring in a mica house seemed the better choice.[28]

The "Strategic" Resource

Mica houses in western North Carolina were hard hit by recessions that affected the mica industry in the early decades of the twentieth century. World War I had created additional demand for the mineral through its deployment of new technologies and, at the same time, had drawn attention to the difficulties of obtaining foreign mica in the midst of war. In response to this urgent situation, the federal government undertook measures to stimulate domestic production of mica but disbanded these efforts once wartime needs were met. As a result, domestic mica production declined dramatically in 1921 and during the first half of the 1920s, then rebounded to nearly 90 percent of wartime levels by the late 1920s before bottoming out in the Great Depression of the early 1930s (see table 1).[29] Companies such as Moth Hill and Doubleback Mountain Mica were able to hold on, barely, while others, like Randolph Mica and John Clay's mica house, went out of business during these difficult times. Sources of employment, upon which communities and women like Nolda Stokes had come to rely, were suddenly gone for good.

With the entry of the United States into World War II, the volatility of the domestic mica industry became a critical issue once more ("Mica Miners Work Double Shifts" 1939; "War Board Wants State to Double Mica Output" 1942). The federal government worked to secure adequate supplies of "strategic resources," minerals such as mica that had vital significance for wartime use, especially aircraft and tank parts, and whose sources were largely foreign (see table 2).[30] In 1939 the 76th Congress of the United States adopted a law whose purpose was "to provide for the common defense by acquiring stocks of strategic and critical materials essential to the needs of industry for the manufacture of supplies for the armed forces and the civilian population in time of a national emergency and to encourage, as far as possible, the further development of strategic and critical materials within the United States for common defense." Public Law No. 117 also appropriated

Table 1. Production of Sheet and Punch Mica, 1915–40

	North Carolina		United States	
Year	Amount (lbs.)	Value ($)	Amount (lbs.)	Value ($)
1915	281,074	266,650	553,821	378,250
1916	546,553	380,700	865,863	524,483
1917	643,476	543,207	1,276,533	753,874
1918	941,200	460,450	1,644,200	731,810
1919	1,021,306	331,498	1,545,709	483,567
1920	1,084,946	405,654	1,683,480	546,972
1921	230,532	51,851	741,845	118,512
1922	544,495	119,767	1,077,968	194,301
1923	1,130,283	188,317	2,063,179	311,180
1924	597,385	108,656	1,460,897	212,033
1925	592,478	105,376	1,793,865	321,962
1926	700,313	150,362	2,172,159	400,184
1927	665,360	114,514	1,512,492	212,482
1928	777,395	129,706	1,681,777	230,956
1929	894,200	150,293	2,035,128	286,321
1930	749,074	112,451	1,465,485	177,307
1931	389,426	51,657	962,953	111,830
1932	127,696	18,322	338,997	45,882
1933	162,672	21,107	364,540	53,179
1934	293,381	38,671	583,528	90,268
1935	512,590	77,598	936,633	191,150
1936	730,446	119,653	1,319,233	203,879
1937	1,044,328	218,176	1,694,538	285,244
1938	632,646	87,879	39,507	139,323
1939	401,170	69,344	813,708	138,963
1940	1,002,646	218,154	1,625,437	291,683

Source: Richard H. Jahns and Forrest W. Lancaster, "Physical Characteristics of Commercial Sheet Muscovite in the Southeastern United States," U.S. Geological Survey Professional Paper 525 (Washington, D.C.: Government Printing Office, 1950), table 8, p. 30.

Table 2. U.S. Imports of Mica and Manufactures of Mica, 1940–65

	India		All Sources[a]	
Year	Amount (lbs.)	Value ($)	Amount (lbs.)	Value ($)
1940	7,152,301	2,352,318	1,654,334	479,861
1945	7,855,086	3,780,456	10,794,736	6,219,286
1950	2,746,811	19,006,642	1,539,752	1,362,385
1955	10,384,327	5,533,990	12,231,904	7,453,589
1960	7,070,016	4,039,264	9,344,551	7,458,219
1965	9,624,686	5,676,554	11,821,704	8,094,411

Source: U.S. Bureau of Mines, *Minerals Yearbook* (Washington, D.C.: Government Printing Office, 1945–65).

Note: Includes unmanufactured mica, block mica, mica films and splittings, and mica cut or stamped to dimensions, shape, or form.

a. Sources, at various times, included Angola, Argentina, Australia, Brazil, British East Africa (now Kenya, Tanzania, and Uganda), British Guyana (now Guyana), Canada, China, Colombia, West Germany (now Germany), the Gold Coast of Africa (now Ghana), Guatemala, India, Japan, Madagascar, Mexico, Mozambique, the Netherlands, Pakistan, Portuguese Guinea, Rhodesia (now Malawi, Zambia, and Zimbabwe), Spain, Sweden, and the United Kingdom.

$100 million for fiscal years 1939–43 to develop domestic mineral resources, under the direction of the U.S. Geological Survey and the Bureau of Mines.

The government program on strategic mica had four distinct components. In addition to mapping the known mica deposits in the United States and making predictions concerning the location of additional deposits, the program included participation in international procurement programs under the Combined Raw Materials Board, research to develop synthetic alternatives to mica, and stimulation of domestic mica production.[31] To stimulate production the federal government established the Colonial Mica Corporation in 1942 to act as its agent.

The purpose of the Colonial Mica Corporation was to directly subsidize mica-mining and -processing efforts and thereby stimulate production. More specifically, this entailed lending money for the exploration and mining of mica deposits; leasing equipment to miners; developing properties with mica deposits; establishing processing and trimming shops; training personnel in trimming and processing mica as a form of direct assistance to mica miners; buying mica at artificially inflated prices; and storing and distributing the mica thus obtained (Skow 1962:152; see also M. Billings and Montague 1944:93–94 and Stuckey 1965:422–23). From 1942 to 1945 the Colonial Mica Corporation leased equipment to 1,188 applicants throughout the United States and collected only about half of the rental fees for this equipment. It advanced funds in amounts of $500 to $20,000 to explore mica prospects and as working capital for mines with confirmed mica deposits—a total of $716,300.31 advanced on 600 mines. While advances were theoretically to be paid back from the proceeds on sales of mica, Colonial Mica received only $208,998.40 from its investments (Skow 1962:153).

But if Colonial Mica failed to break even, it did effectively spur activities in prospecting, mining, and producing mica. Whereas six hundred people were employed in mica production before World War II, the establishment of the strategic mica program led to the employment of eight thousand workers as miners and processors and at higher wages than they previously had commanded (Hatch et al. 1957; Roy 1952; Skow 1962:141–45).[32] The number of working mines in the United States increased several-fold, to an average of 658 by 1944 (U.S. Tariff Commission 1947:34). Equally important, the federal government was able to determine, with a greater degree of accuracy, the extent of mica resources still in the ground (see U.S. Bureau of Mines, *Minerals Yearbook* 1948, 1950; Burgess 1949; Gwinn 1943; Houk 1942; Jahns and Lancaster 1950; Murdock 1942; and especially Lesure 1968).

One of the more significant findings of the mapping project was that the primary site for mica was located in the mountains of western North Carolina, and levels of mica production soared in the region during the war years. Along with subsidizing mining, Colonial Mica helped rationalize mica processing in the mountains by supplying local companies with government mica, manufacturing equipment, and specifications about methods and output of production. Factories expanded, and new companies were founded, to take advantage of the government contracts:[33]

> Basically, they were absolutely committed to government production. That is, they weren't free to pick and choose what they wanted to do. It was just sent to them, and "you do this," which was no big problem. The thing was the terms under which the equipment was provided to you. You wound up at the end of the war only having to pay salvage value for the equipment, and so everybody just got all kinds of good punch presses and machinery that they needed to produce tools and dies if they wanted them . . . anything related to mica production . . . office equipment even. . . . And so, as a result, everybody was pretty well stocked. (interview 22)

Dependent as it had become on the operations of the federal government, the mica industry in North Carolina and throughout the country once again went into decline when the offices of the Colonial Mica Corporation closed in 1945 (see table 3.) However, the loss of war-related production was partially offset by an expanding market for domestic technologies—from heavy equipment such as diesel locomotives and automobiles (interview 16) to household appliances—all of which relied on mica: "After the war, appliances

Table 3. Sheet Mica Sold or Used by Producers in the United States, 1940–49

	North Carolina		United States	
Year	Amount (lbs.)	Value ($)	Amount (lbs.)	Value ($)
1940	1,002,646	218,154	1,625,437	291,685
1941	1,614,863	318,783	2,666,453	566,858
1942	1,654,895	505,634	2,761,844	725,030
1943	1,901,120	1,772,324	3,448,199	3,228,742
1944	814,874	1,530,625	1,523,313	3,262,711
1945	563,990	243,058	1,298,587	737,342
1946	424,791	135,505	1,078,867	217,955
1947	210,816	84,275	415,589	116,110
1948	257,926	44,678	270,042	45,940
1949	507,935	113,058	578,818	125,928

Sources: Jasper L. Stuckey, *North Carolina: Its Geology and Mineral Resources* (Raleigh, N.C.: Department of Conservation and Development, 1965), 418; U.S. Bureau of Mines, *Minerals Yearbook* (Washington, D.C.: Government Printing Office, 1940–50).

Note: Data refer only to block mica and processed mica, or "mica splittings," not to ground mica, scrap mica, or flake mica, all of which are considered "waste products" with different applications.

were a real hit. People coming home from the war . . . a lot of soldiers had money saved up and were getting married and everything. Everybody wanted washing machines and radios and all this, so there was a pretty good market for mica at the time" (interview 22).

Moreover, the dismantling of Colonial Mica did not spell the end of efforts to secure domestic sources of mica but rather a hiatus in government activities that lasted five years. The Defense Production Act of 1950 established a new set of programs that continued the multiple emphases of the past but gave priority to the creation of a stockpile of strategic mica. Although the entry of the United States into the Korean War intensified the demand for mica, the programs of the 1950s were the outgrowth of recommendations submitted to Congress in 1945 by the Army and Navy Munitions Board.[34] In response to these proposals Congress had devised the Strategic and Critical Materials Stock Piling Act of 1946 to authorize peacetime acquisition of minerals deemed vital to the nation's defense (Skow 1962:159–61).[35]

In 1952 the federal government installed "depots" in New Hampshire, South Dakota, and western North Carolina, areas determined by the mapping research of the 1940s to contain large deposits of mica. The depots operated as government facilities, much like the Colonial Mica Corporation, for purposes of inspecting, purchasing, and processing mica. Congress directed that the government amass 25,000 tons of mica and mandated that mica meet strict specifications with respect to quality and the amount of voltage that it could withstand.[36] As an incentive for miners to reopen idle mines and operate processing plants at maximum capacity, the General Services Administration (GSA) instituted pricing systems that increased the value of mica beyond the levels that Colonial Mica had established. A news article that appeared before the new depots opened reflected the success of this strategy: "Miners want to get their share of the millions of dollars the Federal Government is going to pay for top-quality ruby mica. The Government's program is scheduled to get under way July 21. Fifty or more tons of the strategic mineral reportedly have been stockpiled in anticipation of selling to the Government" (Campbell 1952).

With the highest grade garnering $70 a pound, contemporary reporters (Jaeckel 1955; Leinbach 1952) likened mica to gold, and an underground economy soon formed around the commodity. To maximize their earnings from the mica program, for example, some entrepreneurs mined throughout the United States and Canada and then sold to the depot that had the highest prices at any given time—despite government regulations against this form of profiteering.

So there was a lot of people in the '50s and '60s who made a lot of money out of mica . . . that I say most of them should not have done it. They leased mines in Connecticut and New Hampshire and Canada. Canada leased its mines. And they would mine mica there and ship it here to North Carolina and sell it to the government at a very, very high price. (interview 19)

It was stockpiled. I trimmed mica, a little piece not as long as my little finger, not as wide as my little finger, and it was $30 a pound. Then it went up as high as $60 a pound, and I trimmed some that went over that. Everybody in the country brought mica there and sold it. They'd bring it there to sell it, and they'd claim they couldn't buy it; they'd take it to New Hampshire, and they'd get more for it. They'd jump in their cars or any way they could go to New Hampshire. They'd sell it up there and they got rich off of that. (interview 10)

Moreover, as one of the incentives for citizens to provide the government with mica, the GSA had instituted broad standards for the depots to use to evaluate the minerals delivered to them. If only 20 percent of the mica in a particular lot met the criteria for one grade of "strategic mica," the depot would classify the whole quantity at that grade and purchase it. From another vantage point, however, the government standard created new avenues to the acquisition of wealth for those with ambition and resources: "There were a number of mines around here that were extremely high-quality mines, and they never sold a piece to the government. They'd sell it to other miners at a premium price. . . . Say, if they were getting $50 a pound for 'good stain,' the other miners would pay $100 a pound to get the 'good stain' because they only had to mix 20 pounds of that [to make] 100, and they got $50 a pound for the whole lot" (interview 22). Beyond the accounts of casual trading practices centered around higher grades of mica, my informants heard reports of unethical business dealings and outright theft. Those who lived a considerable distance from the government depot were easily swindled out of their stores of mica:

There's mica found down in [the foothill counties]. There are pockets of very fine mica. Some farmer down there runs across that stuff and says, "Hey, this is valuable stuff up at [the depot]—." He didn't know what it was worth, had no idea. He'd bring it to the depot and—this is not firsthand information, this is talk, general talk—he'd bring it up there, and they'd look at him and tell him it wasn't the kind of mica they wanted. But they'd tell him who he could sell it to. They'd say, "Try so-and-so, you might sell it to some individual over here." So [the farmer'd] take it to that individual; he'd buy it for nearly nothing. Then he'd bring it to the mica depot and sell it for that $70 a pound. (interview 19)

Mica was also mined on property belonging to "owners [who] did not know there was mines on it" and therefore had no notion of their losses (interview 22). Those well attuned to the value of this commodity also suffered loss when shipments of mica suddenly "disappear[ed] from the back of somebody's truck" and reappeared days later at the mica depot or the doorstep of a mica buyer. Yet "it was still hard to prove [the mica] was from somebody else's mine," and such acts of thievery often went unpunished—but not unnoticed (interview 22).

In sum, a federal program intended to stimulate regional mining activities had the effect of furthering the careers of entrepreneurs and elites that were able and willing to take full advantage of government incentives: "Lawsy, there were a lot of people just made scads of money out of the mica. But some of them cheated the government. I don't know who it was, because Old Man Vern—as we called him—had charge of the mica depot. And he had to take the rap. He went to prison for it" (interview 19). By contrast, miners and mica workers made comparatively little money from the procurement program because wages averaged $1.20 per hour for mining and less for mica trimming or processing. What they gained, instead, was employment for the duration of the stockpiling program. At the close of this period one miner observed: "I hate to be losing a job, but when I get another one, I hope it's better than this" ("Three WNC Counties Hard Hit" 1962).

The stockpiling program lasted from 1952 until July 1962 (see tables 4 and 5). During that time North Carolina produced an average annual yield of 524,118 pounds of sheet mica valued at $1.67 million, or a cumulative total of 5.75 million pounds and $18.21 million (Stuckey 1965:413, 424). At the height of the program in 1956 more than five hundred mines in North Carolina produced 770,903 pounds worth $2.14 million.[37] The North Carolina depot purchased more than three-quarters of the strategic mica, and western Carolina suffered proportionately with the closing of the stockpile. The end of the program threw nearly two thousand waged laborers and self-employed people out of work, and unemployment in the mica-producing counties of North Carolina rose to 50 percent ("Three WNC Counties Hard Hit" 1962). The smaller mica companies and sweatshop operations that had come to life during the stockpiling program faded just as quickly with the termination of federal contracts. Mining all but ceased in 1963.[38] Then, again, most sources of mica had been exhausted in the waning moments of the procurement program:

> The government was not going to cut it off when they reached a certain amount of mica, they were going to cut it off as of a certain date. They had an amount they wanted, and when they reached that, they said, "As of six months from now, the mica program is ended." And in that six months you wouldn't believe

Table 4. Trimmed Sheet Mica and By-products
Purchased by the General Services Administration
for the Stockpile of Strategic Mica, 1952–60

	North Carolina	United States
Year	Amount (lbs.)	Amount (lbs.)
1952	36,831	55,515
1953	113,270	164,698
1954	139,872	198,812
1955	188,915	236,605
1956	176,942	218,820
1957	152,296	193,272
1958	170,993	238,550
1959	185,202	295,233
1960	150,520	263,987
	1,314,841	1,865,492

Source: Milford L. Skow, "Mica: A Materials Survey,"
Information Circular 8125, U.S. Bureau of Mines
(Washington, D.C.: Government Printing Office, 1962),
table 33, p. 103.
Note: Although the stockpiling program continued until
1962, Skow compiled information only for the years noted.

Table 5. Mica Sold or Used by Producers in the United States, 1950–65

	North Carolina		United States	
Year	Amount (lbs.)	Value ($)	Amount (lbs.)	Value ($)
1950	483,736	102,179	578,818	125,928
1951	464,949	127,204	594,884	160,322
1952	595,331	664,075	697,989	908,135
1953	619,895	1,308,494	849,394	2,153,584
1954	479,221	1,787,197	668,788	2,393,041
1955	553,444	2,745,234	642,113	3,370,397
1956	770,903	2,135,057	887,871	2,757,073
1957	557,607	1,575,099	690,052	2,492,462
1958	521,701	1,721,949	661,344	2,844,469
1959	505,623	1,755,314	706,395	3,419,490
1960	430,193	1,411,440	578,985	2,830,335
1961	390,870	2,237,000	526,007	3,385,760
1962	320,305	867,000	363,016	1,299,278
1963	92,961	12,604	102,961	12,904
1964	242,662	58,481	242,662	58,481
1965	713,293	184,650	716,086	184,986

Sources: U.S. Bureau of Mines, *Minerals Yearbook* (Washington, D.C.: Government Printing Office, 1952–65); Jasper L. Stuckey, "Mineral Industry of North Carolina from 1960 through 1987," Economic Paper 68, Division of Mineral Resources (Raleigh, N.C.: Department of Conservation and Development, 1970), 14.
Note: Data refer only to uncut sheet mica, not to scrap or ground mica.

what people did to get the mica out of these old—. They go in and they'd shoot supporting pillars, anything that had mica in it, to get it out. Because the government, during that period, you know, as they had all along, would buy anything you brought in. So a lot of old mines, as they were abandoned, were left in terribly unsafe conditions. And people were mining twenty-four hours a day, some of them. You know, they were pulling pumps out of them as they went along, and things started to flood as they were still shooting in there. It was a real mess. (interview 22)

By the late 1960s the only sheet mica produced was the by-product of feldspar mining, a reversal of earlier times when feldspar was considered waste material and discarded in the search for mica. In 1967 all of North Carolina produced only 4,500 pounds of mica, valued at $1,000 (Stuckey 1970:14).

Conclusion: A Marginalized Industry

More than a hundred years after Clingman, Persons, Clapp, and Heap commenced their prospecting and mining in the mountains of North Carolina, the mica industry continues, albeit in greatly diminished form. Whereas mica companies in North Carolina once exported mica to foreign countries, most of the mica used in the United States in the late twentieth century came from India, Brazil, Madagascar, or through periodic sales of excess mica from the government stockpile (U.S. Bureau of Mines, *Mineral Facts and Problems* 1985:514; see also Indian Institute 1977). In the words of one Moth Hill worker, "When I told these people that was visiting, that we took through, about all the mica having to come from India, that surprised them so. They couldn't believe that, that there was no mica mined here anymore, because they thought this was mining country. You know, our forefathers mined all the time, brought the mica out of the hills here, and sold it to them. But it's not what they do in that Upper End, there's no mica used from local mines. The mining just stopped" (interview 9). By the mid-1980s, the United States produced just five hundred pounds of sheet mica, about 10 percent of the amount produced during the 1970s (U.S. Bureau of Mines, *Mineral Facts and Problems* 1985:510; Shirley and Allen 1976:2). A decade later, according to the U.S. Geological Survey (2001), domestic production of sheet mica was less than half a metric ton per year.

The United States used 14.7 million pounds of sheet mica in 1953, but in 1983 the country used only 2.2 million pounds (U.S. Bureau of Mines, *Mineral Facts and Problems* 1985:509–10).[39] The changing technologies of the twentieth and twenty-first centuries—the development of solid-state electronics, synthetic forms of insulation, and microchips, among others—restricted the need for mica.[40] Nonetheless, some technologies still require mica parts: the equipment used to deliver radiotherapy to cancer patients, the machinery of the computerized axial tomography (CAT) scan, space shuttles, missiles, radio transmission, "expendable military hardware," and automobile engines. Nothing has surpassed the electrical and thermal properties of mica nor its precision and durability (U.S. Bureau of Mines, *Mineral Facts and Problems* 1985; Indian Institute 1977:45; Jahns and Lancaster 1952:2, 4–5, 16–17; Stuckey 1965:410–13; Anglin ethnographic interviews). Due to continuing demand for mica's specialized properties and the creation of new markets during the late 1990s, U.S. companies *increased* their usage to 5,500 metric tons, or 12.13 million pounds, of sheet mica in 2000. At the same time, consumption patterns have been limited by a dwindling government stockpile, the high costs associated with domestic production (mining/processing), and the limited availability of high-quality mica from international sources (U.S. Geological Survey 1994, 1999, 2001).

When I began my field research at Moth Hill in 1987, *The Thomas Register of American Manufacturers* (1987) listed approximately fifty-five manufacturers of mica products; by 2001, fifty-one companies remain. That list included small mica firms in North Carolina and elsewhere in the United States, as well as conglomerates like General Electric and Westinghouse with their vast inventories of electrical and electronics equipment. Indeed, small companies like Moth Hill persisted by brokering mica products from India and fabricating mica parts for their corporate clients. Yet by the late 1980s Moth Hill Mica Company ran only one shift and employed fifty people, all of whom were subject to periodic layoffs when there was a lull in production orders; ten years later the labor force was reduced to thirty-eight employees. This represents a considerable departure from the 1950s and 1960s, when Moth Hill subcontracted with the GSA and worked three hundred employees on three shifts.

To people working in the mica plants in the late 1980s, it made little sense for their children or other young people to go into this line of work. To paraphrase one of the Moth Hill laborers: You don't make much and there's no future to it, but when we started, that was all we knew to do. Employers and employees, whose experience spanned seven mica companies in western Carolina, told me that mica mining was long since over, mica parts had been almost entirely replaced by plastics, and it was only a question of time before the few remaining factories went out of business (Anglin field notes 1987, 1988). On the other hand, I also heard from informants that, if the United States were to become involved in another war like the one in Vietnam, the mica industry might thrive once more:

Lamar Watkins: They used to run three shifts.

Elsa Watkins: Yeah, honey, they used to have a first shift, a second shift, and a third shift.

[Interviewer]: That's hard for me to believe.

Elsa Watkins: Well, honey, they did. Anytime there's a war, they had all of them. (interview 4)

4. Working "Close Home"

Going to the mica factory, as with any drive in western Carolina, meant travel-ing narrow windy roads dotted with churches, farmsteads, and houses—as well as an increasing array of so-called convenience stores, fast-food restaurants, garages, and other businesses contained, for the most part, in small metal build-ings or trailers. While I drove in and out of the morning fog that settled along the ridges, the road became, by turns, steep and unpredictable, and expansive.

Along the way I passed the small commercial center of Sadieville (population 2,200) and drove through a valley that offered considerably less in the way of car parts, hamburgers, tanning beds, or videos. In their stead were trailers, houses, and fields that ran nearly to the ridge line. Driving farther, I felt the terrain shift. The valley narrowed, and the road followed a path between the river and mountains that had become steeper and more sharply defined. Houses were tucked into flatter sections of land beside the road, and there was a small settle-ment that had the look of a mill village: small wooden houses and trailers placed close to each other with little ornamentation and no room for gardens, yards, or additions. The road took me past churches and schools, some in ruins and others newly refurbished with coats of paint, elaborate stonework, and well-kept grounds beside them.

Just beyond, in a curve of the road that mirrored the course of the river, lay Moth Hill Mica Company. On either side of the road were buildings with grav-el parking lots next to them. The main structure, two stories tall and perhaps one hundred feet long, was built from cinderblock and concrete that had turned a dismal gray over the years. Although the building had windows all around—in contrast to the textile plants in North Carolina—many panes were broken and covered with pieces of cardboard. Fragments of the mica parts made by the factory were everywhere, like plastic wrap shredded into pieces and left to coat the landscape.

Barely visible across the road was a small block building that sat betwixt river and hillside. It once had housed the mill wheel that turned river water into power for the entire factory. Off-limits to me, this building was the locus of "pure mica" operations: remnants of the manufacturing processes on which the company had been founded nearly eighty years earlier. Its neighbor was a slightly larger wooden building right next to the road. Called the "Tea Room" in memory of the years when it functioned as a restaurant, this structure had been converted into a site for asbestos processing at the factory until the state banned those activities. Afterward it became a facility for storing mica and other supplies. The third and final building, a metal warehouse, was located beyond the river and out of view.

In 1987 there was little more to Monroe than these buildings and two old country stores, one of which was abandoned and the other used to store galax leaves and other plant materials collected locally for the floral industry. Several churches of different denominations (Presbyterian, Methodist, Baptist), a few houses, and a post office also marked the settlement. Three or four decades earlier, however, Monroe was a thriving town where you could buy anything, sell mica and farm commodities to local merchants, go to the movies, or eat at a cafe.

Pulling into the parking lot of the driveway was always the hardest part. I smelled the heavy lacquer fumes as I reached the factory. It always felt like a warning: Get out of here if you have the choice. I'd open the car door, make my way through mounds of mica scraps and past a long line of vehicles showing the wear and tear of rural roads. I'd head toward the ramp and the heavy wooden door whose hinges were so worn that you had to lift as much as push it open and enter the factory through the Lower End.

On the side of the room facing the road were two rows of punch presses: tall black metal structures like oversized sewing machines, with slides in front for mica parts to skid into the cardboard boxes placed beneath. Behind the presses were equally tall wooden chairs for women to brace against as they hunched forward over strips of "mica plate" (laminated mica) and pushed their foot pedals. A collection of smaller presses and shorter chairs lined the opposite wall, where the "ring boys" worked. Between the ring boys and the punching operations were rows and rows of 55-gallon drums filled to the brim with "trash," defective parts and leftover scraps of laminated mica. The back corner of the room held an oven, similar to an electric kiln for firing pottery, used to "cure" mica plate in the final stages of its manufacture. Nearby were dies used to cut the laminated mica into particular shapes and sizes and other tools for repairing punch presses. Washers, the end result of workers' labor, were stored in old candy box-

es and larger cardboard containers piled up against the walls and crammed under tables in any space available.

An arched doorway, whose plaster was crumbled from age, led into the main hall of the building. The clock where employees punched in and out was located here, as was the entrance to the offices of the secretaries and the heads of the company. Toward the back of the hall was an old freight elevator, rarely used. A well-worn stairway led to the department "Upstairs" where women, seated at long tables, "laid" mica plate by hand. Below the stairs was a hand-printed sign marking the presence of the men's bathroom, a recent addition built from plywood. Off to the other side was the entrance to the Upper End, the department that produced sheets of laminated mica with machines that looked like ferris wheels of mica flying out onto long conveyer belts. Close by were the "steam tables," the equipment on which newly made mica plate was first dried and the source of one of the factory's more notorious explosions. Huge presses that squeezed excess varnish from the sheets of mica plate, and the drums where varnishes were mixed, were located on the farthest end of this long rectangular room. In the rafters, in the corners, on window sills, and clinging to the screens that partially marked the boundary between outside and interior space were piles of mica dust.

The Lower End was considered the best place to work at Moth Hill. In contrast to the Upper End it had plenty of heat in the winter. The smell of lacquer fumes on the Lower End was minimal by comparison to that in other factory departments—particularly the Upstairs, where dust masks were no match for the varnishes that, as one worker noted, "make you put away your walking shoes." The room on the Lower End was also in good repair: the floors did not flood when it rained, and the lighting was decent. Most important of all, production orders were regular there, and workers hardly ever got laid off.

* * *

It took me a while to come to these conclusions. For days I came in at midmorning and watched workers at their jobs, as they stopped for lunch, and as they carried on conversations all the while. Some of those days I stood awkwardly to one side and tried to stay out of the way while the work went on around me. Other times I helped with the tasks at hand or was given a turn "spelling" a worker so she could take a break from "plate-making" machines that, except for the noon hour, continued running for the duration of the shift. My education started with John Payne's tour through the factory, when I observed far more of Moth Hill's dynamics than I initially realized.

Gertie Russell, the first person I met on that tour, had the job of "feeding the machines"—stocking two pieces of equipment, spaced about twenty feet apart, with flakes of mica—while keeping track of the laminated mica that rolled off the other end. She told me how wonderful it was to be employed at Moth Hill, how generous the Paynes were, and how much she loved to labor in mica. "It's hard work, but it's good work" was the theme she repeated. I wondered then how representative she was of the workers in the plant and whether her remarks might change were I not a visitor passing by with the owner-manager.

Workers Upstairs uttered similar sentiments, but some remarks had an undercurrent. Darlene Stokes, the only female supervisor in the factory, compared the labor involved in making mica plate by hand to "playing cards" on a fiberglass cloth. She spoke of how she "loved taking [the surface] up or down a few 'mills' [millimeters]," skilled labor that required more than visual acuity, and she showed me a finished piece as it emerged from the steam oven. Warning me not to touch lest my hand become enmeshed in the varnish coating, Stokes added she had always wanted to wrap someone up in the cloth and see how tight it would stick. John Payne responded to her aggressive humor by observing that, in that case, he had "better watch out." But Darlene Stokes retorted, "Oh, no, baby. I wouldn't do that to you. You'd fire me."

By way of explaining this mixture of impertinence and intimacy, John Payne told me how he had played in the factory as a little boy and that many current employees had watched him grow up, sometimes taking care of him during their shifts. Their claims on him, as even a first-time visitor could see, were registered not only through threatening jokes but also in manner of address. He was "John" or "John Walter," never "Mr. Payne" (nor had his father been, as I came to find out). Yet this discourse had another dimension, and that was the state of the mica business. Because many corporations were finding less expensive alternatives to mica products, John Payne told me, orders were down at Moth Hill, and he was "working fewer people than this time last year." During any given week one-third of the employees were "off," released into temporary unemployment until production orders warranted their return. Payne had also been forced "to let about five people go," reducing the workforce to its current size of fifty-eight, and he needed to eliminate another five to eight positions. The latter, he hoped, would occur through "retirement and attrition." Consequently, "firing"—unemployment without the euphemisms—was much on the minds of Stokes, Russell, and their colleagues at Moth Hill.

That first day's lessons, twin discussions concerning the perilous state of the mica industry and the political claims of kinship, were reiterated during the course of my fieldwork in the factory. Family ties were a constant theme in workers' conversations, so much so that an observer was not necessarily aware of the selective usage to which such references were put. Virtually everyone, it seemed, was related to someone else at Moth Hill or had had kin working there at some point in the past. Yet for all their apparent arbitrariness and ubiquity, renderings of kin connectedness reflected class differences, factory relations, and changing interpretations of gender (see Batteau 1982; D. Billings and Blee 1986; Bryant 1981; Hall et al. 1987; McKinney 1988; Waller 1988; and Yanigasako and Delaney 1995). These points are best illustrated through what I will refer to as "recruitment stories"—descriptions of the various routes that workers took in locating employment at the factory—and equally the ways that departmental networks and bonds of familiarity operated on the shop floor of Moth Hill. Such explorations lend themselves to further discussion of management directives, the mica business, and the status of production orders. In sum, they allow us to better comprehend the multiple, and often contradictory, meanings of working "close home."

Both Zona Watson and June Robbins made their way to Moth Hill with the aid of female relatives knowledgeable about the plant's hiring practices. Robbins said that her aunt came to visit one afternoon, and the next day they ended up at the factory: "I was about twenty-three years old, and my aunt came over and said, 'Let's go down to Moth Hill and ask for a job.' I said, 'What do you mean?' I wasn't even wanting a job, you know! We went down there and she asked for a job. I didn't even ask, but they told us to come in to work at nine the next day" (interview 5). Robbins was not enthusiastic about the prospect of waged labor, nor did she understand what that work entailed. As she explained it, she mistook "mica plate" for a kind of dinnerware that the factory presumably produced, and she learned the difference the day after their interview with the front office. Forty years later, when I started my field research, June Robbins was still working on Moth Hill's Lower End.

Like June Robbins, Zona Watson "didn't know a thing in the world they did or anything" about Moth Hill. An older relative, Ruby Stewart, who was an experienced mica worker, introduced Watson to the plant. "My half-sister—Harold's mother—lived across the creek there from us, you know, and she had worked there, and then she had quit. She had boys and she raised them by herself. She'd worked mostly at Moth Hill. But she quit somehow or other," Watson told me. "We were pulling off corn up there and gathering in the corn, and she [Ruby] said, 'Let's go up to Moth Hill. They're hiring a lot of people. Let's go up there and get us a job.' And I said, well, I thought, I can go and work 'till Christmas" (interview 7).

The story does not end there. Watson's mother went to Monroe's main store cum post office, which the Paynes also owned, to seek an audience with the Paynes, as many people did; however, she found the interview clouded by misconceptions about her family: "On that weekend Mama went up to the store, Jeter Payne's store—see, that was the nephew—and Royce was in the store. And she said, 'Zona and Ruby been talking about coming and seeing if they can get a job.' And he said, 'Well, tell 'em to come in Monday.' He said, 'But Zona won't work.' Said, 'I don't think she'll work.' Pansy [Zona's sister] had worked there some when she was going to school, in the summer" (interview 7), and her negative comments had affected Royce's assessment of Zona.

Once at Moth Hill, Zona Watson had to overcome Royce Payne's negative impressions, but there she was aided by her half-sister and the "older hands" whom Ruby Stewart knew. They trained Zona and helped her get the work assignment she wanted: "This woman from Cove Creek, she was cutting off plate on that machine, there where I've worked on all these years. She wanted me to cut off for her, and I would. And she'd sometimes rest and go over there and patch [the machine-made mica plate]. When she told Royce she was quitting, she said, 'Let Zona have that machine.' And they did. Junior Willis was there, so that's how I got started. I didn't know a lot of them [at first], but I learned a lot of people, a lot that's dead now" (interview 7). Although Zona had worked at Moth Hill for nearly forty years and was known for her skill on a machine particularly important to mica production, she had followed the pattern of her half-sister in quitting the factory as family circumstances necessitated. Mostly, this meant traveling across country with her husband, Zeyland, when he could not find work in Monroe, and returning to the mica plant as soon as she could.

Pearl Henson (later Roberts) had quite a different experience. She went to Jeter's store of an afternoon and ended up in conversation with Royce's father, "Uncle Dan": "I walked over there because my sister-in-law didn't want me to stay at the store; it was too worldly for us—with all that gang of men and stuff. So I was talking to some of the girls that I went to school with. They were working there. The main owner of the plant, Daniel Payne, came out and started talking to me, and he knew my daddy and all that. He said [my daddy] was the best friend he ever had in his life. And he just kept talking, talking, talking" (interview 10). Pearl went over to Moth Hill because, unlike the worldly general store, it was a respectable place for an adolescent girl to visit. The factory was where her sister-in-law and school friends worked, and even the Paynes knew who she was:

> My sister-in-law come up there [to the factory] and said, "You've got to leave." She said, "Go on and get your shoes and stuff, and go on back to the house and . . . get the washing done. And so [Uncle Dan] said, "No, you can't leave yet. Royce will be here in a minute." About the time I started to leave, here come Royce. [Uncle Dan] said, "Here's Fate Corbin's girl. I want you to put her to

work." Royce asked, "When can you go to work?" I told him, "Oh, Lord, I can't work!" He said, "Yeah, you can. You just fit in for what I want." So I asked him, "What would it be?" and he said, "I want you to take Garland and Junior Stamey's place." They was in service at the time. (interview 10)

Royce and Uncle Dan approached Pearl through their memories of her father and their desire for extra hands. They knew she would "just fit" at the plant and, in the bargain, replace two men off to fight in World War II. As with June and Zona, Pearl was not really looking for a job, but she was familiar with the factory and started to work there immediately. It was a time when, as Royce Payne put it, "Why, we were booming! We had that place plum full" (interview 21).

Local knowledge about the mica factory and the experience of family members created avenues to waged labor for young girls and women who were more than a little ambivalent about these prospects. The efforts of friends and relations meant, in turn, that the Paynes had ready access to labor—new as well as experienced factory hands—and a set of practices by which they could manage the burgeoning workforce of the 1940s and 1950s. Furthermore, through these means the Paynes were able to control the gendered and racial composition of their labor force. Royce Payne and his father preferred to hire white women, inasmuch as they "could hire them cheaper" and, at the same time, acquire workers who "could do any job over there just as good as a man" (interview 18; see also Janiewski 1985; B. W. Jones 1995; J. Jones 1986; Roediger 1991). White women did find work whenever there was mica to be mined, and when the Paynes needed domestic servants, African American women found work too. But Moth Hill employed no people of color and only a few white men. "Never did ask to work in the plant" was Royce Payne's response to my questions about this (interview 18).[1] I suspect that he might have said the same had I asked about the growing Latino/a population that labored instead in agriculture and the floral industry of Clark County.

It was one thing to labor at Moth Hill when it was the largest employer in the county and especially when wartime need for a strategic resource expanded employment opportunities for women (interview 16). It was quite another situation when the labor force was not three hundred but fewer than sixty, and mica wages paled in comparison to those for other kinds of factory work. Nonetheless, Moth Hill was the only factory in that remote rural section and, especially during the peak in unemployment of the 1980s, offered work when little was to be had—except by commuting or leaving Clark County. In the early 1980s, when Frances Stokes needed a job so that she could pay for her son's education, she talked to her father, who was working at the mica plant, "and I prayed about it, and I asked the Lord to help me find a job. Daddy come home one evening, and he said, 'Would you like to go to work down at Moth Hill, and make rings?' I said, 'Well, I'll try it.' They taught me to make rings when I first went to work" (interview 11). Frances Stokes started at a job coded as "male labor" and pulled down higher wages than women typically earned, before she was transferred to the Upper End. Doubtless, her father's intercession on her behalf was part of the reason for that unconventional assignment.

Gertie Russell "retired on the state" shortly before I met her and had come back to Moth Hill via the efforts of her sister, Annie Burleson. Through controversial moves described to me as "telling a tale on somebody," Annie sought to have her long-time work partner, Mae Webb, replaced by her sister. Thus Gertie found her way out of retirement and back in the thick of things on the Upper End. She justified her presence at Moth Hill by being known as a hard worker, as well as by providing personal labor for the Paynes. During the period of my field research, the number of employees fluctuated with the ebb and flow of factory production. What few openings there were invariably went to the sons and daughters, and occasionally siblings and parents, of the extant (or recent) labor force at Moth Hill. This was one dimension of working "close home": "They get somebody in the family, a daughter-in-law, a daughter, or something, and they want her to work up there. Then she gets hired. That stays family, right there. That's all it is, really, Moth Hill family. It's Cove Creek" (interview 6).

Kith and Kin and Bosses

At the plant the language of kinship mediated the actions of employees and managers. Men might have greater access to supervisory roles than women, but as kinspeople and members of settlements in the surrounding area, they were also responsive to the sets of mutual obligations that extended into the factory. For example, Dallas Stamey was Hazel Roberts's uncle and the factory overseer when she first went to Moth Hill. While Stamey was remembered for his strict enforcement of work rules, he was known to Roberts, first and last, as her uncle and someone she could approach with problems or differences of opinion. Similarly, Zona Watson recalled taking complaints about factory policy to the main supervisor: "Yes, I used to tell Dallas Stamey, when he was there, that the women were discriminated against. Because they always worked the men in preference to the women. If anyone was off, it was the women" (interview 9). For Zona Watson, who was the mainstay of her family, this was a bread-and-butter issue. It was also something she could discuss with a neighbor who understood how hard it was to find work and what that meant for the Watson family.

The scenario was different in the late 1980s, when strict supervision of the shop floor had given way to laxity—the result of changes in overseers and successions in Payne family management—but the bonds of familiarity still held. Concerned about declining work orders and possibilities of layoffs, Hazel Roberts prevailed upon Carl Fisher, supervisor of the Upper End, much as Watson had talked to Stamey in earlier decades. For his part, Fisher tried to keep Roberts and her work partner, Frances Stokes, occupied making "stock" when they had long since completed customer orders. Neither Stokes nor Roberts blamed Fisher when he did lay them off or had to send them to the department Upstairs where they hated to work; they knew he'd done all he could to keep them on the Upper End. Outside the factory Roberts and her mother took presents to the wedding reception held in the community for Carl Fisher's son, Jack. When Hazel Roberts fell seriously ill, Carl "looked in after her" at the hospital, as did others from the factory. These were not extraordinary measures, of course, but reflections of broader commitments.

The Paynes themselves appropriated the language of kinship to legitimate paternalistic labor policies, reflected both in methods of recruitment and the informal obligations that they exacted from employees as part of their (equally informal) labor contracts. The significance of referring to the founder of the mica business as "Uncle Dan" and other members of the Payne family by their first names was to invest the power relations of the factory with connotations of family and community. Royce Payne could recite the names and generations of the families that had worked for him, and he thereby consolidated his claims about Moth Hill: "I was talking to a fellow three mile up the road, at a big brick church. He said nearly all the money that went into this church came out of Moth Hill Mica Company. Nearly all of it. And you stop these things and people just have to leave" (interview 16). It was a pact that worked both ways, for while workers experienced the authority of the Paynes in concrete terms, they nonetheless operated upon personal connections with those in charge (see Wingerd 1996:881).

At times this seemed to involve colluding with factory management, as when Gertie Russell observed that factory hands had to intensify their efforts on the job so that Moth Hill could continue, even in the current hard times. "It don't have the money to fix the things that are broke," she said. Russell practiced what she preached to the younger hands. She came in "early of a morning" to sweep the floors on the Upper End and ready the machines for the day's work. Asked about the Paynes' response to her extra hours of maintenance work, Gertie replied, "They don't pay me for it. If I asked them to, they wouldn't let me do it."

As part of their daily responsibilities, Moth Hill workers (including Russell, Annie Sparks, Hazel Roberts, June Robbins, Floyd Wilson, and Franklin Watkins) provided personal services to the Paynes. Floyd took care of cattle that belonged to Eunice (Royce Payne's sister), while Franklin went daily to Eunice's house to get a list of groceries or errands. Once back in the plant, Franklin sought the help of other Moth Hill employees in decoding her spidery writing so he could complete the chores before "dinnertime" (midday in western North Carolina). Hazel Roberts, who had tended John Walter's children before and after her work shift, still offered much sought-after advice after they had reached adolescence. Wally, the oldest, regularly ducked his classes at the local community college and came instead to Moth Hill where he would be "petted." Annie Sparks and her sister, Gertie Russell, brought Royce Payne his dinner when he still came regularly to the plant. "It don't matter none; I enjoyed it" was June Robbins's commentary on her years of driving Royce's wife, Violet, into Sadieville to do her shopping. Others, however, argued that the Paynes expected too much of their hands: "A job is a job, and that's *all*."

Accomplished in spirits of placidity or incipient rebellion, these activities formed the backdrop against which factory hands in turn asked favors of the Paynes and voiced their own opinions. Thus while members of the Payne family enjoyed a heightened sense of position as the owners of Moth Hill, their employees were emboldened to express themselves in ways that might elsewhere result in reprimand or dismissal. The kinspeople who helped Hazel feed and care for the Payne grandchildren after working hours likewise conveyed to Royce her displeasure at being publicly reprimanded. When Royce came to Hazel, asking why she didn't "say anything back" at the time, she responded: "Because you're old and you're foolish. . . . But if you ever do anything like that to me again, I'll lay you out and help you up." He never did apologize, Hazel told me years after the incident, but something of a truce was established. In like manner Darlene Stokes spoke so freely to John Walter Payne that he felt called upon to explain the circumstances to a visitor touring the factory. June Robbins, for her part, "enjoyed" both the opportunity to drive her employer's wife throughout the countryside and to have private discussions with Royce about shop-floor politics. In other words, Moth Hill's employees did not accept without dispute and negotiation either the power of paternalism or the various meanings attributed to kinship.

Given the doubled visions of kinship and waged labor, women's activities took on added significance within the factory. Central members of kin and social networks and, for many years, the primary labor force in mica processing, women engaged in various endeavors that shaped daily life on the shop floor and the character of factory relations. The recruitment stories serve as an important illustration of how, by enlisting neighbors and relatives for openings at Moth Hill, female hands were able to fill the plant with colleagues who endorsed their interpretations of work rules and job assignments. Hazel Roberts noted of the Lower End, "That bunch down there handpicks [their co-workers] and kindly works them over" to make sure they'll "fit in."

This was something that Hazel knew about. When orders got so scarce at one point that the women on the Upper End decided they had to "go hunt us up a job," Frances Stokes traded on her Cove Creek connections and experience making rings on the Lower End to move back in to some of the good steady work they had down there. Hazel, on the other hand, had two problems. She had previously had run-ins with the authority of the women on the Lower End, and she had "kin [there] who wouldn't claim her" because of differences in social and economic standing in their respective branches of the family. As a result, Hazel never did get on the punch presses. Without kinspeople nearby, she told me repeatedly, "You've got to be nice, because you never know when you're going to need help."

In the daily routines of the factory women provided for kinspeople as co-workers. Perhaps the most obvious expression of this came at dinnertime when workers separated into families and ate the meals that female kin had prepared for them. The preparation of dinner was quite noticeable, as women heated food on the steam tables usually used to dry mica plate. An hour beforehand, factory workers pulled out their jars of food and baking potatoes, and the smells of cooking would mix with lacquer fumes. When the factory whistle blew, family members sought each other out in their appointed places, and their kinswomen set out the meal.

Gertie Russell and Annie Sparks, sisters and co-workers, sat together every day—one or the other providing dinner. Tammi Wilson from the front office and her husband, Floyd, one of the "ring boys" from the Lower End, joined Gertie and Annie at their "table," the machine that produced the "flexible" plate. Down on the Lower End, Franklin and Rita Watkins sat together eating the food that Rita had brought. Al Gardner, his sons Jay and Jimmy, and daughter, Vickie, congregated over by the punch machines to eat their dinner, always finishing with a candy bar that Al carefully divided with the aid of his pocket knife. Upstairs, Maxie Stokes gathered her daughters, daughters-in-law, and unmarried son off to one corner of that large room, while the sisters Alma Moody and Darlene Stokes ate and worked together at another table. Downstairs, Hazel Roberts and Frances Stokes, friends almost as close as sisters, alternated days in supplying the meal and sat in their own little spot—outside, whenever the weather permitted, or atop the machine on the Upper End where they made the "red" (mica plate). As their charge, I followed Hazel and Frances to that day's location and exchanged store-bought cookies for the baked potatoes they had made me.

Having "your people to look out for you" meant informal conversations about what was going on in the front office and how best to respond, as when Hazel Roberts conferred with Gertie Russell about production strategies or, early on in my fieldwork, June Robbins warned me of the need to pay another visit to Royce if I wanted to keep coming back to the factory. It could also mean using friends and relations to scout out information about the state of the mica business or other news of Moth Hill. In addition to her own efforts to screen and sort out defective washers, for example, June checked the quality of factory output through reports from her daughter, an employee at a company that used Moth Hill parts in its own manufacturing processes. When her daughter's company experienced problems with the parts or business was down, June Robbins knew about it and told others on the Lower End. News traveled quickly around the Upper End, and beyond, when two workers—men poorly regarded for their arrogance and lackadaisical work[2]—cost the plant $27,000 in defective merchandise that another customer had returned.

They discussed more than the status of production, for women brought the life of surrounding settlements onto the shop floor. If a house burned down or someone was seriously ill or other matters about area churches or local politics were pressing, factory networks efficiently conveyed that information too. Through this process I learned of the problems of a working-class family whose son had been diagnosed with AIDS (Anglin 1997) and the health concerns of Moth Hill workers and their families. When Gertie Russell's husband fell ill, Hazel Roberts knew about it as soon as Gertie's sister did, and Hazel kept in touch all the time that Gertie was out tending to Isa. However, in addition to opening up possibilities for assistance and a general sense of concern, these discussions operated in ways that maintained distinctions between workers. The difficulties that her husband created for Gertie (most notably, his "running around on her" and forcing Gertie to leave her church) were invariably mentioned in the course of conversations about his current state of poor health, and the women accorded Isa little sympathy. From Hazel I heard how Elsa Watkins had disavowed their kin relations, because divorce and other problems of the past had damaged the reputation of the Roberts family. And Hazel said that Elsa also often acted against her in the plant.[3] Similarly, women in the factory related another story involving this class-based logic, that of Billy Johnson, whom they described as a hard worker from a "rough" background and "bad to drink [after a] payday." Thus I learned the delineations of social networks: who were "good, Christian people," which families had higher social status and/or economic resources, which were poor but respectable, and those from whom I should keep a safe distance.

Included in these conversations and informal dealings were messages about gendered relations. Women routinely avoided interactions with men who were not kin. If necessary, they were able, through reliance on relations and female colleagues (kin or no), to assert their independence from male co-workers— even when those co-workers were their superiors. While I did not observe these rules initially, I found them increasingly significant as I became established within the network of women on the Upper End. Hazel Roberts told me quite explicitly to stay away from her boyfriend, Will Stokes, and it became obvious that no one knew quite what to make of my efforts to ask questions of the men working in the plant. I was violating boundaries established through kin connections and gender definitions and getting nowhere in the bargain. Subsequent to these realizations, I sought access through appropriate channels and/or acknowledged my limits. I left Will alone.

Men likewise maintained their distance from women to whom they were not related, although they frequently resorted to teasing as a means of drawing attention. Women were more than able to hold their own in such instances. When Frances Stokes briefly returned to making rings from lacquered mica (melted and slumped over molds), she had to deal with the connotations of a work assignment that had been traditionally assigned to men and the "ring boys" working beside her on the Lower End. To Floyd Wilson's tossing of waste pieces of mica and joking remarks in her direction, she responded in kind and maintained a confident friendly presence that he could not disrupt. To my questions she replied: "Oh, I don't mind the teasing. It helps the time pass faster. This work is boring, boring, boring." And when, for what seemed to be the hundredth time, I was subjected to Franklin Watkins's jokes about not being married, Hazel suggested in a loud voice for everyone to hear: "Tell him we don't take the 'culls.'" This occurred in the public space of the factory, with the shift of workers lined up to punch out at the end of the day; in effect, she had reduced a male supervisor and, by extension, his male colleagues to the status of inferior: a "cull" or animal considered to have no breeding potential and thus removed from the herd. Not surprisingly, no one in line responded to Hazel; however, shortly thereafter Franklin apologized to me for his remarks. I realized then that I could learn a lot from Hazel Roberts, Frances Stokes, June Robbins, Darlene Stokes, and even Gertie Russell about assertiveness as well as workplace strategizing.

Legacies of Change: The Mica Trade and Gendered Factory Labor

While relations of gender, kinship, and class shaped daily life in the factory, these were not invariant structures but rather understandings tied to particular historical contexts and processes of production. Notwithstanding the comments of younger workers that little had changed from the workplace that their parents and grandparents knew, much had changed about the mica industry itself in the decades after the "government program" and the organization of factories like Moth Hill.

The market for mica declined dramatically in the 1960s, because of both the conclusion of the Korean War and the development of new technologies. The invention of a kind of synthetic mica, otherwise known as plastics, provided an alternative form of insulation for many electronics applications. At the same time, rising costs of mica mining and processing—a legacy of government efforts to stimulate domestic production—rendered this commodity more expensive and consequently less attractive to private industry. Even though mica became an important resource once again in the era of the Vietnam War, production never regained the levels of the 1950s and early 1960s. Whatever "pure mica" the military needed was largely (but not exclusively) obtained from the federal stockpiles or by importing it from India and other international sources. The paradoxical effect of government interest in western Carolina mica was that it all but destroyed this regional industry.

As the primary workforce for mica processing, women were directly affected by these changes. From the mid-1960s onward plant operations required far fewer women, and where possible, their jobs were mechanized. The importation of mica from India effectively eliminated the skilled work of sheeting and grading mica, because the Indian government limited mica sales to only fabricated (processed and punched, rather than raw) mica.[4] While menial labor had always been part of women's work in mica, now women almost exclusively performed deskilled tasks. Adjuncts of the machines they tended, women were regarded as an expendable and relatively inexpensive source of labor.

Likewise, men's labor was devalued in the transformation of the mica business from an industry based on the extraction of local minerals to one organized around the expropriation of inexpensive and available labor. Men once had mined mica in small family operations that sold the commodity to local merchants and government buyers, or they had worked for bigger mining operations. "Shortest days you ever worked in" was Lamar Watkins's way of describing his employment as a miner (interview 4). With the importation of foreign mica, however, little work remained in "pure mica," and men found jobs instead as machine operators, "fixers," or supervisors in the factories that remained.

The rationalization of productive processes carried additional implications for gendered relations in the factory. Whereas women once had dominated the workforce, by the late twentieth century nearly equal numbers of women and men worked in mica factories;[5] the result was elevated male authority in the spheres of production. Although men performed menial jobs such as mixing chemicals, sanding and varnishing mica plate, punching out parts, and the like, more than half the men employed at Moth Hill either supervised department operations or engaged in activities that required some skill and/or individual decision making. By contrast, with the exception of two office workers and one female supervisor, women tended machines that made the sheets of laminated mica, operated punch presses, and did other forms of rote work. Even when they "laid mica by hand," which meant assembling mica pieces and coating them with varnish, female employees had little power over the labor process. Indeed, workers Upstairs frequently convened around a long table with its own conveyor belt. Much like they did with the machines running on the Upper End (the department that produced laminated mica), the women placed mica flakes on a lacquered surface as the belt moved steadily forward.

Furthermore, all male employees, regardless of task, earned higher wages than women. Those who served in supervisory capacities were paid still more. In the late 1980s this meant that women were paid the state minimum wage ($3.35 an hour) and men $0.10 more per hour. Skilled male workers earned an additional $0.10, and supervisors $0.20, per hour. Presumably, just as Frances Stokes earned more money when she performed "men's work," so Darlene Stokes received higher pay for her work as a supervisor but less than her male colleague Upstairs. Women workers considered the discrepancy between men's and women's wages as a sign of gender-based discrimination, and it was thus a source of discontent. Hazel discouraged her brother from seeking employment at Moth Hill by telling him, among other things, "the minute you go to work there, you'll be making 10 cents more an hour than me." (Paul Roberts responded, "It's not really like that, is it?") Nonetheless, frustration about wage differentials was tempered by knowledge that the differences were slight and, more significantly, by the realization that everyone in the plant was underpaid.

Beyond outsourcing mica fabrication and, in the bargain, becoming a distributor of foreign goods, Moth Hill intensified its effort to become ever more flexible in its manufacturing practices so that it could maintain a place within the shrinking mica trade. Where this had previously meant that different sections of the factory produced specialized parts on demand, flexibility in the 1980s translated into the practice of shutting down entire departments for weeks at a time, the ubiquitous issue of "getting laid off." This policy had a particularly deleterious effect on women, because they were less likely to have the supervisory positions or the flexibility to move throughout the plant. Even Darlene Stokes was laid off when Upstairs had no production orders, while her colleague, Jimmy Gardner, stayed on to coordinate plans for production and the shipment of outstanding orders.

Consequently, women were more likely than men to face periods of unemployment, as Zona Watson had once complained to Dallas Stamey, and were routinely laid off in three of the five divisions of the factory. Although they were able to draw unemployment checks during those periods, factory workers faced serious economic hardship because unemployment compensation is based on salary, and women received only minimum wage. Worse, health insurance for Moth Hill employees was paid out of their salaries, not by the company, further compounding workers' problems when they were released from waged labor. "It's a lost cause," one woman observed to me in discussing the work plans for her department and her own economic circumstances.

Thus women found themselves in contradictory positions. On the one hand, they derived power from their roles as kinswomen within the workplace. On the other hand, however, they were powerless in the face of dwindling plant operations and changes in mica processing that rendered their labor almost obsolete. Time and again, I was told in answer to my questions about work schedules, "I don't know. It's all according to what [the supervisor] wants me to do. I guess I'll know Friday evening if I'm coming in to work. It all depends on whether they've got orders or not." Perceptions of the marginal and unpredictable character of their employment counterbalanced the kinds of assertiveness that women displayed in their interactions with coworkers and factory managers. It was not fatalism that workers displayed but pragmatism about what was possible in a failing business. Within those concrete boundaries Moth Hill employees worked strategically, as experiences in one factory department illustrate.

Productive Relations on the Upper End

As one of two sites in the plant for the manufacturing of laminated mica (mica plate/micanite), the Upper End contained four large machines for producing different forms of micanite. The department also had presses to squeeze excess varnish from the sheets of plate, steam tables to dry the plate, equipment to mix the lacquers used in various manufacturing processes, and any number of fifty-five-gallon drums for storing the concoctions. Gertie Russell, Annie Burleson, Hazel Roberts, Frances Stokes, and Zona Watson formed a work group that divided into teams to tend the machines. Typically, Annie and Gertie worked "cutting-off" on one machine, Frances and Hazel on another, and Gertie flying between the two to keep the machines adequately supplied with mica and varnish. Zona Watkins came to work only when the factory had orders for a special kind of plate requiring the services of all five women for its manufacture. Orders for this variety of micanite were erratic, and Zona worked less than half the time as a result. When Moth Hill had no orders for the other kinds of machine-made plate, Frances and Hazel had to work Upstairs. Because the department Upstairs was the most susceptible of all to layoffs, workers there resented the addition of Hazel and Frances, whom they considered to be "taking work away" from them. Of the five women, only Gertie and Annie remained on the Upper End all the time.

At the same time, the Upper End had a higher proportion of male to female workers than was typical for the plant. Three male workers ran presses, mixed chemicals, and did odd jobs throughout the department. Two men, and sometimes a third, made specialized mica parts on equipment also housed on the Upper End. Thus while the women worked among themselves, they dealt constantly with male co-workers, as when Billy Johnson and Ralph Shook opened crates of mica or carried sheets of mica plate off to the presses.

In addition to running a furnace that powered the plant, Carl Fisher served as supervisor of all the procedures on the Upper End. He walked throughout the department, making sure that the equipment was running smoothly and assisting at times with operations. Carl Fisher never criticized anyone's performance for the time I was in the plant, nor did he often intervene in their activities. However, as the one in charge of all productive processes, as well as quality control, he was a force with whom the five women had to contend. I never saw anyone directly challenge his authority, although all regularly consulted him about the status of orders.

Carl periodically checked the mica plate to make sure the flakes of mica were evenly distributed and the varnish none too thick or pooled in any spot, as well as to gauge the breadth of the sheet. Telling me that he was "the one who got in trouble if anything was wrong with it," Carl explained the need for these modest efforts, lest customers judge the plate defective by virtue of its thickness or the poor quality of the mica. "They lost a lot of business that way," he noted. Indeed, workers on the Lower End frequently voiced criticisms about the micanite that they had to use for punching parts.[6] Both the speed of production and the quality of the plate had deteriorated in recent years, they said, and this they attributed to the poor supervision of Carl Fisher, as well as management policies that assigned too many tasks to too few employees. At the time of my field research supervisors were responsible for dealing with the front office on the specifications for new orders, assigning orders to workers and setting up the necessary equipment, supervising task assignments, shipping finished orders, and overseeing supplies. The change in management with Royce Payne's retirement only added to the loads borne by departmental supervisors and workers, and questions proliferated with respect to authority over manufacturing processes. There was little time for details, and the standards for factory output were, at best, relaxed.

Within this context women on the Upper End negotiated work assignments with Carl Fisher and looked to each other for support in the daily politics of the shop floor. Thus while Hazel Roberts told me that she had to watch her back because she had no relatives at Moth Hill, she routinely sought the counsel of Zona Watson and Gertie Russell. They were older women whom Hazel considered as second mothers for having "practically raised me" and for being much like her own maternal kin. Beyond her relatives and Cove Creek neighbors, Frances Watkins also looked to Zona and Gertie for advice, and to Hazel for solidarity, amid the unsteady rhythms of the Upper End. Their work experience and collective memories formed the backdrop for a sustained critique of contemporary conditions, especially with respect to issues of job security, occupational safety and health, workloads and standards of production, and gendered hierarchies. Equally important were their involvement in fundamentalist Christianity, their embeddedness in the working-class communities surrounding the plant, and their sense of dignity, aspects of a broader cultural framework through which female employees on the Upper End (and elsewhere) pursued not only bread but roses from their dealings in the workplace. Yet, more than anything, they were realistic about what was possible in the climate of scarcity that characterized Moth Hill. As Hazel put it, "Annie, Gertie, and then Zona, they trained me. And I'm supposed to train the ones that're next, coming up behind, God help me. But, like I say, it's just close home. You need the work and you still need to be close to home, that's the place to be. You're not going to get rich. You're going to make a living; that's all. You don't get no benefits" (interview 6).

5. Life Histories and Local Cultures

IT IS ONE THING to go into a factory, observe what is going on around you, talk with everyone you can—be they employees, supervisors, or owners—and draw conclusions about the various forces at work. However, as I learned by going home with Hazel Roberts and spending time with Zona Watson, getting to know people outside the work setting dramatically changes one's understandings of labor relations and what matters to workers in the factory. It is not simply a question of learning about the cultural forms through which workers contest the authority of managers, although that is an important dimension of this examination. Equally, if not more valuable, is the opportunity to consider the life experiences that women bring with them into the factory and how those broader contexts inform their endeavors in the workplace.

In other words, the concerns identified by women (and men)—members of kin and social networks, local churches, and settlements or "branches," as well as employees with complex work histories—might look quite different from those suggested by a union organizer or a feminist researcher come to investigate working conditions in a small factory. Rather than interpret the former as inconsequential, if not evidence of how workers are domesticated and their interests subverted, we have new questions to consider, new ways to focus our inquiry. Should our emphasis be on how the factory continues to profit by hyperexploiting its labor force? Or on how workers operate to maintain jobs in the face of economic restructuring? Might we look for moments of overt conflict regarding factory policies, instances where employees use local traditions to "humanize" the conditions under which they labor, or some combination of these? Do other settings, outside the factory, constitute "free spaces" where employees and other residents of local communities can address problems of waged work—in conjunction with other, equally compelling interests?

By entertaining questions such as these, we interpret commentaries about "dead-end" jobs from a different vantage point, one that balances workers' pragmatism about the demands they might realistically achieve in an ailing industry and/or economy with their determination to secure or maintain those aspects of factory life deemed critically important. Anticipating the discussions of chapter 6 (paternalism, protest, and back talk), we take more seriously the efforts of women at Moth Hill (or elsewhere) who defy hierarchical constructions of ethnicity, gender, and class without necessarily being able to dismantle those systems (see, e.g., Bookman and Morgen 1988; S. Fisher 1993; Friedenberg 1995; Ginsburg and Rapp 1995; Hall 1986; Kondo 1990; Lamphere 1985, 1987; Lock and Kaufert 1998; Maggard 1998; Milkman 1985; Mullings 1997; Sacks 1988, 1989; Sacks and Remy 1984; J. Scott 1985, 1990; Susser 1996).

Fine-grained analyses of people's lives allow us to appreciate the multiple and even contradictory strategies through which they contest dominant power relations. In answer to Karen Sacks's noteworthy questions (1989:543), we see that working-class residents of places like Pike County determine what is "worth fighting about" from the context of regional traditions and local social networks. We also come to realize that what constitutes a life well lived might involve more than what one does to earn wages or how one responds to bosses and that this represents neither complacency nor defeat. Through her insistence about what was important to her, Zona Watson, in particular, taught me this.

First and foremost in her lessons to me was Zona Watson's emphasis on history and place, grounded in memories of her mother, her family, and growing up on Liston's Branch. Another, more complicated dimension of her sense of place pertained to the early years of her marriage to Zeyland Watson and the difficulties that they encountered in locating sufficient income to start a family and remain in the area where they had been raised. Of comparable significance for Zona was her involvement with religion, exemplified by her ties to local churches and her mother's example of a fundamentalist Christian spirituality that was separate from church settings or preachers. Religious meanings formed the foundation for how she viewed her childhood; her life with Zeyland, their children and grandchildren; and the troublesome business of finding public work. Yet Zona Watson also spoke directly to questions of class: the ways in which her aspirations to become a white-collar worker had been undermined, her experiences in dealing with the Paynes and of being poor while others at the factory were not, and the health problems with which she contended as an elderly woman of lesser economic means.

In many respects Hazel Roberts duplicated Zona Watson's emphases on the importance of family relations and a sense of place, as well as her involvement in fundamentalist Christianity. For Hazel, as with Zona, class was not an abstract concept but something that she dealt with as part of her daily routines and spoke about in those terms. But as an unmarried woman of another generation, Hazel Roberts also articulated perspectives that varied considerably from those offered by Zona. Whereas Zona spoke from the perspective of an older woman who had outlived her husband and was partially retired from waged labor, Hazel still lived with her parents and seemingly had much of her life before her. More mobile and self-reliant than Zona could have been as a young woman in the 1920s and 1930s, Hazel envisioned alternatives to her work at Moth Hill and, indeed, the need for them.

In sum, the stories that Hazel and Zona related, my activities visiting them at home and going off on outings of various kinds, and the opportunity to attend church with Hazel for an extended period of time provided me with a better sense of how these women of different generations viewed their communities, social networks, and the time that they spent at Moth Hill. Most of all, they showed me that, by concentrating on productive processes, factory routines, and management agendas, I had set my sights far too narrowly.

"We've Changed Our Standard of Living": Stories from Zona Watson's Life

Zona Watson, in her seventies when I began my field research, was one of the oldest workers at Moth Hill.[1] Like many of the older women there, she was a widow who supported herself with a combination of social security payments and the wages that she made through her factory work. Zona's soft-spoken ways, her status as a senior (if partially retired) worker, and her intelligence won her the respect of her co-workers—if not Royce Payne. Although her expertise on the machine that produced the "flexible" (mica plate) made her an invaluable worker during the years that this variety of micanite "carried" the plant, orders in the late 1980s called for that manufacturing process far less often, and Zona's status shifted to that of part-time worker.[2] However, this was an arrangement that suited her, for it was sufficient for her to maintain her health insurance; she had chronic health problems from too many years of full-time factory work.

Zona lived by herself on Liston's Branch, just a few miles from the factory. She was raised in that area, and her small wood-framed house sat just a few hundred yards from the site that once had held the log home of her mother's youth and Zona's own childhood: "[My mother's people] were from Liston's Branch. They cleared the land and built a big log house and they had a large family, but they all married and left except my mother. She stayed to take care of her parents; she didn't marry right away. She lived with them till they died. It was some time in the 1800s [that they settled there], 'cause Mama was the next-to-youngest child, and she was born in 1881, so there's twenty years between her oldest sister and her."

Several of Zona's siblings, as well as some of her children and grandchildren, lived on Liston's Branch, and they came together for such things as Sunday dinners and trips to town or church. Zona had not intended to move into the house that her brother had built and left behind for the mills of South Carolina. She'd wanted her family to have its own place, acquired with the money her husband earned prospecting for mica, except that Zeyland had other plans:

> Zeyland had just made a lot of money at the Bald Knob Mine, so we was going to build us a house over there [on the branch/creek]. My brother and his family were moving to Rock Hill, South Carolina, and he wanted to sell the house. I said, "No, we're not going to buy this house. We're going to have us a new one." I'd never lived anywhere but old houses. But Zeyland'd been to Sadieville, and he had his eye on a new Buick. Zeyland always did love new cars. So he spent the money on the car, and we bought this old house with what we had left.

Thus Zona and Zeyland made a home for themselves on Liston's Branch. Zeyland prospected for mica and tried his hand at other jobs, both near and far away, and Zona eventually went to work at Moth Hill. As was true for many in the factory, money was always hard to come by. Zona explained that she had long since gotten used to being poor, and she marveled at the Moth Hill employees who had late model cars and fancy brick houses. As she put it, "I can't seem to save anything."

On the other hand, Zona always made a big garden, with rows of dahlias and other flowers and a host of vegetables that she canned for the winter. She would be outside tending her garden whenever the weather permitted and regardless of whether her adult children offered any help. In so doing, she continued in the tradition of her mother, who kept a large farm going while her husband ran a sawmill:

> [Mama had] milk, butter, and patches of raspberries and she . . . walked to Monroe, to sell them [there]. She tried everything. She'd order seeds, everything from Burpees' Seeds. All the time, back in the years when she went to the fair in Sadieville, she tried to sell everything, to have everything to take.
>
> They always had big cornfields, so they had that to feed in the winter, and they put up hay. The fields that's in timber now, all of these mountain fields,

that was the cornfields where we had to hoe corn. It'd take an hour to do one row from one end to the other. We always had to hoe corn. They'd hire people to help us. . . .

Sometimes she had five or six, the boys—Zeyland and his brothers, you see—we all growed up here together. They'd help hoe and other families' children. . . . We had good times. I didn't think it back then. I thought we was working awful hard, but now I look back on it, we had a good time.

While he "had a mill and always sawed lumber," Zona's father was never successful in his business dealings. Her mother kept the household going, and her family well fed, from the crops and livestock that she raised: "[My mother] kept cattle, cows, chickens, you know, she always had cattle to sell." In the first half of the twentieth century the regional fair and local merchants provided outlets for enterprising farmers like Mrs. Aldridge to sell (or barter) their produce.

Nevertheless, her mother wanted more for Zona and her siblings than to make do on a farm. She saved enough money to put all four of her children through high school and two through college programs—this during the 1920s when money was tight in the local economy. Not only did Zona's mother acquire the funds necessary for textbooks and college tuition but she forswore the local custom of keeping children out of school to help with farm chores during periods of peak production. As Zona recalled, her mother learned the liabilities of that approach through her own experience: "Children had to work, to help [with the farm] work. [My mother] didn't believe in that, you know, but one time she kept me out to help pick beans. She had a big patch of beans that they shelled out for winter beans—and dried. We picked beans all that day, and that night the cows got in and ate the beans and ruined them. She said she never would keep any younguns out of school any more to help do work because she'd had such bad luck with the beans. Every one of us finished [school]."

Zona and her sister Pansy went on to college, Zona to a business school and Pansy to what were then called "normal schools" for educating future teachers. However, as Zona ruefully observed, "I got an education, but I didn't put it to use." The problem was not her lack of initiative but a shortage of jobs during the depression. "By the time you could get jobs, I was married and had the children, and I didn't have a chance to work."

Zona went to Tennessee to attend business college because "I had it in my mind, all I wanted was to be a secretary. . . . I didn't know a thing in the world about it." On completing her courses, she returned to Pike County and, because she lacked the money to return for the final examination, never received a degree. Despite these difficulties and the problems of finding employment during the depression, Zona did work briefly for a lawyer in the county seat.

Twice she worked for six months, periods defined by his ability to pay her. It was enough, however, to show her that she hated being a secretary: "I didn't like the people I worked for. They cussed you and made passes. I just was fed up with that." Zona would have liked to continue her training and become a teacher of "those commercial subjects," had that prospect been available to her. Instead, "it just was real hard times then, and you couldn't get any work."

So she went back to Liston's Branch and was courted by young Zeyland Watson, whom she'd known growing up. They ran off to Tennessee to be wed and thereby avoided her mother's protests against their union. On that occasion Zona "wore the best [she] had," for there was little extra to spend on new clothes. From a discussion between Zona Watson and Gertie Russell I learned, "In those days you were glad if you could get together the money for the license."

Zeyland and Zona Watson, once married, confronted the problems of finding employment yet again. The scarcity of jobs in Pike County meant that they had to leave North Carolina—for the coal mines of West Virginia, the canning factories of California, the timber industry of Washington, anywhere there was work. They followed the lead of neighbors and kin on Liston's Creek and headed first to the coal mines:

> Well, the beginning of that, the coal mining, of going there from here, was one of our neighbors up the creek there, Fred Johnson, went to Coalwood, West Virginia. He moved his family then. His boys, his children, growed up with us and we was all friends. [They] wrote back and said there was work. [Fred Johnson's wife] was Zeyland's [sister-in-law's] aunt, so [Zeyland's brother and sister-in-law] went. . . . They went first, and then Zeyland went, and then his brother-in-law. And then different ones from here went and worked in the coal mines. His brother-in-law never came back here till they brought him back to bury him in Long Hill. [Zeyland would] go and then it would get slack, the work would, or they'd have a strike or something and he'd come back here.

Over the course of eleven years in the 1930s and 1940s, Zeyland, Zona, and their children traveled regularly to West Virginia so he could work as a coal miner. The first time they made it there, they had to share a "sawmill shack" back in the hollow with Zeyland's brother and sister-in-law. The men walked three miles to the mines, and the women stayed behind to deal with their young children, clouds of coal soot, and life in a coal camp. That first year was "hell on Earth, if there was such a thing," the strongest words Zona ever used in my hearing. Although they moved to company housing and things got better, Zeyland never lasted for more than a year at a time. He joined the union and did his share of picket duty, but whenever he could, Zeyland

Watson would take off for the North Carolina mountains. "He was an awful strong man, he could lift a lot, and that's why they'd hire him back after he'd quit and come home," she said.

When little work was to be had in coal mining, and fewer jobs of any kind in western Carolina, Zeyland and Zona traveled out to the West Coast. They learned of employment opportunities out west, the same way they had about the coal mines: "Zeyland didn't have any work, and this friend of his, a neighbor up there, up the little creek, said, 'Let's go to Washington State and work in the timber.' . . . [This Ed] Phillips, he had several brothers out there, and so we packed up the first of January and started west . . . with two cars." They didn't make it all the way across country that first time. Zeyland learned en route that he had been drafted into the army, so they returned home—only to find that World War II had just ended. Despite this setback, they went again, like so many others from Pike County looking for work. Five times in all they drove to the West Coast for its promise of employment in the timber industry.

In between Zeyland worked in the coal mines, or the mica mines if the market was good and he had any luck. Mica mining was Zeyland's first love and an occupation he shared with his father and brothers: "He spent many a day prospecting and digging, thinking he was going to hit the rich vein right away." Indeed, they did find two mines that proved quite productive and commercially successful—in the hands of those with the resources to develop them. One, in particular, they called "the rich man's mine" because "the men that bought it, they really made the money during the war."

Zona briefly found work in a little mica house at the head of the creek, near the old schoolhouse where she had attended elementary school. There they trimmed and sheeted local mica for sale to the Colonial Mica Corporation until it closed in the mid-1940s. Several years later, after Zeyland and Zona returned to western Carolina almost for good, a new government program was under way (the decade-long stockpiling effort), and more jobs were to be found in mica processing. That was when Zona took a job at Moth Hill and encountered Royce Payne's negative evaluations, the by-product of her sister's comments from the years when they were still in school and, more important, Royce's propensity to size up potential workers. Zona worked hard to disabuse him of his prejudices and prove her sister wrong, and she was there forty years later to tell me her story.

One story she told me, with great bitterness, was about how Royce had denied her the opportunity to receive an unemployment check. It was a time when she had left Moth Hill to return to the West Coast with Zeyland, because he was not able to find work in Pike County—or in the state of Washington, as it turned out. The loss of Zona's wages and/or the possibility of compensation made for even harder times:

> Well, then, the next time we went, I had been working at Moth Hill, and I told Royce that Zeyland didn't have any work here, and he thought he'd get work there [in Washington] and I wanted to go. I was going out with him. And I told [Royce] two weeks before; I wasn't going to lie. I never had a job with unemployment, and I [wanted] to get a layoff slip so I could draw. Well, when we got there, it was a real cold late spring, and work in the timber business didn't start up.
>
> And I couldn't draw any unemployment, 'cause [Royce] said I just quit. He did me dirty there. The man at the employment office said that seems a pretty good reason for you to leave, 'cause your family's going, you know. We didn't have the money to come home, and work didn't start.
>
> Lots of people had left and gone to other places and come back to work. I could name different ones he [Royce] let come back to work. I worked there thirty-nine years last November.

But Zona had more to talk about than work histories and her early encounters with Moth Hill. These were the things that I asked her to speak to, background information that helped contextualize her career in mica and comments about the current status of the factory, and she was willing to respond. At the same time, she persisted in telling me about her faith— not to witness or to convert me but to describe the bedrock of her life. Just as talking about her own life meant telling me about her mother's, so Zona spoke about religion.

In the early years Sundays meant walking with her siblings and father to the Presbyterian church in Monroe, three or four miles away: "You had to be ready to go to church on Sunday morning or you had to be real sick." After the Presbyterian Sunday school, over which her father presided as superintendent for about fifty years, they would walk on to the community church designated to host the preacher that week: "Back then, one Sunday they'd have the preaching at the Presbyterian. The next Sunday, they'd have preaching at the Baptist. The next Sunday, they'd have it at the Methodist. So after Sunday school, Papa'd bring us down to whichever church was having preaching, and we had to stop and go there for preaching. We'd want to come on home so bad, and we'd get just so mad. Papa would make us stop for church, for preaching services, and we'd just be a-dying to come on home."

Zona's mother, who had been raised Baptist, stayed behind on Sunday mornings. Perhaps, as other informants described, having people going to more than one church would "split the family." It could also have been, as Zona explained, that her mother's productive activities militated against long sojourns away from the farm: "My mother didn't go [to church] much because she always had too much to do. She felt like she ought to stay there. Sometimes it would happen that she had to churn on Sunday morning. She had to do the milking, and sometimes she had to churn. You know, it'd be the day. And she always cooked us a good Sunday dinner, and we always had somebody with us, and we looked forward to that." Zona's mother kept the farm going and celebrated Sundays by making a big dinner for family and for friends who had come to visit. Staying home from church was no sign of impropriety for, in addition to meeting the obligations of the household, her mother studied the Bible and taught the children her religious beliefs. Moreover, she was well represented at the local church(es) by her children and husband.

In those days, at least, the significance of the church extended beyond the public observance of religious faith. Local churches provided the occasion for residents of different settlements to assemble, whether it was to hear circuit-riding preachers, participate in revivals, or attend "singings" that featured local church choirs. Boys and girls walked together to church, and young couples courted en route: "There'd be a revival or something at the church going about all the time, at one of the other churches, and that's the only places we went at night. That's where the boys and girls walked home together from the churches. They'd go to one or the other churches, to the revivals or singings or whatever they had." Attending church was "something to do" at a time when few residents of Pike County had cars and travel was limited. Young and old alike, they would "walk off these mountains" to "go and fellowship" at area churches. Church revivals—weeklong meetings held in the spring and fall—often lasted all day and into the night, creating a pretext for sharing meals and long conversations as well as listening to various preachers. It was in this setting that Zeyland Watson found an opportunity to court Zona Aldridge.[3]

Not long after she married Zeyland, Zona became a member of the Baptist church on Liston's Branch. It wasn't that Zeyland asked her to do so, for he did not attend church regularly in those days. Neither could this be construed as an act of disloyalty against the church in which she was raised, because the tradition of circuit-riding preachers made for a community-based ecumenism. Zona Watson switched over to Liston's Branch Baptist because, as an adult woman, she could exercise that choice, and the church appealed to her: "I don't know that I liked it any better. But I felt it was a little church, and they wasn't many people to do anything. I felt needed after I went there. And I was the church clerk, for eight years, I believe it was." Along with holding office as church clerk, Zona taught Sunday school for more than twelve years. This was a position in which women's, as well as men's, authority was respected, and what mattered most was knowledge of the Bible and local theology. In so doing, Zona followed the teachings and example of both her parents.

By the time I met her, Zona was no longer teaching Sunday school, although she was still a member of the church. Liston's Branch Baptist Church, with attendance of more than one hundred people and a weekly collection of nearly $2,000, had become quite large by local standards and had nearly outgrown its facilities. Zona went to preaching at the church and local singings whenever she could, but that became more difficult after Zeyland died in the mid-1980s.[4] As was true for many of the older women in the plant, she never learned to drive a car and had to rely on her children for transportation: "I don't go much anymore. I can't go unless somebody takes me and they're not very good to go, my people's not. They go when they take a notion." Even if she could not make it to church, Zona studied her Bible in keeping with the traditions of her mother and her neighbors on the branch. Like her mother, Zona prepared Sunday dinner each week for her extended family and visitors, including Hazel and me: "Well, I still did that when my children was growing up. I always tried to fix . . . a good Sunday dinner for them, if they didn't have anything but potatoes and beans the rest of the week." In addition, Zona Watson quietly discussed her faith with those who were interested in what she had to say. That might mean her relatives, including her sister, who continued on at the Presbyterian church, or the women with whom she worked on the Upper End.

Not everyone in the factory was receptive to such conversations, for church membership, like kin groups and settlements, operated through selective principles; employees drew a distinction between those who were "saved" and those who were not. Among the women of the Upper End, three (including Zona) were members of area churches, while the others worshiped at home. Discussions of religious doctrine, at least the ones to which I was witness, navigated carefully around distinctions between the Pentecostalism of Frances Stokes's church on Cove Creek, the Missionary Baptist tradition with which Zona Watson and Hazel Roberts were affiliated, and the nondenominational Protestant fundamentalism of Gertie Russell and Annie Burleson. Yet if individual churches articulated particular histories and experiences, the collective concerns of evangelical Christianity allowed for a sense of commonality, to which these conversations attested.

By contrast, women on the Upper End were less sparing of the local Methodist church. They referred to this as the "Payne family religion," since Daniel Payne had been instrumental in founding the church and Royce's family had been members for many years. Along with the Presbyterian church in Monroe, it was considered a church of the elite: those more involved with wealth, power, and things of the flesh than with being devout Christians.[5] Perhaps the dwindling influence of the local Methodists, whose congregation consisted of twelve members in 1987, matched the fate of the mica industry. It could also have been, in the late twentieth century, that the vestiges of community-oriented ecumenism no longer encompassed mainstream denominations, with their differences both of theology and social class.

Zona departed from the judgments of her colleagues, doubtless because of her previous experience with both churches. The decline in fellowship was one of the changes she regretted most: Residents of this section of Pike County "go to their own church, once in a while. They count it as 'that's all I need to go,' but they used to fellowship and go to the other churches." In conjunction with the movement away from farming the land and the demise of the mica industry, this comprised a major part of the social transformations to which Zona and others of her generation had been witness.[6] Zona explained, "They've got so they're too busy, I guess. We've changed our standard of living, I reckon, from what it used to be, years ago. See, most everybody used to raise and produce most of what they ate and had on their land. But now they don't do that, you see. The fields where they used to have corn is all grown up, or either set in shrubbery. It's just different. They don't farm, or even garden much, anymore." Such changes represented the further crystallizing of class relations, as well as alterations in specific cultural practices, during the latter half of the twentieth century, and Zona was not alone in expressing a sense of dislocation. Yet the words of Mae Webb, a friend and former co-worker from the Upper End, would hold for Zona as well: "God don't make no mistakes. Everything he does is for a purpose, even if we don't know about it now" (interview 14).

The Tensions of Another Generation: Hazel Roberts's Life

In the stories she told of her life Zona Watson emphasized the significance of working-class communities in the mountains, the travails of her past, and her concerns about the present. Her contemplative approach bespoke the influence of her mother, as well as Zona's status as a woman finished with raising a family and at least partially retired from waged labor. While Hazel Roberts respected Zona as "a second mama" who had "helped raise" her and was a continuing influence in her life, Hazel operated in a very different way.[7] If Zona was quiet and dignified, Hazel was outspoken and activist. Hazel viewed her life as an opportunity to "witness" to her faith and, as a working-class woman in her mid-thirties, confronted head-on the problems of finding a decent job and maintaining her home in the mountains.[8]

It was not that her experiences, apart from the issue of factory work, were idyllic. Growing up in a family where "lightning had split the [family] tree" of her grandparents' generation, Hazel knew firsthand about the lasting effect of such scandals and the politicized nature of family relations. With her father (and brother) Hazel bore the name of the man who had been her grandmother's second husband and who was not her "real" grandfather, while she also experienced her mother's anguish because she had been raised—with her brothers and sisters—in an orphanage/mission school.[9] Although Pearl Roberts was able to turn those early experiences into an opportunity to befriend nearly half of Pike County, "all my friends that I've tried to help out," neither she nor her daughter were oblivious to slights by relatives who considered themselves superior and remained aloof. So "the rich get richer and the poor get poorer" in different parts of their family trees, as Pearl observed, while her daughter showed me that those who are poor "have to watch [their] back[s]" and take care of others in like situations.

Whereas Pearl had been unable to complete her education and instead started work when she was only fifteen, she made sure that Hazel and "a lot of kids got a college education. I've bought sixteen class rings." Hazel also helped put herself through school, working from the early days on and distinguishing herself in the eyes of her teachers: "When I was in grammar school, I was working in the cafeteria. And when I got in high school, I was a teacher's aide, that was grading papers and putting down grades. And then, when I got in college, I worked for a stockbroker." Unlike Zona, Hazel's initial encounters with higher education and the world of business had been positive. She finished her associate in arts degree in twelve months (rather than two academic years), while the stockbroker for whom she worked "treated me like I was kind of special—and he paid me pretty good."

Yet even with the encouragement of her boss, Hazel never adjusted to that urban setting. It was more than two hours' drive from Pike County, she knew few people, and her family was too far away: "In a big city they don't care about you. You could die and be buried for a year before anyone would notice. In Grove, if you're not seen in your yard two or three times a day, someone will call to find out what's wrong. They're not being nosey; they just care." So Hazel returned home just after her brother had completed high school, and together they put in applications at a hosiery mill within commuting distance from her parents' house. Hazel found herself working under the supervision of her brother, but mixed blessing or not, that situation didn't last long: "The doctor told me I couldn't work no more. And I said, 'Yeah, I'll work. If it's the Lord's will, he'll send me a job.' But I didn't know of it."

After her experience with working production and the first of many health problems, Hazel considered going to work at Moth Hill. It was, after all, "a job in the neighborhood" and a place well known to her family. Having heard that John Walter Payne was looking for "a good hand," Hazel approached him. "I said, 'Just hire me and I'll show you a thing or two.'" Bravura aside, Hazel did not expect that much would come of their conversation. "I went to church that Saturday night. I come home, and Daddy said they'd hired me. I thought they were kidding." Only after John Walter spoke with her again and had showed her "how to get in that place" did Hazel take the job offer seriously. Even then she had to deal with the suspicions of Royce Payne, who informed her of his fears that "we'll just get you trained and you'll quit." Hazel responded by telling him that she would stay a year, "after that I won't promise you nothing," but she continued on at the factory for thirteen years.

Older workers, including her mother and Zona, explained their connections with Moth Hill by noting that "there wasn't anything else" to do to earn wages and by describing the boom time of the late 1940s through the early 1960s. In contrast, Hazel started her job when the mica industry and Moth Hill were in a prolonged downturn from which they never recovered. She told me, more than once, that she never intended to stay at Moth Hill but "after you work here for a while, you lose your ambition. And, really, then you make friends, and you don't want to leave them."

Yet her actions belied her words. During the time that I was engaged in field research, Hazel was involved in computer classes at the local community college—even though she had to contend with a teacher who belittled her in front of the class—and attended a summer program in Kentucky for "older" women who showed aptitude and an interest in higher education. Most of all, Hazel wanted to go back to school full time for a "four-year degree" so she could go into business for herself, even in that "dog-eat-dog world."[10] In the meantime she stayed on at Moth Hill, negotiated with Carl Fisher to keep her work as steady as possible, and looked for other jobs with better pay such that she wouldn't always "have to look at the price of everything and set it back down." Hazel tried, without success, to get a job in the predominantly male, unionized minerals company where her father worked until his retirement and in the fall of 1987 drove two counties away to take the civil service exam.[11] Responding to this latter turn of events for her work partner, Frances Stokes commented with regret and pride, "She's going to leave me some day. She's going to take off for the wild blue yonder." Who knows what might have happened had Hazel Roberts not died two years later at the age of thirty-nine.

Hazel talked about getting a place of her own, small enough to take care of easily because she would "rather be out doing things," and she expressed little interest in getting married. She would drive off Sunday afternoons to meet Will Stokes away from the scrutiny of their respective families; however, nothing more seemed to come of their visits. People in the factory used to say that Maxie Stokes would never let her youngest son marry and that Hazel too had an obligation to care for her parents, especially her mother, who had serious health problems.

Just as real a factor was the love of reading that Hazel shared with Zona and Hazel's passion for writing poetry that earned her a trip to Kentucky. "I write better than I talk," she once said by way of describing these activities and deflecting further commentary from me. She knew very well the images of "ignorant hillbillies" that "outsiders" maintained about people from the mountains—and factory hands, in particular.[12] During one midday break, for example, I watched her handle a car filled with Florida tourists inquiring about the factory and the education levels of its employees. "Honey, everyone of them in there's got college degrees," Hazel had responded and then asked if they wanted to go inside. And for her friends on the Upper End, Hazel brought a copy of poems and short stories published by the program in Kentucky, and both Zona and Frances showed their delight in her accomplishments.

None of this could be separated from Hazel's involvement in fundamentalist Christianity and Long Hill, the Missionary Baptist church that she and her brother, Paul, had attended since they were little. Hazel was a Sunday school teacher, as Zona had been, and she worked with Etta Long in teaching the "older women's class." In addition to her commitments to Long Hill, Hazel meditated on her Bible at home and sought every opportunity to witness in public: "The devil knows that when you're at home, you're just around your family. But when you're on a job, you have the chance to witness to a lot of people, so he makes it hard for you. [The devil] gives you all sorts of excuses about being tired, having too much to do, because he knows you're working for God." Hazel welcomed the chance to talk about Jesus' compassion and the blessings of salvation, as well as to counter the glamor and illusive authority of the devil. With respect to those at Moth Hill who were not saved, she saw her role as speaking on these matters and praying on their behalf, rather than condemnation. She also sought the companionship and conversation of fellow believers—Frances, Zona, and Gertie—or Mae Webb, if we were Upstairs, for Hazel respected Mae's knowledge of the Scriptures and viewed her as an elder.

Hazel and Frances talked about the "rapture" or the "second coming," when Jesus would return to bring those who are "saved" directly to heaven. They would not have to die or "be buried in that cold, cold ground," while those who were "lost in sin" would be left behind to suffer endlessly.[13] The immediacy of this belief, the way it was insinuated into every part of Hazel's life, became evident the first time that it was too cold for us to eat dinner (picnic-style) outside, and we took refuge in her car. I saw the sticker on her dashboard that read: "WARNING: In case of the Second Coming . . . driver will disappear!" This message was nothing to be taken lightly, but neither did Hazel force her beliefs on me. Instead, she wanted me to know about the comfort she found in her religious beliefs, and, with Frances, she continued to invite me to church. My fears about becoming enmeshed in obligations I could not honor notwithstanding, I eventually accepted their invitations.[14] Through those experiences I learned about ways that people live their faith and working-class churches minister to their communities. I also learned about righteous anger and the power of dissent.

"At Home in the Church"

> God help us all
> not to fall
> for the Devil's Way
> —Pearl (01/88)

Long Hill Baptist Church was a community institution and a place where working-class people could go to worship in the traditions of fundamentalist Christianity. Long Hill's main building served as the schoolhouse when Zona Watson attended elementary school about sixty years earlier, and for at least a century the church had been responsible for maintaining the community cemetery. While circuit-riding preachers had long since given way to pastors called by God and voted in by their respective congregations, Long Hill still took its part in hosting interdenominational gospel singings with choirs, pastors, and congregants from the various churches in Pike County. "Just for tonight, let's put our denominations in our back pocket and enjoy being in the house of the Lord," was the greeting offered by Harlan Brown, the preacher at Long Hill.

Long Hill ministered to its own congregation through a conservative theology based on a literal interpretation of the King James version of the Bible and an emphasis on the power of personal conviction. In the tradition of Missionary Baptist churches in Appalachia, Long Hill functioned as an independent congregation that fostered exuberance and emotionalism in its religious services and exhorted all communicants to personally attest to their religious faith. The hierarchical organization of church associations and the politics of doctrinal interpretation central to Southern Baptist churches were conspicuously absent (see Dorgan 1987; Humphrey 1981; McCauley 1995; Rosenberg 1989). Thus while Long Hill supported traditions of patriarchal authority through its male leadership, the organization of the church limited that authority lest it compromise the actions of the faithful. Congregations voted pastors and deacons in or out through annual elections that reflected the sentiments of the church membership as a whole, and the gendered sphere of Sunday school classes provided one occasion to air and debate such feelings.

The centerpiece of prayers, sermons, Sunday school lessons, and casual conversation were the experiences of working-class men and women in the mountains. Each week, when Hazel, Paul, and I took our places next to Nola and Ben Forbes in the last pew on the left, other worshipers greeted us with questions about the status of production orders, paychecks, and jobs at Moth Hill. Nola would tell us "Moth Hill girls" of the plans for the coming week in the Lower Building, while Ben and Hazel would commiserate about the goings-on in the Upper End. If Ben or Nola were absent, Hazel would determine the cause and lend her aid and likewise for Parnell Hayes, who sat at the end of our pew.[15]

Deacon Lonnie Fields welcomed us at the start of the service by telling us that he hoped we were "feeling well in body" and by enjoining the visitors "not to make themselves at home, because that sounds like work, but to *be* at home" in the church. He offered prayers that spoke of the opportunity to worship God in his house and referred to Jesus as the "lovely Savior," language that contrasted with Lonnie's blue-collar clothes and his conversational manner away from the pulpit. Even Harlan Brown, the pastor and the only man to wear clothes that were fancier than work attire, referred to his own working-class past. He had worked third shift for about thirteen years, and once was Paul's boss, before he received his calling from the Lord and secured a paying job as the preacher at Long Hill. Harlan exhorted his parishioners to attend church faithfully, saying that because "God gave you strength to go out and work on a job," they owed their Sundays to God.

In similar spirit but with little allegiance to Harlan Brown, Etta Long often used her experiences as a factory worker for her text in the Sunday school class that she taught, with Hazel as her assistant. Etta's stories depicted in concrete terms the connection between her faith and her daily life as worker, mother, and wife, topics that resonated with that group of older, married women. Faith helped Etta endure the rigors of her job and the recalcitrance of her co-workers, to whom she witnessed on a regular basis. Her experience with the "angel of the Lord" en route to work one day offered an illustration of the personal terms through which Etta integrated these separate worlds. As she was driving down the steep and curvy highway one wintry morning, Etta felt the car skidding off the pavement. Suddenly, she felt "the angel of the Lord just grab ahold of the wheel and keep my front tire from slipping into that ditch." The angel brought the car to a halt, and Etta regrouped, making her way to the factory before the start of her shift. As Etta conveyed it, hers was an encounter with the hazards of country roads and, simultaneously, with Jesus as comforter and support amid such difficulties. Nothing was vague or abstract about Etta's experience and her testimonial to it.

Other stories similarly recounted tales of personal traumas and events, grounding Sunday school participants in the themes of fundamentalist Christianity and its relevance to their lives. As an example of the power of prayer in her life, Hazel described her brush with death some years earlier. She was in the hospital, and doctors had told her that she would not survive her illness. Her family refused to believe the prognosis, because six years earlier she had been diagnosed with cancer but had lived through it, and they felt sure that "God would work another miracle." Hazel got very angry at everyone—her brother, her parents, the doctors and nurses—and told them all to leave her alone. Afterward she had a change of heart; she prayed for hours and felt God answer her prayers. Hours later, when she woke to the sound of the telephone, Hazel told her family that everything would be alright, that God was in the room with her and she would be well again. To her doctor's amazement she did recover completely.

Chief among the themes considered in Sunday school was God's grace and power, in this world and the next. In a discussion about going to God in prayer, one woman commented, "I don't know what the lost do when they're in trouble. I really honestly don't know." When contrasted with the tricks of the devil and the temptations to which sinners surrendered, these narratives presented the agency of the individual in securing her salvation and assisting in the salvation of others. Louise Roscoe, an elder in the class, told a joke to this effect: "There were two devils—one was sitting around doing nothing, and the other one was working furiously. The first devil asked the second one why he was so busy. And he said, 'There's a woman down there just a-praying her heart out.'" The sinful world was an arena in which to act, to testify, and to engage the saving powers of the Lord. However, all would come to naught "if you weren't right with God," as Etta taught us on many Sunday mornings, for "your prayers wouldn't get past the ceiling."

On the few occasions that Etta allowed her actually to lead the class, Hazel emphasized the importance of charity and good works as expressions of faith: "We have to send something up the road. If you don't help nobody now, then when it's your time, you can't expect nobody to come and help you when you ask." Those sentiments were acted upon in prayer requests on behalf of members of the Sunday school class and others absent from Long Hill, as well as in the actions taken by the church. In monthly business meetings the congregation discussed the needs of working-class families from the surrounding area and apportioned resources accordingly. The networks thus engaged provided money and goods, not simply moral support. Disabling illness, fires that destroyed homes, unemployment—the membership of the church dealt with all of it. Of the many discussions that I witnessed during which Long Hill "voted money" to people who had been burned out and lost all they owned, Parnell Hayes's bout with cancer best exemplified the force of church networks and Baptist rhetoric.

A contemporary of Hazel's and deacon of the church, Parnell found out about his illness by experiencing ten seizures one Sunday. Doctors who treated him in the hospital told him that he had a brain tumor and would not live long. When members of Long Hill Baptist Church learned of his crisis, they voted money toward Parnell's medical bills, grown immense with the surgery and adjuvant treatment that his doctors had ordered.[16] They prayed for Parnell and his family and visited him in the hospital. No one held out much hope that he could be made well. As Hazel said to our class, "We can't ask for God to heal Parnell. We can just ask that God's will be done."

To the amazement of the congregation a very frail Parnell returned to church two weeks later. He had always been a slender man, but now he was emaciated and looked decades older. Standing beside the pastor and the other deacons, Parnell greeted us before the service, and he sought the opportunity to come before the church so he could explain what had gone on. His was an emotional address that presented his life-threatening illness in theological terms, affirming his connection with the church and lamenting his condition as a disabled laborer. Parnell thanked the church for its gifts of prayers and money but mentioned his worries about putting too much of a burden on the church. He added that he wanted to take on the job as janitor and groundskeeper for Long Hill, because he was no longer able to hold a regular job. This last was what hurt the most, he told us, for he was used to working fourteen- or sixteen-hour days. It had been his life.

What Parnell planned to do with the rest of his days was to testify to visitors at home and in the hospital, where he returned regularly for treatment. His illness he understood to be a punishment from God for the wickedness of his kin, who refused to attend church even after Parnell had been made deacon. Rather than being bitter about this, Parnell was jubilant in his faith: "I'm ready to go right now if that be the Lord's will. I'm glad it was me." With tears in his eyes he told the congregation, "You-uns are my brothers and sisters." Long Hill was his family, and it was there that he came home. Once Parnell had finished, Harlan told us that there would be no preaching that day. Parnell had given a better sermon than he could, and anyway we needed to assemble outside for the picture that Parnell had asked to have made.

Scores of personal testimonies fill my field notes from Long Hill. Many of these spoke to the omnipotence of God, as contrasted with the actions of sinners and the faithful. Thinly veiled criticisms of preachers who had succumbed to their own self-importance, for example, were offered to counter Harlan's authoritarian discourse and his habit of referring to himself as "God's man in the pulpit." Etta, for one, gave a lesson based on the example of Jim Bakker: "Sometimes preachers get to thinking they're too important. Look at Jim Bakker leading the PTL, asking us for money, and all the time he was up to his eyeballs in sin. And now the IRS is after him. . . . There's some of us take the notion to get our hips up and quit the church, but even if we did, everyone of us, the church would still go on. There's none of us is indispensable." If preachers and other authorities could at times be called into question, God remained supreme and churches would continue their missions.[17] Another Sunday school class on the Book of Job consolidated these teachings by conveying the dangers of "rash speaking," or talking back to God. "Words is like boots," Etta observed on another occasion. "Once we've said them, they go marching out of your mouth, and you can't call them back. And then you have to ask for forgiveness, which is the hardest thing to do."

When Brother Lonnie opened services one Sunday with another reference to Job, declaring that "we are filthy before God," Etta, Hazel, and the other members of the class expressed their agreement. The god of this Missionary Baptist church could be portrayed as being jealous and chastising, as well as "lovely." Those who disregarded him would burn in the eternal fires of hell. Thus the rhetoric and practices of Long Hill Baptist Church summoned forth contradictory images of the need to submit to God's authority, symbolized by the church, and the importance of individual acts of faith and testimony.

In his study of coal miners in West Virginia, David Corbin contends that notions of God's perfection provided miners with the moral authority to speak against the wickedness of coal operators—and company preachers. An incident from the life of Mary Harris (Mother Jones) illustrates his argument: "Mother Jones best expressed the miners' feelings about the company church when a local justice of the peace questioned her about holding a union meeting in a 'House of God [a company church] with everyone carrying a gun.' Jones quickly retorted, 'Oh, that isn't God's house. That is the coal company's house. Don't you know that God Almighty never comes around to a place like this?'" (qtd. in Corbin 1981:153). Coal miners could articulate their grievances through the language of their faith, as a contest between sinners and the righteous. Not every church could claim to be God's house.

The preacher at Zona's church spoke in similar terms on that Sunday that Hazel and I came to visit. He kept repeating to the congregation that "I'm thinking you need to remember who you are. You're the children of God." The responsibility of the saved, he told us, was to witness to their faith through their actions and to oppose the sins of this life. By so doing, the children of God would attest to their status and attain their heavenly rewards.

Such interpretations easily carried over to Moth Hill Mica Company for, as Harlan Brown once asked the members of Long Hill Baptist Church (located barely a mile from the factory), "Did you ever know anyone who got rich *except* by dishonesty?" Yet just as sin and the devil would not be destroyed until the second coming, according to fundamentalist theology, so mica workers and coal miners were forced to contend with an imperfect world and the sinners' seemingly being in charge. What the congregants had nonetheless was a discourse of righteousness and the faith to live that out through their own deeds (see also McCauley 1995:16–17).

In addition, through my weekly meetings with the members of Long Hill, I learned about the importance of church as "home." Parnell's oratory before the church and the comments exchanged each week in Sunday school were powerful reflections of the ways that religious belief and kin and community affiliations combined to provide visions of a meaningful life. "Being at home in the church," the phrase used in place of "making oneself at home," meant sustenance in the immediacy of religious belief. It meant making do with whatever the circumstances were, as Parnell so eloquently testified, knowing you were not alone. Amid the contradictions of economic restructuring and a social system whose informality meant that kin or neighbors often experienced class differences as personal slights, and suffered deprecating remarks from employers, "being at home" was no simple matter.

We might finally consider the narratives related in this chapter from the vantage point of Marx's well-known statement that "people make their own history, but they do not make it just as they please; they do not make it under circumstances chosen by themselves, but under circumstances directly found, given, and transmitted from the past" (1972:437). The unevenness of circumstance; the extent to which people draw upon the past even as they work to fashion new possibilities for themselves; the differences of gender and generation, as well as ethnicity and class, that inform specific events and the local perspectives concerning them—the life stories of Zona Watson, Hazel Roberts, and Parnell Hayes illustrate all this. Their narratives suggest a view of history and culture not as static shapeless forms but reflections of the myriad lives created and sometimes endured in particular material contexts. While certain interpretations may prevail and be taken as "fact" or public knowledge, they neither suppress nor fully conceal the disagreements rooted in differences of experience and social location. When people act upon such disagreements and make specific claims for themselves, they challenge existing relations of power and indeed create alternative histories or other, more viable worlds.

6. Paternalism, Protest, and Back Talk

The idea that there is a "fundamental opposition between capital and labor" does not explain the multiplicity of forms that resistance to control may take nor why there is resistance at one time and not at another.
—Caroline White, "Why Do Workers Bother?"

At any time, forms of alternative or directly oppositional politics and culture exist as significant elements in the society. We shall need to explore their conditions and their limits, but their active presence is decisive, not only because they have to be included in any historical (as distinct from epochal) analysis, but as forms which have had significant effect on the hegemonic process itself. That is to say, alternative political and cultural emphases, and the many forms of opposition and struggle are important not only in themselves but as indicative features of what the hegemonic process has in practice had to control.
—Raymond Williams, *Marxism and Literature*

IN HIS LANDMARK STUDY of Central Appalachia, John Gaventa (1980) argues that the dominance of coal companies was based on their ability to overwhelm regional cultures with the legacies of industrialization: waged labor, conspicuous consumption, "progress," and corporate power. According to Gaventa, because residents widely accepted the value of coal mining for local and regional economies, coal operators found it easy to undermine any challenges to their preeminence. Only the terms under which miners labored were subject to disagreement, and coal companies manipulated local governments, news media, and elites to render miners powerless in these matters. People in Central Appalachia were not inherently fatalistic or passive, in other words. Instead, the coal industry's monopolization of power and cultural legitimacy had forced people into quiescence:

The pattern is one in which challenges by the people of the [Appalachian] Valley to the massive inequalities they face have been precluded or repelled, time and again, by the power which surrounds and protects the beneficiaries of the inequalities. The unitary nature of the power and the transferability of its components among various aspects of community life liken the powerlessness in the contemporary Valley to that of the coal camps of earlier years. The pattern serves now, as it did then, to maintain and strengthen the absentee-dominated social and political order which was established in the "colonization" of the region in the late nineteenth century. (1980:252)

Efforts by laborers and local citizens to challenge such injustices were "repelled, time and again," in the ascendancy of multinational corporations and their recolonization of the mountains.

Gaventa's analysis is an important corrective to the "culture-of-poverty" perspective, for he argues that power relations in Central Appalachia can be understood from the vantage point of political economic structures and historical factors, and not as a response to hypothetical deficiencies (whether cultural, psychological, or genetic) in the region or its inhabitants. Left undisturbed in Gaventa's schema, however, is the notion that the forces of industrial capitalism had defeated the people in Appalachia and had mostly reduced their cultural traditions and political practices to defense mechanisms (see also H. Lewis, Johnson, and Askins 1978; Whisnant 1980, 1983).

More recent scholarship, including work by Gaventa, suggests alternative readings of the vibrance of political structures and citizen activism in the face of economic restructuring, but this does not yet have the weight of the older arguments for academic circles or popular audiences (see, for example, D. Billings, Norman, and Ledford 1999; Black 1990; Couto 1993; S. Fisher 1993; Gaventa, Smith, and Willingham 1990; Hall 1986; R. Lewis 1987; Maggard 1998; S. L. Scott 1995; Seitz 1995; Smith 1987; Trotter 1990; White 1994; Yarrow 1990). Appalachia seemingly offers more dramatic appeal when cast as the victim of forces beyond (or possibly within) its control, a place outside the American dream (cf. Duncan 1999; Harrington 1962; Schenkkan 1993; Stewart 1996). Rather than dwell further on why that might be so, in this chapter I follow Gaventa's lead in examining the complexities of power in Southern Appalachia. The analysis offered here, however, emphasizes the range of possibilities for contesting power, the roots of protest in particular social configurations, and the centrality of local cultures and histories to these endeavors.

Following the work of Antonio Gramsci (1971) and Raymond Williams (1977), I refer to "hegemonic" and "counterhegemonic" processes in speaking about the means by which citizens dispute, refashion, and at times overthrow dominant political orders (see also Wolf 1990 and Trouillot 1995).[1] Viewed from this vantage point, power is neither one dimensional (meaning that one either has this resource or does without it), nor is it fixed in time.

Through his notion of "militant particularism," or place-based protest, Williams argues further that politically subordinate peoples draw upon lived experience and cultural practice to articulate their concerns as citizens or laborers and, in so doing, challenge the foundations of social hierarchies (R. Williams 1989; see also Harvey 1996).

Such forms of political engagement make use of tradition in self-conscious and even arbitrary ways. Calling upon the work of Gayatri Spivak, I consider these forms to be instances of "strategic essentialism," or the representations of cultures and identities produced by subaltern peoples "in a scrupulously visible political interest" (1985:342–43). This approach purposely leaves open the questions of whose political interests are being represented, in what ways, and by whom. As Spivak and other feminist scholars have made evident, relations of gender, ethnicity, race, nationality, and not simply class inform disparate visions of political action, as well as access to authority within spheres of protest (see, for example, Bose and Acosta-Belen 1995b; Fernandez-Kelly 1983; Hossfeld 1990; Kingsolver 1998; Lamphere 1987; Milkman 1985; Robnett 1996, 1997; Rowbotham and Mitter 1994; Sacks 1988; Sacks and Remy 1984; Schneider and Rapp 1995; Sparr 1994; Susser 1997; Turbin 1987; Zavella 1987).

The framing of industries and labor processes in gendered and racial/ethnic terms, assumptions made about women's and men's capacities to perform skilled versus unskilled tasks, the value accorded certain categories of work, and the positions adopted regionally and nationally concerning workers' rights—Marx would include all this as part of the "circumstances given" to members of the working class, and Gramsci and Williams would incorporate it under the rubric of "hegemony." Examined in conjunction with the history of particular work settings, this broad set of conditions holds profound implications for the prospects of dissent, complicity, or combinations thereof.

For example, because North Carolina is a "right-to-work" state, workplaces by law must remain open to employees (including supervisors) who choose not to participate in labor organizations. Even in industries with well-established relationships to organized labor, North Carolina has no "closed shops," where jobs belong to union members and the union alone has the power to settle labor contracts and/or grievances. That this should be the case illustrates the political authority of industries like tobacco and textiles, which have played so vital a role in the state's economy (see Frankel 1984; Hall et al. 1987; Janiewski 1985; B. W. Jones 1995; Wingerd 1996). Given laws of this sort, and national disregard for the problems of blue-collar laborers, it is vital that we not limit studies of agency/activism to the activities of organized labor or formal confrontations as gauges of oppositional consciousness and political efficacy. In many instances, including workplaces like Moth Hill, the resourcefulness of workers, and the informality of their strategies—whether formulated as "backtalk" (Stewart 1990), "hidden transcripts" of resistance (J. Scott 1990), "negotiated loyalty" (Zahavi 1988; Wingerd 1996), or activities augmenting formal lines of protest (Robnett 1997; Sacks 1988)—constitute the means necessary for achieving pragmatic victories. This chapter is directed toward a broader conceptualization of political praxis.

To characterize Moth Hill Mica Company as *paternalistic,* then, is not to suggest that the setting is all powerful or that, in fundamental ways, it demarcates the social world of factory employees. Rather, the term depicts a particular approach to the management of labor, the organization of productive processes, and the creation of profit. In an ideal sense a paternalistic factory regime is "rooted in workers' dependence on a specific employer," the efforts of employers to regulate workers through their families, labor-intensive methods of production and profit seeking, and the negligible involvement by state and federal governments in orchestrating or overseeing labor policies (Burowoy 1985:98, 99). In practice, however, workers within the factory, as well as other constituencies (families, residents of local communities) less directly affected by factory policies, challenge those strategies. Zahavi's concept of "negotiated loyalty," wherein "wary opponents" sort out sets of obligations and expectations through daily interactions and workplace struggles, captures well these counterhegemonic activities (1988:99–119; Wingerd 1996:883).

An initial tour of Moth Hill would easily support the idea that paternalism is an archaic system, an outgrowth of agrarian practices and southern tradition. For two members of a younger generation of employees, working there was like "going back one hundred years" (Jeff Franklin) or, at the very least, "stepping back into the '20s" (Frances Stokes). Yet closer scrutiny of that factory's history provides a different reading, consonant with Douglas Flanning's 1992 argument that southern paternalism represents a modern industrial approach to labor shortages and oscillations within regional or national economies. Daniel Payne and his backers responded to fluctuating demands for mica in the early to mid-twentieth century by creating different processes and products from mica; sending company representatives across the country to sell their products to clients in various industries and to the U.S. government, as well as to international buyers; and by relying upon a labor system sufficiently flexible in size and technical capacity to respond to the dynamism of the market.[2]

Amid the cycles of the mica industry, the factory owners established their

own version of benevolence by bringing such amenities as a small movie the-
ater and a restaurant to the town of Monroe and operating one of its local
stores. "We've meant a lot to these people," Royce Payne told me, and he talked
about the significance of providing "the only payroll in the whole county"
during the late 1920s, when mica was still booming, and into the 1930s with
the Great Depression (interview 16). The alternatives to mica work, as Zona
Watson's life history reveals, were either to leave the North Carolina mountains in search of jobs elsewhere or remain in the county and on the farm.

Because of concerns about the plight of laboring peoples in the South and
its growing interest in mica as a "strategic mineral," the federal government
did intervene at specific moments in the affairs of this and other mica companies. The Code of Fair Competition for the Mica Industry was approved
in 1934 as part of the National Recovery Act. The code established child labor laws and set minimum wage levels and maximum hours for the mica
industry. Differentials remained between the wages earned by northern
workers and their colleagues in the South, but the new laws substantially
reduced the disparities.[3] The code also set forth the right of mica workers to
"organize and bargain collectively" (National Recovery Administration
1934:298–99, 312). Workers at Moth Hill, however, never realized the promise of the wage-and-hours provision. Noting that her husband and their kinspeople were members of the United Mine Workers of America and walked-
picket lines when they were in the coalfields, Zona maintained that getting a
union started in western Carolina would have been all but impossible:

> In the South there's not too much union labor. There never has been. That's
> why a lot of the . . . like the hosiery mills and a lot of those things moved them-
> selves to the South from up in the northern states, the New England states. . . .
> [The employees] might have wanted one. But the people they worked for,
> now, like Moth Hill and them, they was all against it. You know, 'til they never
> had it. (interview 7)

Compared to the coal miners of Central Appalachia, mica workers had
scant bargaining power both because of the cyclical nature of this industry
and the depressed regional economy. Exceptions came as a result of programs
administered by the federal government to facilitate production of mica for
wartime use. Throughout the 1940s, when the Colonial Mica Corporation
was in operation, and during the federal stockpiling program of the 1950s and
early 1960s, prices for mica increased dramatically, and laborers—both miners and mica processors—were in great demand. Nevertheless, the transience
of federal programs and their stimulation of local industry offered laborers
little in the way of lasting support. Mining stopped, factories closed, and those

who continued to find work in mica received the minimum allowable by state and federal law. By contrast, the stature of companies like Moth Hill, which weathered the shifting tides and maintained substantial workforces, grew.[4] That Royce Payne became an influential member of the county's chamber of commerce during the 1950s is telling.

The sole evidence of efforts by mica workers to organize comes from a case taken by the National Labor Relations Board (NLRB) against a small company producing ground mica.[5] What makes the case interesting is that it occurred right at the start of the boom cycle of the 1950s, and local entrepreneurs may have considered it as a way to set an example for mica laborers and would-be organizers. Despite warnings by the plant superintendent that he would "get shed . . . of the men that were working there that joined up with the Union," the employees voted 25-23 to unionize the factory (Case no. 34-CA-168:775). The superintendent made good his promise by firing the four union organizers and intimidating other employees in the factory. In response, union representatives contacted the NLRB to contest the legality of the company's actions.[6] The NLRB argued the case twice before the federal courts and ultimately prevailed. Yet in the two and a half years that it took the NLRB to win the case, the company succeeded in destroying the fledgling union. If this was all that could be said about dissent in western Carolina, we might conclude, with Gaventa, that the coercive actions of their bosses forced mica laborers into submission.

But my experiences at Moth Hill suggest otherwise. Early on in my field research I heard Bonnie Lou Watkins and Terri Watkins, two factory workers Upstairs, talking about the benefits of unions. Their discussion centered not around Moth Hill, where "they leave you alone, but they also don't pay you anything." Rather, it concerned the factory that employed Bonnie Lou Watkins's children: "You really have to *work* there, and the supervisors and bosses watch you like hawks." Terri and Bonnie Lou talked, as Zona did, about how businesses came south to North Carolina because they could work two people for the price of one worker up North. The gist of this conversation was that unions were helpful when employees were forced to "work production" and follow tightly regimented routines but not in places like Moth Hill where employees had greater autonomy and the future of the company itself was in question. At Moth Hill work-based networks took the place of formalized dissent and provided the means for women to negotiate the politics of the shop floor. In the words of Hazel Roberts, "I guess you've already figured it out. Around here, the hands boss themselves."

My attention specifically to women's participation in work networks at Moth Hill is based on three premises: the centrality of women in kin and social networks, the historic and now-waning significance of women's labor in mica processing, and the relative inaccessibility of male factory workers to me, except through established alliances with their kinswomen. While men undoubtedly do participate in work networks in other factory settings, I saw little evidence of this at Moth Hill. This I attribute to the fact that men tended to work alone—as supervisors, skilled laborers, or unskilled laborers who were shifted to one task or another around the plant. In those instances, such as with the "ring boys," male workers labored together and had opportunities for camaraderie. However, this sociability did not spill over to breaks or dinnertimes, when male workers would go off to visit their kinswomen or head off alone to sit in their trucks.

An equally significant reason for focusing specifically on women's practices within the factory is the need to redress the silence about gendered relations of protest in Appalachia. The realm of union activism, especially in relation to coal mining, has been defined in masculinist terms such that when women appear, it has been primarily as flag wavers or great figures in history. Maggard has referred to this as "the Mother Jones syndrome," the exception that allows further neglect of the way that women, families, and communities have supported and made possible the coalfield wars of the twentieth century (1986:100, 102, 107; see also Giardina 1987; Moore 1990). Gaventa's study, for example, does not mention women—not as wage laborers, coparticipants in labor disputes, or even as householders reproducing labor for the mines (see Tullos 1989). Such omissions not only marginalize women, they signal the minimizing of Appalachian culture discussed earlier. If women exist primarily within the context of families, and families are defined as being part of privatized worlds, then regional traditions can be seen as tantamount to conventions that inform personal identities and private lives. The realm of political economy affects them, but they remain outside it.

Yet we have other models for thinking about gendered relations of protest and the writing of Appalachian history (see S. Fisher 1993; Hinsdale, Lewis, and Waller 1995; Maggard 1998; Moore 1996; S. L. Scott 1995; Seitz 1995; Smith 1998; Yarrow 1990). My study follows in the spirit of Jacqueline Dowd Hall's 1986 work on female textile workers and labor activists in early twentieth-century Elizabethton, Tennessee. Through the "gender-based symbolism of their protest style," Hall writes, the female strikers of Elizabethton "expressed a complex cultural identity and turned it to their own rebellious ends" (1986:372). If we substitute the formalized protest of Hall's account with informal resistance in the absence of unions, we can say much the same of the mica workers at Moth Hill.

During my time in that factory I witnessed women maneuver shop-floor politics and productive processes so that they could maintain some control over the conditions of their labor even in that problematic setting. I watched factory hands directly confront management with their concerns about occupational safety and health, as well as other aspects of factory policy, and I heard stories recalling previous such encounters with supervisors and owners. I also experienced firsthand the agency of Moth Hill employees in responding to the presence of someone who was a stranger and therefore not accountable to them. Had Hazel Roberts, Zona Watson, Frances Stokes, Gertie Russell, and Annie Burleson not brought me into the social networks of the Upper End—and their churches and homes apart from the workplace—I surely would not have lasted eight months at Moth Hill. Given that turn of events, I was better able to appreciate the ways that female factory workers, in particular, appropriated cultural forms of authority to make factory life more tolerable and to selectively contest the dominance of the Paynes.

Lest this account appear too heroic, I must also note that, by working to maintain the profitability of the plant and thus the future of their own jobs, Moth Hill employees supported the paternalistic approach of the Paynes. Yet even here I heed the suggestion offered by del Alba Acevado in her discussion of Latin American women's labor: that we view women as "active agents, albeit in contradictory ways, in the making of their lives" (1995:77). With these ideas in mind, we return to the Upper End.

Dissent and Complicity

As with the other factory departments, changes in the mid-1980s greatly affected the Upper End. These changes included decreasing the labor force by half and stretching out workloads among existing employees. In the absence of contracts with the military and strict federal guidelines for quality control, the company decided that it did not need to staff production processes so carefully. According to Al Gardner, "The lawyers doing the taxes said they had too many hands," so the company laid off the "extra hands."

Three of the five women on the Upper End were in their sixties and seventies, which reflects Moth Hill's strategy of hiring back or maintaining "old hands" and relying on their skills. This saved the company time and money for training new workers. It also meant that workers like Zona, Gertie, and Annie remembered the practices of the past and the implications of current labor policies. Where once a machine like "the flexible" had taken six people to run it, now three women did the work. Moreover, downsizing drastically reduced the ratio of female to male workers in this department. These tensions informed the talk and activities of women on the Upper End.

A significant part of the conversation on the Upper End centered around the employees' notions of women's responsibilities to their families and what they referred to as "women's lib." Gertie Russell started one discussion with this observation: "The Bible doesn't talk about it [women's liberation]. A woman's place is in the home, not working, but I have to work. The first woman to go in and get a job should have had her hide tanned." Yet she and Hazel Roberts went on to talk about how waged labor was a reality for most of the women they knew. At other times they spoke critically of neighbors or acquaintances who "never *did* work" and instead relied on husbands "to keep [them] up." My sense of these and other conversations, in which Gertie spoke of having "married too young" and Hazel communicated her desire not to marry, was that they framed women's place within the factory and their families in a language of defiance. The women did not dispense with conventions, but neither did they fully agree with them. So it was that Gertie Russell expressed satisfaction when she told about how God had given her husband, Isa, cancer as a punishment for his having "run around on her" in earlier years.

Conspicuously absent from conversations on the Upper End—or, indeed, any of the other factory departments—was any discussion of race. This was in part due to the hiring practices of the Paynes, who did not hire African American workers for mica processing once Moth Hill became a factory rather than an informal operation run out of the springhouse. Indeed, given well-established racialized labor hierarchies in western North Carolina, and the small population of African Americans dwelling in Pike and Clark counties after divisive events in the early twentieth century,[7] it could be argued that women did not talk about race relations because the area had been effectively segregated (see D. Billings and Blee 2000; Frankenberg 1995; Harrison 1995; Inscoe 1995; Janiewski 1985; J. Jones 1986; B. W. Jones 1995; Roediger 1991; Turner and Cabbell 1985; and B. Williams 1989).

June Robbins, from the Lower End, once alluded to the multicultural settlement called Redding, whose population had declined in the late twentieth century but remained a symbol of the county's more racially diverse past.[8] However, June could tell me very little about what the residents there did for employment, much less other details about life in that settlement.[9] Hazel Roberts made few remarks in public on the topic of race, other than to declare to her co-workers that she planned to vote for Jesse Jackson and the Rainbow Coalition in the 1988 presidential elections.[10] Whether her comment was truth, audaciousness, or simply intended for my benefit, Hazel displayed an attitude of tolerance even as she cautioned me not to make an issue of race relations within the factory. That convention was upheld on the Upper End.

Within the network of the Upper End the five women displayed their loyalties to one another through frequent consultations about various matters related to both work and family. Hazel went to Gertie for guidance when a male co-worker was harassing her. Gertie suggested she "knock him to the ground, that he'd have a hard time getting up, and he'd deserve it." While Hazel did not specifically act upon this advice, it surely had an effect on the men who worked within earshot of their female colleagues. Frances and Hazel also conferred with Gertie about their efforts to remain employed at Moth Hill, despite the scarcity of orders on the Upper End.

Of all the women on the Upper End, Hazel was the most openly critical of the Paynes. But by her own account she went directly to John Walter Payne to discuss her concerns about job security, just as she had previously approached Royce to air grievances about work relations in a former department. When faced with problems on the job, Gertie and Annie likewise appealed to management, whom they knew through personal interactions and family or community connections. Zona too had gone to Royce Payne so that she might counter his negative views about her capacities as a worker and undermine any potential discrimination against her with respect to layoffs and work assignments. In so doing, she and her colleagues adhered to the implicit contract embedded within paternalistic systems wherein factory owners and upper-level supervisors interact directly with individual laborers and respond, often in limited ways, to the employees' concerns.

All five women also talked about problems in management, most notably the decline in interest and responsibility that attended recent changes at the factory. As Hazel put it, "When my mother and Zona went to work, Moth Hill was really something. Now it's just a job in the neighborhood." A problem that employees throughout the factory frequently mentioned was that Moth Hill was "a family-run business," operated by relatives who disliked and distrusted each other.[11] "I never saw a family who got along so poorly," June Robbins once observed. The primary issue, however, was that the Paynes were more interested in making money than they were in investing in the factory or their hands.[12] So the equipment was poorly maintained, and the owners paid little attention to the safety of workers.

Annie Burleson spoke at length of the fires that had occurred in the factory—three or four in the twenty-two years she had worked there—and noted how dangerous it was with all the solvents stored haphazardly on the Upper End. She pointed to the piles of lacquer dust that had been allowed to build up on the machines, as well as the mica "trash" spread throughout the room, and wondered aloud when the next fire would occur. Gertie had been working at Moth Hill when a steam table exploded:

Oh, it was critical, wasn't it, Isa? It went through up through there. It was like a big blockbuster [a large, high-explosive bomb], they said. The boys that was in the army, and heard the blockbuster, said it sounded like one. And every light went out but one back there behind where me and Annie cuts off back there [now]. There was just one little tiny light there. And there wasn't a water pipe, there wasn't a light line, there wasn't a window, not even a window sash left in that whole building. Windows and the window sashes was clean across the highway. (interview 12)

The explosion occurred right after a massive two-day effort to meet an order for mica plate. "Had the steam table not blowed up until the next night, it'd have gotten the whole gang of us" (interview 12).

Hazel had witnessed two fires during her thirteen years at Moth Hill. She added that she saw no point in trying to evacuate the building in the event of a fire: "There are so many older people in here that if you hollered 'fire,' chances are most of them are gonna have a cardiac arrest." Nor would there be any way to escape the fallout from an explosion, once all the chemicals ignited. "And if you run from here to Grove [three miles away], chances are you're still gonna get blown off the map" (interview 6). These and other stories suggested that factory workers were keenly aware of their hazardous working conditions, and they alerted newer workers to these problems.

That workers like Hazel and Annie did not confront management about this could be construed as evidence of fatalism or passivity. I would suggest that they were exercising judgment about the efficacy of this kind of complaint, for they knew that the Paynes changed operating procedures only when the state forced them to do so—in the aftermath of safety inspections, for which the company received advance notice, and as a result of the imposition (and enforcement) of new laws. As Annie Burleson put it, "They obey them [the state inspectors]. Sometimes it might cost them a lot."[13]

Moth Hill had even dropped its insurance policies rather than comply with additional safety measures that their insurers required. Royce Payne offered this account of how Moth Hill was "operating now, after seventy-nine years, without any insurance":

Well one [insurance agent]—he got this idea. He said, Now, when you close this place up of an evening, shut all the windows and doors and go home over the weekend. You come in here Monday morning, this place is full of fumes from evaporation, and somebody strikes a match or something, and kaboom, the whole thing will blow up." He says, "You'll have to take every one of these drums [of solvents and lacquers] out of here, every evening, and put them in an explosion proof building" [that] we didn't have and bring them back the next

morning. We said, "You go to the devil. We ain't going to do it." Well, they can-
celed the insurance. (interview 16)

The barrels remained in the building, despite the loss of insurance and negative reports by state inspectors.

Other occupational hazards concerned the women of the Upper End. All
five women recounted their experiences in getting mica flakes lodged in their
eyes. The flakes were nearly impossible for doctors to extricate and, coated
with abrasives, they caused infections as well as inflammations. However,
when injured, workers were left to their own devices to obtain medical attention. John Walter Payne threatened to dock Hazel's pay once when she
attempted to drive an injured worker to the doctor.

Just as pervasive was the problem of lacquer fumes. Hazel and Frances were
more aggressive than their colleagues in voicing their complaints. In addition to telling me that I had ruined my health in coming so regularly to the
factory, they observed that a number of Moth Hill employees had been diagnosed with tuberculosis and other lung diseases that they thought were
attributable to inhalation of mica dust and lacquer fumes. "People who work
at this plant don't need to be embalmed," Hazel told me. Ed Payne (another
of the owner-managers) tried to close off the Upper End one afternoon because, he said, the "fumes were overpowering." Hazel retorted, "What do you
think we're breathing?"

Workers from other departments expressed their concerns about the fumes
and lacquer dust, hazardous materials that they were forced to inhale during
the course of their work. This was why the department Upstairs was the job
assignment that workers tried most to avoid. Contamination by the vapor-
ized lacquers (whose specific contents were not made known to employees)
was heaviest there and became almost unbearable in the wintertime.[14] Dorthy Hollifield, who worked Upstairs, claimed that she had different reactions
(nausea, insomnia, lethargy, headaches, etc.) to particular varnishes used in
fabricating hand-made plate. Although wearing a mask did not eliminate these
problems, Dorthy felt it reduced the side-effects to a more tolerable level, and
she was one of the few workers to routinely use this equipment.

Hazel and Frances hated being sent Upstairs and spoke of "having [their]
walking shoes put away," another way of describing how the fumes in that
department intoxicated and disabled them.[15] In more than one conversation
they asserted that Moth Hill was well known to local doctors for the occupational safety and health risks that it posed. The doctors knew, as Hazel put
it, that after people work at the mica plant, "they don't have any lungs left
and they're not human anymore." Gertie claimed that the fumes never both-

ered her, but she opened the windows when the air quality noticeably wors-
ened and occasionally even she would admit to feeling bad. Zona noted that
some processes for making laminated mica, no longer used on the Upper End,
produced even worse fumes. Of toluene, an ingredient in many of the varnishes and employed in cleaning equipment, she simply said, "I've been using it all my life and it never hurt me." Theoretically, the state had restricted
the use of this solvent, but it was difficult to tell this from the day-to-day
operations of the factory.

In a poorly lit section of the Upper End, the Paynes posted the list of hazardous materials that the State of North Carolina required them to post;
however, they did not otherwise address the possibility that lacquer fumes
or mica dust constituted occupational hazards from which workers might
be protected. Royce had gone so far as to explain to me how mica, unlike coal
or cotton fibers, could not cause pneumoconiosis, but neither the medical
literature at the time nor the state health department supported his argument
(see Berry et al. 1976; Churg and Wiggs 1985; Davies and Cotton 1983; Dreessen et al. 1940; Mihailov and Berova 1968; Morgan and Seaton 1984; Pimentel and Menezes 1978; Sahu et al. 1985; Shanker et al. 1975; Skulberg et al. 1985;
Tat and Simonescu 1972). Instead, the occupational risk that the owners were
most willing to discuss was the amputation of fingers by punch presses that
"double-tripped," because the installation of guards had solved this problem long before.

But if the factory owners thought that mica dust was harmless, their employees argued otherwise. From Zona's perspective the respiratory problems
that eventually killed her husband were attributable to his years in the mica
mines—many of them spent working for the Paynes.[16] Elsa Watkins also
worried about her husband, Lamar, whose lungs were filled with "60 percent
dust" from mining mica and sanding mica plate at Moth Hill. Elsa's own
problems with skin irritations and respiratory ailments caused her to con-
sult a doctor routinely, and she considered having her lungs x-rayed by her
own physician because she did not trust the physical exams required by the
State of North Carolina.

Annie Burleson was the only one on the Upper End to regularly wear a
mask as protection against the dust and fumes. The only kind of mask available to the workers was a dust mask that offered little defense against minus-
cule mica parts or airborne resins. As June Robbins found out one day when
she was working with extremely dusty materials, dust masks were difficult
to come by when you really needed them. June looked around, to no avail,
and she enlisted her supervisor, who was equally ineffectual in his efforts.
Finally, they located an old, frayed mask underneath notebooks and other

supplies at Arval's desk; while she was not satisfied with this arrangement, June used it for lack of a better alternative.

Given the company's evident disregard, workers took action to render their work environment less hazardous, if not hazard free. Women, Upstairs and down, swept constantly to keep the dust to a minimum. Gertie entered the factory early to do maintenance work that would help her sister and co-workers, even if it was not remunerated by the Paynes. On the Lower End, where punching operations filled the air with dust, women brought aprons and pillow cases to cover their laps and clothes while they worked. The presses that women operated had makeshift cardboard covers, attached with masking tape, that they were constantly adjusting to keep scraps of plate and dust from flying in their faces. Such practices partially compensated for the lackadaisical approach of the factory management, and workers kept talking to each other, as well as to the Paynes, to make clear their dissatisfaction with this state of affairs.

In addition to matters of health, frustrations about the wage scale and the differential between men's and women's wages were equally topics of conversation for the women of the Upper End and other factory departments. Given the status of orders and the directives from management, they voiced their pessimism about receiving increases in wages. Royce would just tell his employees they could "raise out of their seats and leave," so who could blame younger generations of workers for looking elsewhere? Indeed, many cautioned their children against working at Moth Hill, for "a young person couldn't make enough there to make their [car or house] payments" (interview 11). After a visit with Royce Payne one afternoon, June Robbins conveyed the news that the owners were worried that the state would increase its minimum wage. If a pay hike were forced on them, Royce told her, the plant might have to shut down. In the more cynical estimations of workers like Terri Watkins, however, this was a familiar ploy: "Every time they've had to raise the minimum wage, [the Paynes] threatened to close, but they've kept on going. That's what Mae Webb has said" (interview 27).

The only worker who attempted to secure a wage hike was Arval Gardner, the supervisor from the Lower End. He made his complaint as an underpaid supervisor forced to do the work of two, and he threatened to quit within a few months if the Paynes did not accede to his request. June Robbins told me to watch, that nothing would come of his bravado, and she was right. On the appointed day Arval went to the front office to pick up his final paycheck. He was crestfallen that his challenge had failed, but as June put it, "You told them you were going to quit. They just took you at your word." Arval quickly regrouped by noting that he would stay on since the Paynes had not located his replacement. While a departmental supervisor might have harbored the belief that his position gave him bargaining power, women workers, in particular, were under no such illusions. They recognized that, while long work histories made them valuable to the factory, they were not irreplaceable. Their strength came through social networks and strategic maneuvering within the factory.

Through their interactions on the shop floor, Hazel, Gertie, Frances, Zona, and Annie sustained their friendships and engaged in what Stewart (1990) aptly calls "backtalk," an oppositional discourse that recognizes the position of the speaker and the limits of authority. Within the context of Moth Hill, gender, class, position in kin or social networks, and years of experience at the factory defined authority. Traditions of evangelical Christianity, with their emphasis on righteous anger and the power of personal testimony, gave speakers added credibility. Although far removed from the bolder, more openly confrontational actions of unionized labor, these practices provided a forum in which women could and did articulate complaints to one another and to management.

One of the most powerful examples of resistance that I witnessed occurred during a discussion between Frances Stokes and Ed Payne. Their discussion, occasioned by the visit of the state health department to conduct physical exams of factory workers and x-ray their lungs, was on the topic of occupationally induced lung disease.[17] In a jovial tone of voice Frances told Ed that the X rays would reveal all the damage that she and her co-workers had been doing to themselves by working in the plant. Ed countered, saying that no evidence existed that mica dust was harmful. To this familiar response Frances rejoined by asking, "But what about all that paste?" She kept smiling and did not back down even as Ed tried to distract her from a controversial subject. And when Ed offered a rhetorical question, "But, now, who's ever turned up with a problem?" Frances provided names of Moth Hill employees diagnosed with lung diseases and the local doctors who would back her assertions. She was well informed and insistent in making her claims. Ed did not cut her off, nor did he assert his status as a factory owner, and the jovial tone of both participants kept it a conversation between "friends" rather than a hostile confrontation. Yet Frances made her point, loud and clear, by back talking the company line.

In the more structured settings of major corporations, where employees and CEOs do not meet, and layers of hierarchy convey labor policies, workers have no room to express their objections directly. They file grievances through union stewards or ask labor relations boards to handle them. In rural Appalachia, where generations of workers and elites have known each other, and community ties are woven into the fabric of family and individual histories, no such formal recourse exists. Instead, the well-known practice was to voice your dissatisfaction and sometimes vote with your feet. To have workers interfere with productive processes, and, Arval notwithstanding, to lose well-trained hands, would disrupt factory operations, as the Paynes well understood. Thus speaking your mind was more than grumbling, more than the frustrations of a malcontent. It was an effective form of protest.

At the opposite end of the spectrum Gertie's hard work to "save money for Moth Hill" may be interpreted in light of Caroline White's observations about female factory operatives in British electronics factories (1989:65–66). Denied classification as "skilled labor" in the gender-stratified world of blue-collar work, and thereby stronger means to articulate interests or grievances, women in the electronics factories appropriated the language of management objectives in carving out their own terrain. At Moth Hill concern for the profitability of the factory and the competence of the current managers fueled Carl Fisher's quietly sardonic remarks that "John Walter don't know what he's talking about" in describing factory processes to me and that it was "a good thing he ain't around here more" to oversee factory operations. Gertie expressed similar concerns when she observed, "The hands have to work harder to make more money for Moth Hill, so the company'll keep going," and when she compared Royce Payne unfavorably to his father, Daniel Payne. In the workers' eyes Uncle Dan had been the one with the intelligence and business sense to build that factory into something noteworthy; the others had simply squandered it.

Lest Gertie's comments be seen as simply justifying her own exploitation, I should add that Gertie tied her concern for the profitability of the company to a critique of labor processes. In particular, Gertie complained about stretch-out practices that forced her and her sister Annie to work too quickly and without adequate attention to the quality of output: "We're the only ones who run two [machines]. The other ones won't. It'd be better if we'd only run one because we can do a better job at it. If I save $10.00 worth of plate [because it meets production standards], that's $10.00 for the company and $10.00 for me." That Gertie's efforts preserved the status quo in the factory, in addition to the well-being of her department and her own seniority, may be considered evidence of the fine line that she and her co-workers traversed between activism and complicity.[18]

Gertie's objections to changes in the plate-making operation, remarks from the Lower End about the declining quality of the materials that they were forced to use (the output of other factory departments), and comments made throughout the plant about returned shipments of defective parts reflected employees' discontent with the outcome of their labors. Workers on the Upper End expressed frustration about changes in productive processes and relations both through back talk and hand-written signs reading: "This machine runs 100 miles an hour" and "On Strike." Because Moth Hill Mica Company was much celebrated for its past accomplishments—once considered an example of entrepreneurial savvy and the benefits of industry for Pike County—protests like these were a way of showing the Paynes how they had failed to measure up to their own traditions. Moth Hill was causing its demise through its labor practices and quality of production.

Local Cultures and Questions of Solidarity

Equally important, workers drew upon their own readings of cultural practices and kin or community ties to make claims in the context of productive regimens and to domesticate factory life. Working "close home" meant more than a "job in the neighborhood," for employees recognized loyalties that extended beyond the walls of the factory. Moreover, they exercised prerogatives underwritten by local custom and the memories of those whose families had labored there for generations.

Thus not only did workers get "laid off" at Moth Hill when orders were down, they also "laid out" for a variety of reasons: to tend to their gardens, visit relatives, meet doctors' appointments, go shopping or to the beauty parlor, or simply because they needed a break from the factory. It was also accepted practice to take off in the middle of a workday for these kinds of reasons. When the frosts of the fall came, many workers left their jobs early or stayed away entirely so they could dig up potatoes and harvest the last of the vegetable crops or tend to "Christmas trees" and other cash crops. Leaving early or laying out did not require formal permission from the managers but simply that employees notify the front office of their plans. As June Robbins told me, "Getting off work is one of the parts of this job which makes it good."

Another strategy was the work slowdown that occurred on Friday afternoons. Employees stopped working on their machines, ostensibly to clean up their sections of the factory because Moth Hill had no janitorial service. They swept floors and cleaned bathrooms, in addition to closing up supplies and washing down the plate-making machines. However, common practice was to operate slowly, if at all, to this end. Workers read magazines, conversed among themselves, and set about the business of getting ready to leave for the weekend.

These activities not only "stole back time" from the company, they brought family life into the factory (Lamphere 1985:523). Visits by the kin of Moth Hill employees extended the social networks in which co-workers participated and consolidated their knowledge of lives enacted outside the factory. In the evenings Gertie and Annie's kin would come early to pick them up from work, and they would talk with everyone there about the day's activities. People who had previously worked at Moth Hill, and some who wanted jobs, might stop in during the middle of the day.

When Gertie's husband fell ill again, her son brought the news to the Upper End. Hazel was there to hear Roger tell his mother that Isa "was eat up with cancer" and to care for Gertie as she slumped over the table. She also knew enough about Roger's flare for the dramatic to converse later with Annie on this topic, and both women consulted with Gertie to find out the real diagnosis (benign tumor in one lung). While Gertie stayed home to tend to Isa, because "you have to take care of your own people," Hazel took Gertie's place running the two machines and looked after her through evening phone calls. Gertie returned to the Upper End as soon as she could, for, in her sister's words, "whenever you've got an illness, you've got to scrimp and save and *do* it." In the meantime her colleagues at work looked after her interests.

Beyond helping co-workers in time of need, women celebrated life-cycle events, particularly birthdays and wedding anniversaries. When Gertie and Isa celebrated their fiftieth anniversary, for example, workers brought her a present and later visited the Upper End to see photographs marking the festivities at home. Celebrations also took place within the factory and involved members of various factory departments.

One example was a "household shower" organized for Belle Stokes, who worked Upstairs. Women from the Upper End and Upstairs brought a huge assortment of foods—biscuits and gravy, eggs, meat, preserves, and other breakfast foods—to the factory, enough to feed everyone from their respective departments. They fixed plates and sent them to the "ring boys" on the Lower End and everyone in the front office. After breakfast Belle opened presents—Tupperware, linens, and a clock, among them—provided her by the female cohort from the two factory departments. An older widowed woman about to move into a new trailer, Belle was clearly pleased and a bit embarrassed to be receiving the kind of attention normally reserved for new brides.

Celebrations, and the allegiances that they reflected, symbolized the arbitrary use of social networks and cultural practices, much as Spivak (1985) argues. The group most conspicuously absent from the household shower were the women of the Lower End. June Robbins expressed interest in the event and told me she had not been informed about it or she would have come along. She revised her statement later to tell me that she didn't really know "that bunch Upstairs," and that it didn't much matter to her. I was confused by June's response, as well as by the fact that some men working on the Lower End had been invited but none of the women.

When Alma Moody had a birthday party, neither Hazel nor Frances would attend, and they scooted me downstairs with them. I was not sure at the time whether this was a response to Alma's uncertain feelings about me or a way for Frances and Hazel to protest their poor treatment Upstairs, since Alma's sister was in charge of the latter operations. It seemed all the more confusing when Alma told me later that her husband was Frances's uncle; however, I realized this made her an aunt by marriage and not necessarily kin.

It would appear that special occasions classified and/or clarified relationships within and between departments: who was kin and who was not, who was a friend and who merely a co-worker, who was trustworthy and who was not. Some of the "ring boys" from the Lower End were kin to women working Upstairs, while, to my knowledge, none of the women were related. Moreover, two men who had not been invited were supervisors on the Lower End. Presumably, the women from the Upper End and the people in the front office were invited for reasons of diplomacy because they were forces with whom the women Upstairs had to contend.

Whether this interpretation holds or not, the household shower and the birthday celebrations also served to illustrate the central roles that women played in forging work-based networks. While men garnered power as supervisors and skilled laborers, kin networks and factory celebrations contained the men's authority. Like kinship, inter- and intradepartmental solidarity had limits, which I often witnessed without fully understanding the underlying reasons. What I came to understand was that the limits to solidarity were based in part on class: those whose families had successful farms or enjoyed more secure employment in other venues and whose children and grandchildren aspired to white-collar jobs—and those factory workers who supported families solely or primarily on their earnings from Moth Hill.[19]

Just as the tensions of class could fragment workers into disparate concerns and, occasionally, antagonistic associations, differential susceptibilities of factory departments to temporary layoffs and problematic working conditions at Moth Hill sometimes served to divide workers. Although values of egalitarianism and cooperation formed the basis for women's negotiations within and between departments, the networks themselves reflected the selective allegiances and hierarchical organization of the social world in which factory workers lived (see Sacks 1988; Zavella 1987). Worker-based networks, in other words, embellished upon the notions of class, gender, kinship, and production politics maintained by diverse constituencies within the plant.

Thus Hazel Roberts found herself isolated from a co-worker who refused to acknowledge their family ties because of differences in social and economic standing and perhaps in part because of Hazel's former difficulties in the department where her colleague still labored.[20] Reversing this same logic, Hazel disclosed that she was "kin to the Paynes but [she] wouldn't claim it," for she did not want to assert a different status or set of claims within the factory. Yet, although she and Zona Watson "weren't much kin" in terms of blood relations, their families shared similar locations and were part of the same community. "We may be poor and such, but we've got a lot" was the way Hazel's mother once described it. Zona had taken care of Hazel when she was young and served as a mentor for Hazel's involvement in the life of her church as well as her educational aspirations. They were, I would argue, kin in the ways that mattered and looked out for each other both at home and at work. Gertie Russell, Frances Stokes, and Annie Burleson likewise identified as working-class people with few resources apart from their earnings at Moth Hill, and they valued the "good Christian people" with whom they worked on the Upper End. Annie told me, "Any one of them here would do *anything* for me."

Through social networks enacted within the factory, women brought the concerns of their communities onto the shop floor and redefined these concerns from the vantage point of their daily experiences as wage laborers. The regional culture of Southern Appalachia and the life histories (of generations) of workers provided the means by which such translations were effected, in various ways and to differing ends. This was the context within which women on the Upper End, and elsewhere in the plant, articulated visions of social justice even as they labored for the Paynes. While the Paynes undoubtedly exploited their workforce and, in Hazel's view, worried about their profits to the last nickel, they did not subdue their employees.

Conclusion:
An Anthropology of Gender,
Labor, and Place

Silences enter the process of historical production at four crucial
moments: the moment of fact creation (the making of *sources*); the
moment of fact assembly (the making of *archives*); the moment of
fact retrieval (the making of *narratives*); and the moment of
retrospective significance (the making of *history* in the final
instance).
—Michel-Rolph Trouillot, *Silencing the Past*

THE FOUNDATION for this study was the recognition of Southern Appalachia as a region whose history belies myths of a simple farming area barely
touched by the forces of modernization. The combination of its long history of capital accumulation and its vibrant cultural traditions has rendered
Appalachia a region distinct, but not completely different from, the rest of
the United States. The complex history thus envisioned reflects the importance of economic, social, and political ties that linked nineteenth-century
Southern Appalachia to the lowland South and the centers of industrial capitalism in the North. In the nineteenth and twentieth centuries, and now into
the twenty-first, Southern Appalachia has participated in economic and
political activities of global as well as national significance.

In other words, I have told the story of the mica industry as a means of
illustrating the power of history and contemporary political-economic forces
on a quiet rural area in the mountains of North Carolina. The crumbling
building that I passed several times before realizing that it was not abandoned
but housed an operating mica factory seems an appropriate symbol of the
past and continuing dependence of a rural community on factory employment. While vestiges of subsistence farming may be seen in the practices of
making summer gardens, planting cash crops, and tending small numbers

of farm animals, the conventions of waged labor are equally embedded in the traditions of the region.

The mica industry is important too in its reflections of the gendered dimensions of this history. An enterprise that built on traditions of petty commodity production and agricultural labor in Southern Appalachia, the mica industry incorporated women's labor into factory regimes. While the rationale offered for this arrangement might be that such labor was both inexpensive and available, factory owners also recognized that women's productive contributions were important and reflected considerable skill, as had been the case in productive ventures on family farms. What factory work represented was the transition to waged labor, not the emergence of women's productive activities. The story of mica reveals the dependence of rural communities on blue-collar work and the centrality of women's labor within this industry.

Equally significant, the story of the mica industry reflects the dialectic between factory work and regional culture. The members of rural mountain communities carried cultural traditions into factory settings as ways of articulating and humanizing their routines as hired hands. While generations of neighbors and kin found their way to mica houses or other factories that developed on the heels of the mica industry, family histories and local custom assimilated the experience of blue-collar work. When work became problematic, either because too little was available or because labor practices were exploitative, workers drew upon the strength of community networks and traditions of interdependence to see their way clear.

Zona and Zeyland Watson traveled across the country in search of jobs, and returned home again, via kin networks. When Zona's brother faced difficulties in his work and his marriage, he returned to Liston's Branch from South Carolina to live with his siblings. And when Parnell Hayes's health failed him, his "true brothers and sisters" brought food and helped pay his hospital bills.

At the same time, the context of proletarianization recast regional culture and community relations in terms of class hierarchies wherein kin did not always consider themselves peers, nor were they necessarily responsive to the claims of family, and community loyalties often aligned with class affiliations. In their recruitment of members from specific settlements and kin groups, local churches reflected this organization of constituencies around class relations. Working-class churches offered theologies that situated biblical interpretations in terms of the trials and tribulations of "common" labor and provided locations where blue-collar workers could "be somebody."

Gender, Class, and Regional Culture

In comparable fashion definitions of gender in rural Southern Appalachia signified the interweaving of regional cultures and working-class lives. Women used the imagery of labor and management to describe their marriages and families and to bolster a spirit of rebelliousness and liveliness among their co-workers. The women were not asserting gender consciousness per se. Rather, an amalgam of gendered, classed, racial or ethnic, and regional consciousness privileged their identification as white, working-class, and "good Christian" women from rural communities back in the mountains. Further, the discourse in which women daily engaged in the mica factory framed their enactment of gender relations in other settings.

Examples of conversations with women at Moth Hill serve to illustrate these points. Gertie Russell spoke quite frankly about the problems in her marriage and said of her husband, "He's mean and spiteful, but I love him." She observed at another point that, in marrying him, "I married too young. I ended up trading one household with all of its burdens for another with more of them. I just didn't know anything different but hard work." Her parents had led a trying life, as Gertie knew all too well. When her father worked away from home, she had been the one to take care of farm chores, hard work that she thought she would get away from by marrying Isa. Like Zona, Gertie had to run away with Isa, bypassing her mother's disapproval. In Gertie's telling of the story, her mother's warning—that marriage would only bring more troubles into her life—had proved true. But, as she remarked on the occasion of her fiftieth wedding anniversary: "I've been in shit and high water up to my neck. But when I said, 'I do,' it was forever. It's not like these marriages today, when you get married one minute and turn around and get divorced after the first bit of trouble." June Robbins spoke similarly of marriage, commenting that it was just like getting another job, with another boss. According to June, men were the ones who wanted to get married and who advised women to do so because "it was good for them." June told me I was smart to remain single and that I should not listen to those in the plant—including the supervisors on the Lower End—who recommended that I do otherwise.

Hazel Roberts explained her status as an unmarried woman by saying that she had dreams that she wanted to realize. She was saving money to return to college one day, something she could not do if she were married. If she and Will were to marry, any time she might manage to save a little money, he would be after her, saying, "Aw, honey, let's get us a new truck." When

Hazel talked about her aspirations to co-workers in the plant, Frances Stokes's father, Dale Moody, told her that she was old enough to let go of her dreams. Those were fighting words for Hazel, and she spoke of Dale as an irascible old man who simply wanted to spoil life for others. Moreover, as a single woman, Hazel was not alone in the plant. At least two other women at Moth Hill had never married, and eight or more widowed women lived by themselves. Although men might advocate marriage as the preferred arrangement for women (and men), many women resisted this in their own lives—and other women supported them.

These themes were reiterated at Long Hill Baptist Church, albeit in slightly different fashion. When it came time in Sunday school to deal with St. Paul's injunction that wives obey their husbands, the teacher for the older, married women's class expressed her dismay at having to contend with this passage. Etta Long's response was to reinterpret the saying as admonishing wives and husbands to care for one another. "And if your husband's not a Christian, you're supposed to make sure he knows that you are one," as her own grandmother had done. With respect to the passage about women as "unto a weaker vessel," Etta said that did not mean that men were supposed to treat women as their inferiors. "We are weaker when it comes to physical strength, you know." Etta's closing remarks—uttered in relation to the idea of "dressing up"—stated well the sentiments of the class about their identities and concerns as women: "I think God wants us to take care of ourselves."

The women of Long Hill Baptist Church also had to deal with the problems of husbands who would be authoritarian if left to their own devices. The pastor, self-identified as "God's man in the pulpit," supported those pretensions, regularly dispensing proclamations about the "weaker sex." The preacher filled his commentaries with paradoxical themes, reflecting women's dual nature as temptress and bedrock of morality. On Mother's Day, before he handed flowers to all the mothers and adult women (who "would someday be mothers too"), Harlan Brown remarked that "today, you don't know if your wife is stepping out on you. Fifty percent of marriages end in divorce." Nevertheless, "a good Christian woman has led many a man into the church," as his own wife had done. Women are the most important contributors at church, he told us, and the ones "who do the work in their homes." But if they were important forces in family and church, women still did not merit the trust of their husbands or pastors.

The arrangements of the Baptist church, where men held the most powerful positions as deacons, preacher, and choirmaster, mirrored that distrust. By contrast, women could aspire only to become church secretary, treasurer, and Sunday school teachers in the women's and girls' classes. That women were blocked from the highest ranks within the church did not mean they acceded to a position of subservience to male authority. Not only did Etta exegete St. Paul in a fashion that was unfamiliar to me but one of the more devout members of the Sunday school class argued against the presumed authority of all male preachers—based, in Baptist theology, on divine inspiration or "calling by God." Louise Roscoe contended otherwise: "I don't believe half of them are called." With the rest of the Sunday school class Etta gave her assent to this criticism, noting, "Well, when God makes a possum, he makes a tree. When God calls a preacher, he makes a church." In other words, the church had an excess of preachers—a situation that suggested that many were pretenders, only claiming to be called to the ministry by God. And—who knew?—perhaps their pastor was one of them. Criticisms such as these illustrated women's recourse to theological interpretations and their separate (gender-segregated) involvement in religious traditions, lest preachers or other church members usurp too much authority.

Although such actions did not topple the foundations of patriarchal domination, the dismissal of that overly authoritarian pastor from Long Hill was evidence of the force of women's dissent. In addition to other problematic actions, at a community singing Harlan Brown had overstepped his bounds by making satirical remarks about "women preachers" and wives who "nagged" their husbands and gave them "sermons." Such comments were the last straw for Etta Long, Louise Roscoe, and the majority of the congregation at Long Hill, so they "voted him out."

The power of dissenting practices was equally apparent at Moth Hill, through the ways that women countered management demands in their actions on the shop floor. They slowed down and stopped work through myriad means: refusing specific assignments, taking added time to punch parts or lay mica plate, "spelling co-workers" at their jobs, and leaving presses and other machines to take unscheduled breaks. After a particularly hard morning spent operating a press, for example, Frances Stokes could stop and say, "I've done enough work for today." Employees argued directly with managers and supervisors about working conditions and strategized separately to make their tasks more bearable.

When Arval, supervisor on the Lower End and the dispenser of cleaning supplies for all the departments in the factory, sent Gertie a new broom along with his concerns that it might be too big for her to use, the women on the Upper End laughed off his comments. Gertie and her cohort told Jay, Arval's son and messenger in this instance, to bring *all* the women new brooms, despite his father's tendencies toward frugality. Jay was also to notify his father that "we're WOMEN down here!" The able-bodied and determined women of the Upper End, in other words, refused his patronizing treatment. Jay returned shortly with the brooms and the Upper End's victory.

Thus the story of mica illustrates the ways that women's identities are partially constructed in terms of class relations and the experience of waged labor, which was normatively part of every non-elite woman's life in Southern Appalachia. Recognition of the interconnections between gender, class, and ethnicity serves as a corrective to regional literature, whose presentation of gendered identities is framed in terms of stereotypes and omissions. At the same time, the lens of waged labor also restricts visions of women's—and men's—lives in Southern Appalachia. Factory work was not necessarily the most important dimension of women's lives, as my informants repeatedly tried to tell me. Kinship connections, religious beliefs, and community ties and traditions were important activities in their own right, not simply as a rebuttal to the alienating conditions of factory jobs. That local traditions were endowed with connotations of class did not diminish their significance but meant rather that the contours of regional culture had been strategically altered to reflect those experiences. Moreover, such traditions were not set apart from the daily interactions that rural residents had with various media and their presentations of American popular culture. If distinctive, Southern Appalachia was not a world apart from the contemporary United States.

As Hazel once declared, "Mountain women are strong! We could scratch a living off a rock if we had to." We should construe factory labor, and women's productive activities in general, as part of a larger concern: to lead good lives in a poor economy. To see this undertaking exclusively in economic terms, or questions of labor relations and militancy, is to miss the point. Equally problematic is the romanticizing and decontextualizing of "good lives" as relics of an egalitarian pastoral past, which is the enduring myth of Appalachia.

Afterthoughts: Histories, Silences, Representations

This book has been as much a reflection on what counts as "knowledge," whose voices matter, as it has been about Appalachia. The making of history, as Michel-Rolph Trouillot (1995) and others have noted, is an arbitrary process through which the experiences and imaginings of elite people are writ large (see Bond and Gilliam 1994; Wolf 1982). Their letters are collected and housed in archives, their biographies represented in the official accounts of the day, their interpretations given weight. Thus Thomas Lanier Clingman and Royce Payne enter the historical record, and their preoccupations become a way of envisioning "Pike County" or "the Blue Ridge Mountains." It is far more difficult to locate those like Zona Watson, who may be wise and articulate but nonetheless stand at the social margins. The narratives of their lives are recast according to the conventions of census takers and are otherwise largely ignored. Official accounts of places like Appalachia may talk *about* Zona Watson or Hazel Roberts—all too often representing them as "broke-headed hillbillies," to use Gertie Russell's evocative phrase. Less frequently are poor and working-class women able to come forth as authors or inter-locutors on their own terms, and so they were justly concerned about what I might say regarding my time with them.

In this text I have tried to place Zona Watson, her colleagues at Moth Hill, and their forebears long retired from mica work, in dialogue—or perhaps competing discourses—with Royce Payne and other factory owners, in or-der to present a slightly more conflictual version of the histories of western Carolina. I have combed the federal censuses from the late nineteenth and twentieth centuries for whatever insights they might offer about the resi-dents who lived in Pike and Clark counties and how they made their lives. I have called upon the methods of ethnography and oral history to create an alternate set of records that emphasizes the experiences and reflections of these people on the margins and illustrates how memories of "the past" inform ways of acting in the present. Still, this account has far too many gaps. Although we may have a better sense of how white working-class men and women lived and earned their living in mica, we know very little about the people of color who resided in the same counties. The silence of the mica workers on issues of race was striking, especially in comparison to their ver-bosity on matters of social class, gender, and local culture. In my field re-search informants cautioned me to keep my distance from the Latino mi-grant workers laboring in a warehouse nearby the plant, and they said little about the African American men and women who lived in Pike County. Given the racialized hierarchies of Moth Hill, I could not counter these omissions. Thankfully, this is not the final word on Pike County or South-ern Appalachia. There are other histories to be written and, just as impor-tant, stories yet unfolding.

My final apprehension in offering this interpretation of the western Caro-lina mountains is that it might be taken as further evidence of a way of life that is anachronistic and/or dying out. In many respects, however, the expe-riences of mica workers and other blue-collar laborers in Appalachia are no different from those of their counterparts in other parts of the United States and "offshore," other places where people face the rigors of economic restruc-turing. In Appalachia, as elsewhere, the gainfully employed create their own strategies for resistance and selective compliance with those for whom they labor. Yet others fight for the right to work, while all endeavor to live with dignity amid the contradictions of the changing centuries.

Notes

Introduction

1. See Reeves (1998) for one response to Adams's work.

2. Mica is useful in such a wide variety of applications because it has several valuable properties. As a translucent material that can be split into very thin sheets, it will emit light but not heat. Even after receiving high-voltage currents over a long period of time, high-grade mica will not conduct electricity and so constitutes an ideal insulating material. Furthermore, it retains these properties under conditions of extreme heat and cold. Chapter 3 provides additional detail of mica's characteristics and examines regional, national, and international political economies and the local history of mica.

3. This argument finds its mooring in the work of feminist anthropologists, sociologists, and labor economists, including Beneria and Feldman (1992); Beneria and Sen (1986); Beneria and Stimpson (1987); Bose and Acosta-Belen (1995b); del Alba Acevedo (1995); Fernandez-Kelly (1983); Fernandez-Kelly and Sassen (1995); Kondo (1990); Lamphere (1985, 1987); Leacock and Safa (1986); Milkman (1985); Mullings (1997); Nash and Fernandez-Kelly (1983); Rowbotham and Mitter (1994); Sacks (1988, 1989); Sacks and Remy (1984); J. Scott (1985, 1990); Sen (1980); Sparr (1994); Susser (1996); and Zavella (1987).

4. See Foucault (1979); Gramsci (1971); Harvey (1996, 2000); Marx (1972, 1975); Roseberry (1989); Schneider and Rapp (1995); J. Scott (1985, 1990); B. Williams (1989); and Wolf (1990, 1999) for their analyses of power, counterhegemony, and the potential for resistance.

5. See Gaventa (1980) for one of the earliest, albeit pessimistic, readings of Appalachian activism. See also Couto (1993); S. Fisher (1993); Gaventa, Smith, and Willingham (1990); Hall (1986); H. Lewis (1976); R. Lewis (1987); Maggard (1998); Moore (1990); Seitz (1995); Trotter (1990); White (1994); and Yarrow (1990).

6. All proper names used in this text are pseudonyms.

7. I am indebted to feminist scholars and their contributions toward a history of gender, as well as to those working to reconstruct a gendered history of Appalachia. See, for example, Abel and Folbre (1990); Barney (1996, 2000); Baron (1991); Becker (1998); Clinton and Silber (1992); Dublin (1979); Folbre (1991); Fout and Tantillo (1993); Groneman

and Norton (1987); Hall (1986); Hall et al. (1987); Helly and Reverby (1992); Jensen (1980); J. Jones (1986); Kessler-Harris (1982); Maggard (1986); Mann (1993); J. W. Scott (1986); Smith (1998); Tilly and Scott (1978).

8. See Mitchell (1991); Pudup, Billings, and Waller (1995); Puglisi (1997); and Inscoe (2001) as recent collections of essays on the new histories of Appalachia.

9. For missionaries such as Stephenson, Dawley had the following response: "Yet with conditions such as these, our good religious workers, missionaries and educators, who know in a vague way that some such conditions exist, collect and spend thousands of dollars to build schools and academies, literally to feed these poor children upon the alphabet. Then they marvel because they do not get results" (1912:183; see also 266–67).

10. Through a careful examination of the writings of the settlement workers in eastern Kentucky, Tice (1998) makes the important point that the "quare women" who came to do "uplift" work differed among themselves in terms of politics, motives, and practices. Becker (1998), on the other hand, documents the way social reformers transformed mountain crafts into a form of sweated labor.

11. Under the rubric "antipoverty programs" I include current efforts to replace welfare with temporary programs of financial assistance and worker training with their problematic consequences for the U.S. poor generally and Appalachia specifically (Rural Policy Research Institute 1999; Zimmerman and Garkovitch (1999).

12. Many of the community studies of Appalachia from the 1950s and 1960s and into the 1990s recounted the traces of folk culture that endured despite the incursions of the modern world. See, for example, Beaver (1986); Hartman (1957); Hicks (1992); Mathews (1965); Pearsall (1959); J. Stephenson (1968); and Stewart (1996). For examples of studies and/or narrative accounts that document problems in Appalachian life and, in some instances, suggest ways to offset or remedy these deficiencies, see Ball (1968); Cattell-Gordon (1990); Caudill (1963); Duncan (1999); Ford (1962); Goshen (1970); Harrington (1962); Horton (1984); Hull (1997); Looff (1971); Swasy (1990); Vance (1965); Van Shaik (1989); Verghese (1994); and Weller (1965).

13. See Eaton (1973) as an example of the folklorist tradition and Sheppard (1935) as a representative of the culture-of-poverty approach. Both texts, written in the 1930s, reflect the philosophy of the local color school.

Chapter 1: Relocating Appalachia

1. Questions about the contexts of free and unfree labor, moreover, are not confined to the past. See, for example, Couto (1993), R. Lewis (1987), Maggard (1998), Setzer (1985), Smith (1987), Trotter (1990), White (1994), and Yarrow (1990).

2. Central to this debate is the question of whether present conditions are considered to presage massive changes in political economic structures, including the reorganization of transnational spaces around the "hypermobility" of capital, or to reflect long-term consequences and crises of capital accumulation (see, for example, Blim 1992; Castells and Portes 1989; Gordon 1988; Harvey 1989; Kearney 1995; Patterson 1998; Susser 1997).

3. These resources include U.S. Census Bureau (1880, 1883a, 1883b, 1992a, 1992b, 1997), Center for Improving Mountain Living (1992), U.S. Department of Agriculture (1999), Mountain Resource Center (1998), North Carolina Chamber of Commerce (1998), North

Carolina Child Advocacy Institute (1998), North Carolina State Data Center (1986), and North Carolina Office of State Planning (1998). The chambers of commerce for both counties, archival material from the local public libraries, and clippings from area newspapers also provided information.

4. I consider the two counties as one unit that I compare at two points in time. This approach is justified by my need to disguise the identity of these counties, lest I undermine the anonymity and confidentiality of those who participated in this study. Perhaps more important is that my research included participants and settings within both counties and that participants in this study moved frequently across county lines in the course of their daily lives. Thus the 1990 figures cited here constitute an average of the values listed for the respective counties. In keeping with the conventions of anthropology, I also use pseudonyms to refer to the proper names of places, institutions, and people.

5. These figures are rough approximations because of problems of misclassification and/or missing information on the part of enumerators, as well as any errors in calculation that I may have made.

6. In addition to omitting information about female heads of household, the census classifies slightly less than 1 percent of male household heads as having "no occupation" or lists them with no information other than their names. Because different enumerators used different methods of classification, it is incorrect to simply assume that "no occupation" refers to those instances when household heads were without gainful employment while the latter reflects the errors of the census takers. There are yet other questions to be entertained about the 1880 census. An enumerator did, in fact, list a number of the women heading households in one particular township both as "farmer" and as "keeping house." It is not clear whether this departure from the conventions of census taking was due to the orientation of the enumerator (whose participation in the census was confined to this township) or whether it also reflected the perspectives of those whom he interviewed. However, this was the exception that confirmed the rules of census taking within the remaining townships.

7. The listing of 151 more farms in the agricultural census than appear in the population manuscript schedule lends credence to the notion that some households headed by women were indeed organized around agriculture and suggests the likelihood that some male-headed households combined artisanal and professional work with farming (U.S. Census Bureau 1883b:30–101, table 5).

8. One might also speculate that in some cases parents gave younger sons title to the land in exchange for the sons' commitment to provide the parents with board and care until their death, as Dunn found in Cades Cove (1988:181).

9. As both McKenzie (1994) and Crawford (1991) note, more significant than total amount of acreage is the proportion of improved acreage (tilled land, hay fields, and pastures) to that which remains unimproved (woodlands, forest, old fields). Salstrom (1991) also suggests that self-sufficiency be examined from the vantage point of farm acres per capita, as well as in terms of total acreage. Following Salstrom's 1991 discussion of declining levels of food production and reduced living standards in late nineteenth-century Appalachia, and in lieu of more detailed information about individual farms in Pike and Clark counties, I consider farms with holdings of less than one hundred acres as marginally viable.

10. Many of those who appeared to be landless in the 1880 census were sons and daughters who would, upon marriage or through inheritance, come to have farms of their own. The census could not capture either the dynamic relations of landownership generally or changes in access to land that occurred during the life of an individual and family. See Dunn (1988) and D. Billings and Blee (2000).

11. In some cases artisanal and professional households included younger generations of family members listed as "farmers" and/or servants identified as "farm laborers."

12. All told, the 1880 census identified a little more than 4 percent of households as being involved in mica work, including mining, dealing, and wage labor. For the most part the connection involved mica prospecting and mining—whether by the head or another member of the household.

13. As Groneman and Norton (1987:3) have noted, domestic work was the primary form of paid employment for women in the late nineteenth century. Following the research of B. W. Jones (1995), McCurry (1992), and Whites (1992) on the significance of female slaves to agricultural production, we might speculate about the use of female servants—particularly women of color—as field labor on Appalachian farms.

14. The census identified some female heads of household as having an occupation, whereas other heads were not so identified. Likewise, some listings recorded the occupations of younger generations (U.S. Census Bureau 1883a, n.6).

15. Among the women heading households were those described as "married," "widowed," "divorced," and "mother." It is not clear whether this last referred to women who had never been married. As Turbin (1987:51–52) has observed, the living arrangements of "never-married" women were quite complex in the nineteenth century and included living in households headed by other women, living as self-supporting boarders in still other households, living in households with siblings (married or unmarried), and living as adult children in the households of their parents. The 1880 population schedule for Pike and Clark counties records all these arrangements.

16. Fifty-four percent of households of color (some identified as black, some as mulatto, and others of multiple race) were organized around nuclear families, 30 percent consisted of multiple generations and perhaps unrelated people, and 16 percent were headed by women.

17. Eleven percent of these households were involved in mica. In a few instances people of color, residing as servants in white households, worked in mica for their employers.

18. This figure should not be confused with the 11 percent of households that kept boarders—a strategy with economic and social implications in this predominantly white area.

19. Other local colorists such as Margaret Morley (1913:160) described her travels through the North Carolina mountains as "a journey back into the history of the past." For critiques of the local color school, in its past and present variations, see especially Batteau (1990); D. Billings (1974, 1999); Billings, Norman, and Ledford (1999); S. Fisher (1977, 1983); R. Lewis and Billings (1997); H. Lewis, Johnson, and Askins (1978); Lyon (1992); Mason (1993); Norman (1993); H. G. Reid (1996); Shapiro (1978); Tice and Billings (1991); Whisnant (1980, 1983); C. Williams (1961); and Wilson (1995).

20. Curiously enough, the number of full-time farms increased by 8 percent and the

amount of land in farms increased by 23 percent in the period from 1992 to 1997 (U.S. Census Bureau 1997). The most plausible explanation appears to be the purchase of land and the establishment of farms by new residents and/or second-home owners. It is equally possible that county residents, having experienced success in agriculture or other economic ventures, might transform their profits into farms and farmland.

21. See also U.S. Census Bureau (1992a, 1992b, 1997), Mountain Resource Center (1998), and North Carolina Department of Commerce (1998). In 1992 Pike and Clark counties produced 1.24 million pounds of tobacco and $1.14 million worth of forest products and Christmas trees (U.S. Census Bureau 1992a, 1997).

22. According to the 1992 census of agriculture, two-thirds of farm operators in Pike and Clark counties described their principal occupation as other than farming, and *all* worked off the farm at least part of the time (U.S. Census Bureau 1992a).

23. The owner of two "cut-sew-finish" facilities, located in Pike County and neighboring Mountain County, attributed his company's loss of contracts—and therefore the need to lay off 95 percent of company employees—to jobs sent off-shore after passage of NAFTA ("Company Lays Off Workers" 1997).

24. *Service,* as the term is used here, does *not* include domestic labor. Manufacturing jobs still accounted for one-quarter of the available jobs; construction work accounted for 8 percent. The vast majority of jobs, however, were in service (26 percent), wholesale and retail trade (18 percent), and local government (16 percent), the latter encompassing educational systems as well as county offices. Finance, insurance, and real estate accounted for 4 percent of the jobs, while 3 percent were in transportation, communication, and public utilities (U.S. Census Bureau 1992b; Center for Mountain Living 1992; Mountain Resource Center 1998). Manufacturing generated $52 million in revenue for 1990, while services produced earnings of $57 million (Regional Economic Information System 1990).

25. The "mothballing" (long-term shutdown) in January 1999 of a large minerals-processing plant by its multinational parent corporation, allegedly in response to the Asian economic crisis of the 1990s, seems further indication that this pattern will likely persist into the future.

26. Official measures of unemployment reflect only those people who are actively seeking jobs and/or are employed; unofficial estimates also include the long-term unemployed and "discouraged" job seekers, who have given up their efforts to find work. In other words, official measures grossly underestimate the number of people who are unemployed (Couto 1992, 1994).

27. Per capita income in western North Carolina, and Southern Appalachia in general, is higher than that reported for Central Appalachia, which experienced significant losses of jobs in manufacturing and mining in the 1980s and 1990s. Indeed, compared to Central Appalachia and the United States as a whole, Southern Appalachia has *succeeded* in retaining its manufacturing base, although this appears to be changing in 2000–2001 as a result of the international economic climate. In 1989 per capita income in rural Southern Appalachian counties was 73.1 percent of the national average, while in rural Central Appalachian counties it was 60.0 percent (Couto 1994:83, 87–89, 96–97; 1992:12). According to ratings given the 399 counties of Appalachia by the Appalachian Regional Commission, Pike and Clark counties fell in the middle of a five-point scale that ranks economies from severely distressed to strong (Couto 1992:2, appendix).

28. According to one set of estimates, more than 16 percent of those employed in Pike and Clark counties were "underemployed," defined as receiving less than $7 per hour, or $14,560 per year, in 1995. This is in contrast with the average annual wage of $24,374 for North Carolina and the national average of $27,440 (Mountain Resource Center 1998).

29. Although 15.3 percent of the population—and 16.6 percent of the children—of Pike and Clark counties lived in poverty, the rate for North Carolina as a whole was 12.5 percent in 1990 (North Carolina Child Advocacy Institute 1998).

It is hard to compare these figures with those from the 1880 census, where the only measures of poverty were the few households that listed "paupoors" as residents within them and the inhabitants of poorhouses. The census shows seven households with paupers, and fourteen paupers in all. What sense, however, are we to make of the household of nine children left alone by the death of their mother and the imprisonment of their father? And what are the economic implications for the numbers of households whose heads and/or other occupants are characterized as "maimed" or having other serious disabilities?

30. Indications of the elite status of a small number of county residents would include households whose annual income exceeded $100,000 (1.3 percent), and farms with 500 acres or more (1.4 percent), in 1990 (U.S. Census Bureau 1990c, 1992b). Additionally, at least some of the nearly three thousand partners in or proprietors of area businesses (which generated $160 million in 1992) would fit the description of elites (U.S. Census Bureau 1992a).

31. Scholars of Appalachia have for some time been engaged in analyses of social class and processes of class formation in the mountains. These issues, however, have not been fully theorized. The primary points of departure in the discussions to date are the significance of indigenous elites in shaping the political-economic contours of counties from their inception; the stratification of wealth, status, and landholdings in the nineteenth-century mountains; the proletarianization of rural residents by the end of the nineteenth century; and processes of local state formation. See Batteau (1982); D. Billings and Blee (2000); Conti (1979–80); Dunaway (1996); Inscoe (1989); Mann (1992); McKenzie (1994); McKinney (1995); Pudup (1989, 1991); and Salstrom (1991).

32. On the complexities of race and ethnicity in Appalachia, see D. Billings and Blee (2000); Cabbell (1985); Finger (1984, 1995); Hatley (1991); Hill (1997); Inscoe (1989, 1995, 2001); R. Lewis (1987, 1994); Lucas (1997); Manning-Miller (1993); McCurry (1992); Perdue (1979, 1985, 1998); Puglisi (1997); Sprague (1993); Trotter (1990, 1996); Turner and Cabbell (1985); Turner (1985); Wilson (1998); Wilson and Beaver (1999).

33. Latinos/as are heavily employed in agricultural production, where they are hired to do the difficult and poorly remunerated work of farm labor. While wages for farm laborers increased in the 1980s and 1990s, they did not keep pace with nonfarm wages—and the rates paid to undocumented and migrant laborers fell well below the reported averages (U.S. Department of Agriculture 1999). Doubtless, they have helped subsidize the resurgence of farming in western North Carolina (see notes 20 and 21).

According to the Census Bureau, the relatively small size and "unusual distribution" of Latino/a populations in western North Carolina make it difficult to create reliable population estimates (U.S. Census Bureau 1998). Other factors that might prove critical in determining the size and composition of Latino/a populations are, first and foremost, the likelihood that some in-migrants are undocumented workers who are reluctant to engage with government representatives; and second, the response of local communities to Latino/a residents. In other words, given the anti-immigrant climate at the national level and the possibilities for localized expressions of racism, many Latinos/as might wish to go unnoticed in the public sphere. With respect to the latter issue, western North Carolina is unfortunately not unique.

34. Until the 2000 census, the Census Bureau mandated that only one racial or ethnic group could be used to classify a given member of the population. Had multiple racial or ethnic markers been available in earlier censuses, some Euro-American and African American inhabitants of Pike and Clark counties might also have identified themselves as part Cherokee. The Bureau of Indian Affairs (BIA) has developed the notion of "blood quantum," which requires that a person have a certain percentage of "blood" (or ancestors belonging to a particular tribal group) to claim that heritage. Moreover, the BIA allows a person only one affiliation with a federally recognized tribal nation—a rule that forces Native Americans to choose between ancestries (Jaimes 1994).

35. Excluding households containing single people and "non-family" households, 11.1 percent of the households in Pike and Clark counties were headed by women, a figure considerably less than the 16.5 percent reported for the nation at large (U.S. Census Bureau 1990b).

36. In Pike and Clark counties 11.6 percent of *all* families lived below poverty level, a rate that more than doubled (23.5 percent) for single-parent families (75 percent of which were headed by women). The median income for female-headed households with children younger than eighteen was $13,516, slightly more than (107 percent of) the poverty threshold of $12,675 for a family of four. Moreover, for female householders living alone, the median income was $5,490, or 87 percent of the poverty threshold of $6,311 for a single person (Mountain Resource Center 1998; North Carolina Child Advocacy Institute 1998; U.S. Census Bureau 1990c).

37. The 1990 *Census of Population* (1990c) does report differences in income for female-headed households. The distribution was as follows (percentages total more than 100 due to rounding):

Income in 1989	Female Householder	All Households
less than $5,000	10.2%	10.6%
$5,000 to $9,999	16.5	13.0
$10,000 to $14,999	22.8	11.6
$15,000 to $24,999	28.7	23.9
$25,000 to $49,999	18.4	30.5
$50,000 or more	3.5	10.4

38. This speaks, as well, to the significance of other income sources, including transfer payments (social security, disability, welfare) and personal and/or business investments. Couto (1994:96–97) notes that, while transfer payments comprised 14.6 percent of the personal income for the United States as a whole, such payments made up 18.4 percent of the income in 1989 for people in Appalachia. Moreover, this constituted an increase, both at the national and regional levels, over the figures reported for 1979. One indication of personal and/or business investments is the information reported in the 1992 *Eco-*

nomic Census on proprietorships. According to that census (U.S. Census Bureau 1992a), women-owned firms—defined as sole proprietorships, partnerships, and subchapter S corporations—constituted 28.6 percent of the area businesses in Pike and Clark counties.

39. The absence of reporting and regulation is, indeed, the very basis of "informalization" (Portes and Castells 1989; Portes and Borocz 1988; Beneria and Stimpson 1987; Fernandez-Kelly and Garcia 1989). See Tryon (1917) for her efforts to determine the value of one historical variant on informal economic activities, namely, the production of "household manufactures" in the United States from 1840 to 1860.

40. See also Stewart (1996), who argues along similar and equally problematic lines.

Chapter 2: Questions of Authority

1. "That Sheppard woman" is Muriel Sheppard, author of *Cabins in the Laurel* (1935). See also Watkins (1985) and Anglin (1992).

2. Arguments against such "culture of poverty" approaches to Appalachia have been articulated by Batteau (1990); D. Billings (1974); Billings, Norman, and Ledford (1999); Couto (1975); E. Fine (1998); S. Fisher (1977, 1993); Gaventa (1980); H. Lewis, Johnson, and Askins (1978); Maggard (1994); H. G. Reid (1980–81); Waller (1988); and Whisnant (1980, 1983).

3. This name is a pseudonym, as are all proper names in this ethnography. In keeping with the ethics of anthropological research, I have endeavored as much as possible to protect the anonymity of my informants and the setting of this ethnography. It is partly for reasons of confidentiality that I have waited some years before presenting my fieldwork on western Carolina mica in one book.

It is also important to note my decision to alter the content of field notes or transcripts from taped interviews as little as possible, lest I sanitize and thereby misrepresent the perspectives of the women and men who spoke with me. This means that I did not edit out the grammatical errors that occur in any verbatim account; more important, the flow of their words and expressions remains intact. I hope that this will allow the reader to be more, rather than less, attuned to what my informants had to say. The liability of this approach is that it can feed into a "culture-of-poverty" motif, for those inclined to interpret Appalachia in this way. I am not sure, however, that transforming my informants' words into the sterile language of academic texts is any less an injustice.

4. That my parents had died only a few years earlier and that I was a single woman like Hazel Roberts provided the impetus for her mother to say that she had "decided to adopt [me]" as she had other "strays," John Walter's children included. The generosity of Hazel Roberts was matched only by that of her mother.

5. My concerns intensified when I heard from Hazel, as we readied ourselves for the evening meeting at her church, that Muriel Payne had received complaints from a worker on "Royce's end" and an anonymous call challenging my identity as a researcher and college teacher. While Hazel would not identify the people involved, she clearly knew who they were and was affected by their questions about me. On the spur of the moment—in the midst of the church service—I showed Hazel my student identification card from the New School, my faculty ID from the college where I was teaching, and my North Caroli-

na driver's license, so that she could know that I was who I said I was. The corroborating evidence clearly made a difference, and Hazel suggested that I show my identification to other factory workers. I followed her advice.

6. The only place to which I was denied access was the "pure mica department," which was housed in a separate building and managed by Muriel Payne. However, I was able to talk with one worker from that department, inasmuch as his skill in machining equipment brought him to other parts of the factory. I met a female employee from "the building across the road" through Long Hill Baptist Church, which I attended for most of my fieldwork. Through these means I heard a little about the activities of the pure mica department.

7. Forty-one women and men, approximately 80 percent of the labor force, worked in the "mica plate" division of Moth Hill. Of these, I interviewed twenty-seven workers, representing two-thirds of the main division and slightly more than half of all employees in the factory.

8. Some employees' reluctance to have me visit at their homes was not reserved for me alone but extended to all who were not connected in networks of kin, church, and neighborhood. Because workers lived in different settlements, they were not responsive to the idea of home visits by co-workers.

Chapter 3: Carolina Mica

1. I am, of course, referring to the modern mica industry developed by Euro-American elites, both residents of Appalachia and venture capitalists from elsewhere in the United States. Woodland Indians, ancestors to the Cherokee and other Native American tribes, mined mica for ceremonial use and for trade. North Carolina mica has been found in burial mounds associated with the Adena complex of the Ohio Valley. Elaborate grave goods, including ornaments made from mica, are indicative of Late Adena sites that are about two thousand years old (Fagan 1995:403, 406; Griffin 1978:243; see also Sterrett 1923:19).

2. For their analyses of eastern Tennessee and eastern Kentucky, see also McKenzie (1994) and D. Billings and Blee (2000), respectively.

3. According to Tryon, homemade manufactures include "1) wearing apparel and household textile supplies; 2) household implements, utensils, furniture, necessities, and comforts; and 3) farming implements, building materials, and general supplies" (1917:188).

4. For the importance of homemade manufactures to western North Carolina economies, see Tryon (1917), Deyton (1947), and Hughes (1976). On the value of women's labor in agriculture see Mann (1992) and Anglin (1995), whose perspectives depart from those of McKinney (1992) and, to a lesser extent, Dunn (1988). See chapter 1, note 6, on the limitations of historical records for tracing women's involvement in economic activities.

5. See Bynum's discussion of the practice of apprenticing indigent children in North Carolina (1992:88–90, 99–103). The apprenticeship system served as a form of social control that marginalized poor women and their children, orphans, and particularly families of color. It also functioned as a social welfare program, an alternative to the poorhouse, and a means by which to lay claim to the labor of indigent children. With respect to this

last point, it might be argued that the formal system of apprenticeship, organized through the courts, had its analogue in the informal practice of recruiting the children of poor relations to labor in the households of their more prosperous kin, in return for room and board and the promise of an education (see also Hughes 1976).

6. According to Inscoe, on the eve of the Civil War 1,877, or 10 percent, of the households in western North Carolina owned slaves. Of these, 38 percent owned 1 to 2 slaves; 45 percent owned 3 to 9 slaves; 12 percent owned 10 to 19 slaves; and 5 percent owned 20 or more slaves (1989:84). The corresponding figures for Southern slaveholders as a group are 26 percent (1–2 slaves); 41 percent (2–9 slaves); 20 percent (10–19 slaves); and 14 percent (20 or more slaves) (Inscoe 1989:85).

7. For more than thirty years Clingman wrote speeches, articles, and letters pertaining to the mountain region of North Carolina. He collected these writings and published them in 1877 (see also Inscoe 1989).

8. It is important to distinguish Clingman's claims—and, indeed, much of the early scholarship on Appalachia—from the much more complex issue of ethnic and racial identities in Appalachia. As I noted in chapter 1, the population of nineteenth-century Southern Appalachia included Italian migrant laborers, Cherokee, freed slaves, those listed in the census as "Mulattos," Anglo-Americans from a variety of ethnic origins, and no doubt others. This stands in contrast to the myth of the mountaineer of "pure Scotch Irish" ancestry. See Craddock (1884), D. H. Fisher (1989), Fox (1901), Kephart (1922), and Weller (1965) as examples of this stereotype. See the responses of Batteau (1990), D. Billings (1974), R. Lewis and Billings (1997), Shapiro (1978), C. Williams (1961), and Whisnant (1980) to these representations.

9. Clingman was also a proponent of reestablishing the North Carolina Geological Survey, which had been initiated in 1852 and disrupted by the Civil War. That initial survey did not extend to the western part of the state (Clingman 1877:116–20; Kerr 1867:6–13).

10. The term *modern* is important because it calls attention to the efforts of Persons, Clingman, and others to transform mica mining from an informal economic activity into an extractive industry. It also acknowledges that nineteenth-century Euro-Americans were not the first to mine or trade in mica. What Clingman (1877:131) took to be evidence of "a party of Spaniards" searching for silver ore were, instead, excavations and tailings from mica mines established by Native Americans "in a very systematic and skillful way" at least three centuries earlier (Kerr 1875:301; Stuckey 1965:414).

11. In his letter to "Messrs. Avery and Carter" concerning the mica deposits of western North Carolina, Clingman ended by saying: "No other mineral of much commercial value has yet been found in the mica veins, but it is to be hoped that at some point or other the beryls found may occur in the form of emeralds. . . . I need scarcely remind you that the emerald ranks next in value to the ruby and the diamond" (1877:131). See also Stuckey (1965:416–17) and Sterrett (1923:167–68).

12. Mining companies and entrepreneurs, not simply households with informal ties to the burgeoning mica industry, commonly used "groundhogging" mining practices— in which "timbering is sparingly used, and pillars are left only where they are absolutely needed to keep the mine open." Among other things, this meant that mica miners often worked in dangerous conditions. Yet, as Sterrett observed, "Some mines can be worked

only by such methods. The deposits may not be rich enough to warrant the expense necessary to equip the mine with proper machinery and [to] timber it carefully and may pay only 'good wages' to the lessees" (1923:21).

13. Even so, mica mining remained a risky venture. Deposits of vegetable matter or iron ore marred many mica blocks, or they contained rifts and cleavages from the shifting of the mountains millions of years ago. As a result, they could not be used for glazing or as an insulating medium.

14. Production figures for the mica industry were first recorded by the federal government in 1880. These figures covered the United States as a whole, and data specifically on production in North Carolina were not available until 1900. However, by 1880 North Carolina had overtaken New Hampshire as the major domestic source of mica (Stuckey 1965:412–13).

15. The decline in production was attributed to the increase in imports of Indian mica and to changes in technology (U.S. Bureau of Mines, *Mineral Resources* 1890:614–15). Increased use of furnaces rather than fireplace heaters meant less need for sheet mica in stove windows. Moreover, manufacturers preferred Indian mica for use as insulating material in generators because it was easier to process into the thin, even sheets that they needed.

16. The invention of micanite in 1888, which was available commercially by 1894, addressed one of the major technical limitations: the small size of most mica crystals. Micanite consisted of mica splittings bound together with varnishes or resins. Through these means large sheets of mica could be "built up" from small pieces of mica (Chowdhury 1941:237–41; Skow 1962:31).

17. India's emergence as a major mica supplier also affected the market in Canada (Spence 1912:18–20, 27–37).

18. Although I do not have figures for the nineteenth century, this is well established in sources on twentieth-century mica production. For example, in 1938 mica workers in North Carolina earned thirty cents per hour for an eight-hour day—improvements in working conditions wrought by the National Recovery Act of 1934. Before this, workers in the South were paid as little as seven and a half cents per hour to process mica, and ten cents to mine it, while working fifty to sixty hours a week (National Recovery Administration 1934:298–99). However, in 1938 unskilled adult male workers in India were paid $3 a month, and skilled workers received $5 per month. Women and children labored alongside men in mica processing, and their wages were not recorded. The NRA had outlawed child labor in the U.S. mica industry (Labour Bureau 1972:8–10; NRA 1934:298; U.S. Tariff Commission 1947:63). The Labour Investigation Committee of the government of India in 1944–45 documented the deplorable working conditions of mica processors, and subsequent legislation sought to address these excesses (Labour Bureau 1972).

19. Urban (1932) examined this issue by looking at the production costs and output associated with two mines in North Carolina. He found, in one mine, that the cost of mining and sheeting mica totaled $39,766.02 (including $9,455.87 in mining supplies) for $49,975.22 worth of mica recovered. In other words, while the rock was valued at $3.93 a ton, profits were meager because the costs of mining and sheeting were $2.75 per ton (1932:8–10).

20. See Leith (1931) on the subject of minerals and world politics. See also Rajgarhia (1951) for problems within the mica industry of India.

21. The invention of the transistor radio later eliminated these parts and therefore these applications for mica; however, the use of mica in radio transmission continued unabated.

22. According to the U.S. Tariff Commission , mica was a critical or "indispensable" element in commutator segments for motors and generators; commutator V-rings for motors and generators; armatures (high temperature and high voltage); airplane spark plugs; radio tubes; transformers; and radio condensers (1938:14–22).

Mica was considered an important, but not indispensable, part of appliances such as electric flatirons, toasters, stove windows and lantern chimneys, fuse plug covers, insulation in rheostats and the starting boxes of trolley cars, neon lights, and telephones. Because its technical requirements were not so demanding, the telephone industry partially replaced mica with other, inferior insulating; however, "telephone repeating stations," integral to long-distance service, required mica condensers similar to those used in radio transmission (U.S. Tariff Commission 1938:23–26).

23. The subtext of this conversation was that laboring in the confines of the springhouse with a male co-worker was not appropriate for a young white girl. Nonetheless, Daniel Payne wanted someone to operate a punch press, labor traditionally assigned to an unmarried woman or a young girl, so he found a female employee. It is likely that she had been working as a maidservant in his prosperous household. Daniel Payne surely would have found a precedent for this approach in his father's own household, which, according to the 1880 census, had included two African American (male) "hirelings" whose purpose was to "dig mica" (see Anglin 1995, ethnographic interviews; U.S. Census Bureau 1880).

24. B. W. Jones's (1995) discussion of racially stratified, gendered work within the tobacco industry in the North Carolina Piedmont provides a useful point of comparison.

25. In at least two instances women who worked in mica early in the century were still working in the early 1960s. See chapter 2 for a description of the informants.

26. One such place that my informants named was the Randolph Mica Company, a mica house that started at the turn of the century and fell victim to recession in the 1920s.

27. Liza Roberts, who went to work when she was twelve, as many of my informants had, noted that workers were initially paid by the pound of finished mica. In 1914 she received fifteen cents per pound for the mica that she trimmed and split in the mica house. When she worked independently, however, she could sell sheeted mica to the mica houses for $7.50 a pound (interview 30).

28. Women typically left the labor force, at least briefly, upon marriage. Some never returned; however, most of my informants waited until their children were school age and then went back to work. Of these six informants, only Ruby Johnson left mica work permanently after marrying. Her husband's employment in construction and engineering for the State of North Carolina made it both possible and necessary that she quit work, because his work initially required that they relocate.

29. See Wray (1931:209) on the shipments of mica on the Clinchfield Railroad during the late 1920s.

30. Gwinn suggested that "mica of military grade" be used in place of the less clearly defined term *strategic mica*. Under this rubric he included "all sizes and qualities of mica used in the manufacture of equipment for the armed forces" (1943:3). More specifically, this referred to "transmitting, receiving, and trimmer condenser films, radio-tube bridges and supports, cigarette films and nose washers for airplane spark plugs, and magneto

condenser films" (1943:4). Put another way, "almost all strategic mica is consumed in the production of aircraft and tank magnetos, spark plugs, military radios, and sound detection equipment" (U.S. Bureau of Mines, *Minerals Yearbook* 1942:1467).

31. The mapping program consisted of joint research conducted by the U.S. Geological Survey and the North Carolina Surveys. Researchers from these agencies visited and sampled about two hundred mines and prospects between 1943 and 1945 (Stuckey 1965:422; see also Lesure 1968; Skow 1962).

The Combined Raw Materials Board included Great Britain, the United States, and other Allies. Brazil and India were the principal sources of mica to which the Combined Raw Materials Board directed its attention; however, Angola, Tanzania, Argentina, Colombia, Madagascar, Mexico, Spain, and Peru were likewise included in these efforts (M. Billings and Montague 1944:92–93; Skow 1962:148–51).

Bell Telephone Laboratories, General Electric Company, Sylvania Electric Company, and Owens-Corning Fiberglass Corporation were some of the better-known companies involved in developing synthetic alternatives, as were government agencies and universities. Although initial efforts were only partially successful in "growing" flakes of synthetic mica, the research eventually succeeded in providing synthetic forms of insulation as alternatives to the elusive mineral (Hatch et al. 1957; Roy 1952; Skow 1962:141–45).

32. In conjunction with efforts to double and, in some instances, quadruple the prices paid for domestic mica—thereby remunerating self-employed miners and processors at rates much higher than before the government program—the minimum wage increased from thirty cents per hour in the late 1930s to forty cents per hour in 1943 for particular industries, including mica (U.S. Tariff Commission 1947:35; see M. Billings and Montague 1944:94 and Skow 1962:153–54, 197–98, on changes in price schedules for domestic mica).

33. Not everyone was enthralled by this opportunity. The head of Doubleback Mountain Mica declined the opportunity to work with Colonial Mica: "He just did not trust the government. He was still bitter about income tax or something. But he felt that once he did that, the government would take over the company and he would lose it. He just did not think that it could possibly be as good a deal as it sounded like" (interview 22).

34. The munitions board further recommended that the government allocate $3.5 million to purchase 500 tons of block mica and 3,000 tons of mica splittings, with purchasing carried out through the procurement division of the Treasury Department. With the advent of World War II these figures were revised upward to 700 tons of block mica and 4,000 tons of mica splittings (Skow 1962:147).

35. The federal government also renewed its efforts to explore foreign and domestic sources of mica. The Defense Minerals Administration, renamed the Defense Minerals Exploration Administration in 1951, loaned money for up to 90 percent of the costs of mica prospecting. "Repayment, without interest, was required only if the project was certified as a discovery or development from which commercial production might be made" (Skow 1961:160).

36. As the reports by Burgess (1949), Gwinn (1943), Houk (1942), and Jahns and Lancaster (1950) make evident, research was undertaken in the 1940s on the technical properties of mica to clarify the characteristics of "strategic grades." This information was integrated into the pricing schedules for mica, and recommendations for which kinds of mica to target for purchase, as part of the federal procurement program.

37. Stuckey 1965:418. According to Skow (1962:161), the Defense Minerals Exploration Administration executed 297 contracts offering financial assistance to those involved in exploring or developing sources of mica. Although the total value of the exploration contracts was $1,670,878, the government advanced only $997,317. Sixty-eight contracts resulted in "certificates of discovery or development," with a value of $507,385.

38. In 1963 North Carolina produced 92,961 pounds of sheet mica, valued at $12,604 (see table 5).

39. By 1986, however, U.S. imports of sheet mica increased by 49 percent to 4.0 million (U.S. Bureau of Mines, *Minerals Yearbook* 1986:1).

40. See U.S. Bureau of Mines, *Minerals Yearbook* (1980, 1982, 1983), U.S. Geological Survey, *Minerals Yearbook* (1994, 1999), and U.S.Geological Survey (2001) for estimates of domestic demand for mica through 2000.

Chapter 4: Working "Close Home"

1. The remarks of Royce Payne on this point are worth quoting at length:

> Crabtree Iron Mines, they had a section up this side of Crabtree that was all Negro houses . . . black houses . . . and they called it "Africa." There was a lot of black people worked over there.
> [Interviewer]: Were there any black people that worked over at your . . . in your mines?
> Not . . . Yes, in my mines, yes.
> [Interviewer]: In the mines, but not in the—
> No, not in the plant. Never did ask to work in the plant. (interview 18)

2. Joe Shelton and his son, J.T., got jobs at Moth Hill through the interventions of kinswomen who were employed elsewhere in the factory (Upstairs). The Sheltons' sloppy work habits—and the fact that they replaced an older, well-respected worker named Ben Forbes—won them no praise from female co-workers who mostly shunned them. After the incident with the defective parts, Forbes got his old job back and peace was restored to the Upper End.

3. "Lightning split the tree" was Hazel's way of describing what had happened to her father's side of the family. Her paternal grandfather had left a trail of broken relationships behind him, and Hazel's father took another man's name when his mother remarried. Besides the question of respectability, there was the issue of differences in socioeconomic standing between the respective families and the aspirations of the younger generations of Watkinses. Elsa Watkins could have put in a word for Hazel when she got ready to retire from the punch presses, a steady job to which Hazel aspired, but she did not. Instead, she complained to John Walter Payne that Hazel Roberts was leaving her shift early (and presumably having someone else punch out for her).

4. Although Indian mica was said to be superior to domestic mica, its main advantage derived from savings on the costs of labor. Rather than continue to "gamble" on the mica veins of North Carolina, Moth Hill's customers found it far easier to let companies in India bear the risks of mining and to capitalize on the meager wages paid to Indian workers.

5. The ratio of women to men in the main division of the factory was 25 to 15, not counting John Walter Payne and Ed Payne in the front office.

6. One afternoon's exchange on the Lower End provides a graphic illustration. As June Robbins sorted through washers that Elsa Watkins had punched from the Upper End's bad plate, June's supervisor reminded her not to be too thorough in her work. The way Al Gardner put it was, "Royce said if you mash anything too hard, it will break." While June did not fully agree with this approach to quality control, she conceded the larger point: "You have to use what's lying around here. You can't let it go to waste." There were few alternatives, given the limited investment of the Paynes.

Chapter 5: Life Histories and Local Cultures

1. This section is based on three interviews (interviews 7–9) that I conducted with Zona Watson during a period of five weeks, as well as on field notes from 1987 and 1988.

2. Even then Zona's contributions were considerable. She knew how to "cut off on the flexible," which was liable to tear and pull apart if not handled correctly. Once, when Hazel hesitantly offered to try her hand again at this task, Zona responded, "Oh, no, I can do it. I've cut 500 sheets in a day."

3. At Long Hill Baptist I heard: "They always said when you was growing up, 'If you want to find a husband, go to church.'"

4. They had been married for nearly fifty years when he died from lung cancer, a disease that Zona and Zeyland attributed to his years in the mica mines.

5. The Presbyterian church fared slightly better than the Methodist church in the conversations on the Upper End but was likewise considered the church of lawyers, doctors, and summer visitors—along with people like Zona's sister, who maintained her ties with the church in which she had been raised.

6. Annie Burleson described how she had come back to Pike County after World War II to farm. She could take her children to the fields and leave them on a quilt in the shade while she worked. Annie raised cabbage and chickens and other cash crops, in addition to the food that she produced for her family. She told me that a lot of people in the county were truck farmers back then, "but now all they grow in Pike County is trees."

7. They were also "branch kin," indirectly related through the overlapping of kin and social networks (interview 6).

8. This section is based on recorded interviews with Hazel Roberts (interview 6) and her mother, Pearl Roberts (interview 10), as well as field notes from 1987 to 1988. My knowledge of Hazel Roberts came not from an oral history primarily but through my interactions with her—at Moth Hill, at her parents' home, and at church.

9. Hazel's mother, Pearl, had been sent to the orphanage on the death of her father and the subsequent nervous breakdown of her mother. In Pearl's words, "Mama was too sick and had a nervous breakdown, and I couldn't stay with her because she was with her grandma, and my grandma and grandpa. I couldn't stay there because it was too far back in the mountains. . . . I tried to get what schooling I could, but I didn't get much. I stayed down at [the orphanage] and tried to work to help others" (interview 10).

10. Her brother even set up an office so that she could be an accountant and work at home. Hazel explained the liabilities of this situation and her desire for greater autonomy from her family:

It's just like [my brother] Paul, bless his heart, he loves me to death, he would go through fire for me. He'd lay down there in that road and die for me. He has got that building right there fixed up for an office. I mean he had power put into it, he paneled it, he carpeted. But he cannot understand that you cannot have an office at home. Because Daddy means well, but he is nosey. And if you're doing somebody's, say, their income taxes, that's between you, them, and God. But Daddy says, "I'm your father, it's different." And then he gets to sitting there and talking like to you, he gets to bragging, and then I might as well have just put it on TV. He cannot understand that. The location is another thing I don't like. If I'm going to go into something, I want a good location, and this is not the best location. Mama, she tends to be friendly; I would never sit down long enough to find out what they wanted. But they can't understand that, and it causes hard feelings and fights at dinner. (interview 6)

11. Of the company where her father worked, Hazel noted: "It's not the greatest place in the world to work. It's not the cleanest. But they have got some benefits, and they do sort of take an interest in their hands" (interview 6).

12. Hazel was particularly critical of "Florida people," who "buy land and dare you to look at it, or breathe the air around it."

13. While the preacher at Long Hill focused on the punishments meted out to those lost in sin, Hazel did not discuss this. Her concern was to show the power of God in her life and to pray for those who did not know this. She was not militant about converting others.

14. I spent seven months (from November 1987 until June 1988) attending services at Long Hill Baptist Church and visited Zona's church, Liston's Branch Baptist, and the Church of the Fellowship, the Pentecostal church that Frances attended on Cove Creek. I stopped going to Long Hill when people began to ask me about getting baptized and becoming a member of the church. While I had valued my experiences as a visitor, I felt uncomfortable with further involvement, and I realized I could not remain a visitor (bystander) any longer.

15. The congregation of approximately sixty members included four major kin groups of three or four generations. Not everyone was related by marriage or blood ties. As was the case for Paul and Hazel, Ben and Nola Forbes attended Long Hill because it was the church in the neighborhood, not because their families had long-standing ties there. Perhaps the lack of kin, in conjunction with their work experiences, intensified the connections between Hazel, Ben, and Nola.

16. In the monthly meeting that followed the sermon, John Roscoe suggested that the church give Parnell Hayes a thousand dollars because his insurance would not cover all the medical bills, and it would be some time before he received disability payments. If Parnell needed more than that, "then we can vote it again. We have the money, and like we said in Sunday school, money's the easiest thing to give."

17. Hazel also offered her own criticism, based in part on her experiences in the hospital. She told the older women's class, "When I was in the hospital, the preachers would come round and ask me to confess my sin, and then I could be healed." When a member of the class protested, "That wasn't Baptist preachers, was it?" Hazel responded that indeed they were.

Chapter 6: Paternalism, Protest, and Back Talk

1. The interpretation of hegemony that Raymond Williams offers is a conceptualization that refuses to "equate consciousness with the articulate formal system which can be and ordinarily is abstracted as 'ideology.' . . . Instead it sees the relations of domination and subordination, in their forms as practical consciousness, as in effect a saturation of the whole process of living—not only of political and economic activity, nor only of manifest social activity, but of the whole substance of lived identities and relationships" (1977:109–10).

2. The different processes and products that Daniel Payne pioneered included ground mica, to be used in making paint, Formica, cosmetics, and the like, as well as oil-drilling equipment; laminated mica or mica "plate," formed into sheets through hand labor or machine processes and sold in that form or fabricated into components, according to the requirements of the customer; and "pure" mica, obtained from international sources and, to a lesser extent (in the late twentieth century), local mines, to be sold in the form of specialty parts.

3. The text of the code includes a description of wage levels in the South—western North Carolina—as seven and a half cents per hour for the sheeting of mica and ten cents for mica mining. The proposed rate increase would bring wages up to twenty-five cents per hour for workers in the South and thirty cents for workers in the North (National Recovery Administration 1934).

4. According to Royce Payne, Moth Hill maintained a workforce of three hundred until the early 1970s. The war in Vietnam created a need for expendable military hardware, and orders for production remained strong at Moth Hill.

5. Mica grinding, as the term implies, is a form of processing that is mechanized and more routinized than that involved in sheeting mica and/or producing mica plate. Moreover, the labor force employed in mica grinding is exclusively male. While Moth Hill did have a small grinding operation, its principal concerns were the mica plate and pure mica divisions. In terms of labor force, production process, and scope of operations, the company in the NLRB suit was quite different from Moth Hill. An important similarity, however, was that production was organized around kin ties and local social networks.

6. The actions of the superintendent reveal a great deal about the nature of mica company paternalism. He not only fired the four workers but did so by challenging customary rights through which workers controlled their own labor. For example, he fired one worker who failed to get permission to leave work, although it was an accepted practice that employees could leave work as needed and that others would fill in for them. In another instance the superintendent coerced the support of a plant foreman, both in the firing of the foreman's son and efforts to foreclose on a loan granted the younger man by the mica company (see National Labor Relations Board 1950; *Federal Reporter* 1952).

7. Not only were fewer employment opportunities available to African Americans, with the closing of the ironworks in the late 1920s, but several incidents of racial violence occurred in the 1930s and 1940s. In one instance, about which it is difficult to get definitive information, a mob threatened violence against an African American prisoner working on a road crew in Clark County. The situation became so volatile that the prison crew was quickly transported out of the area, and the national guard dispatched to quell the

ensuing riot. Shortly after this event many African American residents left the area; however, multiracial communities persisted in both Pike and Clark counties.

8. African Americans—former slaves and their descendants—settled Redding in the nineteenth century, but it was also home to Native Americans, whites, and people of mixed ancestry. Until the time of integration, children from the settlement went to their own school or the small school established in Monroe for African Americans. The minimal information available on this and other multiracial settlements in Pike and Clark counties is indicative of what Darlene Wilson terms "familiar patterns of historical trail-blurring" (1998:59).

9. June Robbins knew that one man from Redding worked in a garage in Sadieville and told me that she assumed that the women made their living as domestics.

10. There was one volatile event, a confrontation between Hazel and her brother and father, when the latter two made racist remarks at the dinner table (see Anglin 1992). The remarks were occasioned by the presence of Latinos walking through Monroe on a Sunday afternoon, a situation that Hazel's brother likened to "dynamite a-waitin' to go off." In the discussion that later ensued around the dinner table, Hazel's brother and father spoke of African Americans, as well as Latinos, in pejorative terms. Hazel stopped it abruptly by asking her father, "Daddy, *what* are you a-goin' to do if you die and go up to heaven and find out Jesus is *black*?!" She stared at her father, and the conversation went no further.

11. Of Eunice Payne, sister to Royce and co-owner of Moth Hill, Pearl Roberts noted: "She's a multi-multimillionaire, and her son can't even come home and bring his family. But she's gone buggy" (interview 10).

12. Royce once explained to me that Moth Hill had to make $2 million in profits each year to meet the minimum requirements of the Payne family.

13. Annie Burleson noted that the company had done well in its most recent dealings with the state: "They passed real good on the last inspection, except for not having fire drills and not having someone watching out for safety. They commented on the housekeeping. It was real good. Tammi Wilson told us beforehand and I cleaned up. I swept that place from one end to the other" (interview 25).

14. A number of employees asked to be transferred out of particular departments, or stopped working at Moth Hill altogether, because of the ubiquity of the lacquers. Frances Stokes's mother and Gertie Russell's husband were among those who quit their jobs at the plant. Their stories formed part of the knowledge base of employees who contested the Paynes' position on the harmlessness of the exposure.

15. My own experience was that I became intoxicated after a very short period of exposure (for I kept my sojourns Upstairs to a minimum), and the headaches lasted for hours afterward. Hazel knew that her persistent sinus infections and headaches were work related.

16. In Zona's words: "Most of the men around here died from silicosis. Two of Zeyland's brothers had that. They'd worked in the mines all their life, and Zeyland drilled an awful lot in these old mines. He'd come home with his hair just matted with that old drill dust and his eyes and nose all covered with just dry rock dust. They'd supposed to have water on the drill, but they never had it. They drilled dry, and that's dangerous because that rock dust gets down on your lungs. There's no way of moving that. It's more dangerous than coal dust" (interview 7).

17. They received X rays every eighteen months—formerly, it was every twelve months—to check for "dust" and cancer. A van serving as a kind of mobile health clinic (complete with X-ray equipment and health-care technicians) drove up near Moth Hill's entrance, and employees lined up outside to have their exams. Positive findings (evidence of lung disease) were rarely reported. The one case that *had* been found, some years before, was a diagnosis of lung cancer attributable to cigarette smoking. The workers did not trust this testing situation, as it occurred under the auspices of the company.

18. Gertie Russell's stance is also a reflection of earlier years, when she desperately needed a job: "Then, after the war, I went to Moth Hill and put in an application early in the summer, didn't I? Me and Jean went down there. They called me to go to work, but I was pregnant and I couldn't go to work. I cried, because I wanted that job so bad I couldn't stand it" (interview 12).

19. My response to a reviewer who found this statement surprisingly mechanistic is that, depressed wages notwithstanding, there were important distinctions *between* Moth Hill employees with respect to their positions in the local economy. These differences also made for different degrees of respectability, different aspirations (and educations) for subsequent generations of their families, and different patterns of sociability. As Mary Wingerd (1996) notes of the mill workers at Cooleemee, one group of Moth Hill employees saw themselves as representatives of "a better class," an incipient middle class. To their colleagues with fewer economic resources, they were simply factory hands who had "got above their raising" and were no longer trustworthy. My point is that, within the factory, there was no one social positioning but a range of possibilities that reflected gender, generation, class, geography (in the sense of rural settlement), religious affiliation, personal/ family histories, and social networks.

20. Of this relative, Hazel's mother said, "The worst thing in the world are kin who used to be poor and then got rich," because they looked down on those who had fewer material resources.

References Cited

Abel, Marjorie, and Nancy Folbre. 1990. "A Methodology for Revising Estimates: Female Market Participation in the U.S. before 1940." *Historical Methods* 23:167–76.

Adams, Shelby Lee. 1999. "Sunday Best." *New York Times Magazine*, April 4, 1999, pp. 40–47.

Anglin, Mary K. 1992. "A Question of Loyalty." *Anthropological Quarterly* 65:105–16.

———. 1995. "Lives on the Margin: Rediscovering the Women of Antebellum Western North Carolina." In *Appalachia in the Making: The Mountain South in the Nineteenth Century.* Ed. Mary Beth Pudup, Dwight B. Billings, and Altina Waller. 185–209. Chapel Hill: University of North Carolina Press.

———. 1997. "AIDS in Appalachia: Medical Pathologies and the Problem of Identity." *Journal of Appalachian Studies* 3:171–87.

———. 1999. "Towards a Workable Past: Dangerous Memories and Feminist Perspectives." *Journal of Appalachian Studies* 6:71–99.

Asad, Talal. 1986. "The Concept of Cultural Translation in British Social Anthropology." In *Writing Culture: The Poetics and Politics of Ethnography.* Ed. James Clifford and George E. Marcus. 141–64. Berkeley: University of California Press.

Associated Press. 2001. "Eric Rudolph Remains Free Three Years After Hunt Began." <http://www.lexis-nexis.com>. January 29.

Ball, Richard A. 1968. "A Poverty Case: The Analgesic Subculture of the Southern Appalachians." *American Sociological Review* 33:385–95.

Bannister, Cowan, and Co. 1869. *The Resources of North Carolina: Its Natural Wealth, Condition, and Advantages, as Existing in 1869, Presented to the Capitalists and People of the Central and Northern States.* Wilmington, N.C.: Bannister, Cowan, and Co.

Barney, Sandra Lee. 1996. "Gender and the Construction of Appalachian Otherness." Paper presented at the Tenth Berkshire Conference on the History of Women, Chapel Hill, N.C.

———. 2000. *Authorized to Heal: Gender, Class, and the Transformation of Medicine in Appalachia.* Chapel Hill: University of North Carolina Press.

Baron, Ava. 1991. *Work Engendered: Toward a New History of American Labor.* Ithaca, N.Y.: Cornell University Press.

Batteau, Alan B. 1982. "Mosbys and Broomsedge: The Semantics of Class in an Appalachian Kinship System." *American Ethnologist* 9:445–66.

———. 1990. *The Invention of Appalachia.* Tucson: University of Arizona Press.

Beaver, Patricia D. 1986. *Rural Community in the Appalachian South.* Prospect Heights, Ill.: Waveland Press.

Becker, Jane S. 1998. *Selling Tradition: The Domestication of Southern Appalachian Culture in 1930s America.* Chapel Hill: University of North Carolina Press.

Beneria, Lourdes, and Catharine R. Stimpson, eds. 1987. *Women, Households, and the Economy.* New Brunswick, N.J.: Rutgers University Press.

Beneria, Lourdes, and Gita Sen. 1986. "Accumulation, Reproduction and Women's Role in Economic Development: Boserup Revisited." In *Women's Work: Development and the Division of Labor by Gender.* Ed. Eleanor B. Leacock and Helen I. Safa. 141–57. South Hadley, Mass.: Bergin and Garvey.

Beneria, Lourdes, and Shelley Feldman, eds. 1992. *Unequal Burden: Economic Crises, Persistent Poverty, and Women's Work.* Boulder, Colo.: Westview Press.

Berry, J. P., P. Henoc, P. Galle, and R. Pariente. 1976. "Pulmonary Mineral Dust." *American Journal of Pathology* 83:427–56.

Billings, Dwight B. 1974. "Culture and Poverty in Appalachia: A Theoretical and Empirical Analysis." *Social Forces* 53:315–23.

———. 1999. "An Introduction." In *Back Talk from an American Region: Confronting Appalachian Stereotypes.* Ed. Dwight B. Billings, Gurney Norman, and Katherine Ledford. 1–20. Lexington: University Press of Kentucky.

Billings, Dwight B., Gurney Norman, and Katherine Ledford, eds. 1999. *Back Talk from an American Region: Confronting Appalachian Stereotypes.* Lexington: University Press of Kentucky.

Billings, Dwight B., and Kathleen Blee. 1986. "Reconstructing Daily Life in the Past: An Hermeneutical Approach to Ethnographic Data. *Sociological Quarterly* 27:443–62.

———. 2000. *The Road to Poverty: The Making of Wealth and Inequality in Appalachia.* Cambridge: Cambridge University Press.

Billings, Dwight B., Mary Beth Pudup, and Altina Waller. 1995. "Taking Exception with Exceptionalism: The Emergence and Transformation of Historical Studies of Appalachia." In *Appalachia in the Making: The Mountain South in the Nineteenth Century.* Ed. Mary Beth Pudup, Dwight B. Billings, and Altina Waller. 1–24. Chapel Hill: University of North Carolina Press.

Billings, M. H., and S. A. Montague. 1944. "The Wartime Problem of Mica Supply." *Engineering and Mining Journal* 145:92–95.

Black, Kate. 1990. "The Roving Picket Movement and the Appalachian Committee for Full Employment, 1959–1965: A Narrative." *Journal of the Appalachian Studies Association* 2:110–27.

Blim, Michael L. 1992. "The Emerging Global Factory and Anthropology." In *Anthropology and the Global Factory: Studies of the New Industrialization in the Late Twentieth Century.* Ed. Frances A. Rothstein and Michael L. Blim. 1–30. New York: Bergin and Garvey.

Bond, George C., and Angela Gilliam. 1994. "Introduction." In *Social Construction of the Past: Representation as Power*. Ed. George C. Bond and Angela Gilliam. 1–22. New York: Routledge.

Bookman, Ann, and Sandra Morgen, eds. 1988. *Women and the Politics of Empowerment*. Philadelphia: Temple University Press.

Bose, Christine E., and Edna Acosta-Belen. 1995a. "Colonialism, Structural Subordination, and Empowerment: Women in the Development Process." In *Women in the Latin American Development Process*. Ed. Christine E. Bose and Edna Acosta-Belen. 15–36. Philadelphia: Temple University Press.

———, eds. 1995b. *Women in the Latin American Development Process*. Philadelphia: Temple University Press.

Bryant, F. Carlene. 1981. *We're All Kin: A Cultural Study of a Mountain Neighborhood*. Knoxville: University of Tennessee Press.

Burgess, Blandford C. 1949. "Guide for Buying Domestic Muscovite Mica." *Mining Transactions* 184:453–57.

Burowoy, Michael. 1985. *The Politics of Production: Factory Regimes under Capitalism and Socialism*. London: Verso.

Bynum, Victoria E. 1992. *Unruly Women: The Politics of Social and Sexual Control in the Old South*. Chapel Hill: University of North Carolina Press.

Cabbell, Edward J. 1985. "Black Invisibility and Racism in Appalachia: An Informal Survey." In *Blacks in Appalachia*. Ed. William H. Turner and Edward J. Cabbell. 3–10. Lexington: University Press of Kentucky.

Campbell, Robert F. 1952. "Franklin Plugs for Branch of GSA Purchasing Agency." *Asheville Citizen Times*, July 13, 1952.

Carson, Jo. 1989. *Stories I Ain't Told Nobody Yet*. New York: Orchard Books.

Castells, Manuel, and Alejandro Portes. 1989. "World Underneath: The Origins, Dynamics, and Effects of the Informal Economy." In *The Informal Economy: Studies in Advanced and Less Developed Countries*. Ed. Alejandro Portes, Manuel Castells, and Laura A. Benton. 11–37. Baltimore: Johns Hopkins University Press.

Cattell-Gordon, David. 1990. "The Appalachian Inheritance: A Culturally Transmitted Traumatic Stress Syndrome?" *Journal of Progressive Human Services* 1:41–57.

Caudill, Harry. 1963. *Night Comes to the Cumberlands*. Boston: Little, Brown.

Center for Improving Mountain Living. 1992. *County Development Information*. Cullowhee, N.C.: Western Carolina University.

Chowdhury, Ramani R. 1941. *Handbook of Mica*. Brooklyn, N.Y.: Chemical Publishing Co.

Churg, Andrew, and Barry Wiggs. 1985. "Mineral Particles, Mineral Fibers, and Lung Cancer." *Environmental Research* 37:364–72.

Clingman, Thomas L. 1877. *Selections from the Speeches and Writings of Honorable Thomas L. Clingman of North Carolina, with Additions and Explanatory Notes*. Raleigh, N.C.: John Nichols.

Clinton, Catherine, and Nina Silber, eds. 1992. *Divided Houses: Gender and the Civil War*. New York: Oxford University Press.

"Company Lays Off Workers." 1997. *Mountain County Times*, December 17.

Conti, Eugene. 1979–80. "The Cultural Role of Local Elites in the Kentucky Mountains: A Retrospective Analysis." *Appalachian Journal* 7:51–68.

Corbin, David A. 1981. *Life, Work, and Rebellion in the Coal Fields: The Southern West Virginia Miners, 1880–1922*. Urbana: University of Illinois Press.

Couto, Richard A. 1975. *Poverty, Politics, and Health Care: An Appalachian Experience*. New York: Praeger.

———. 1992. *Beyond Distress: New Measures of Economic Need in Appalachia—A Report on Economic Trends and Social Issues*. Knoxville: Commission on Religion in Appalachia. October 28.

———. 1993. "The Memory of Miners and the Conscience of Capital: Coalminers' Strikes as Free Space." In *Fighting Back in Appalachia: Traditions of Resistance and Change*. Ed. Stephen L. Fisher. 165–94. Philadelphia: Temple University Press.

———. 1994. *An American Challenge: A Report on Economic Trends and Social Issues in Appalachia*. Dubuque, Iowa: Kendall/Hunt.

Craddock, Charles E. [Mary Noailles Murfree]. 1884. *In the Tennessee Mountains*. Boston: Houghton Mifflin.

Crawford, Martin. 1989. "Political Society in a Southern Mountain Community: Ashe County, North Carolina, 1850–1861." *Journal of Southern History* 55:373–90.

———. 1991. "The Farm Economy, the Market Economy, and Antebellum Social Relations in a Southern Mountain Community: Ashe County, North Carolina, 1850–1860." Paper presented at the Annual Meeting of the Southern Historical Association, Fort Worth, Tex.

Davies, D., and R. Cotton. 1983. "Mica Pneumoconiosis." *British Journal of Industrial Medicine* 40:22–27.

Dawley, Thomas R., Jr. 1912. *The Child That Toileth Not: The Story of a Government Investigation That Was Suppressed*. New York: Gracia Publishing.

del Alba Acevedo, Luz. 1995. "Feminist Inroads in the Study of Women's Work and Development." In *Women in the Latin American Development Process*. Ed. Christine E. Bose and Edna Acosta-Belen. 65–98. Philadelphia: Temple University Press.

Deyton, Jason Basil. 1947. "The Toe River Valley to 1865." *North Carolina Historical Review* 24:423–66.

Dirks, Nicholas B. 1990. "History as a Sign of the Modern." *Public Culture* 2:25–32.

Dorgan, Howard. 1987. *Giving Glory to God in Appalachia: Worship Practices of Six Baptist Subdenominations*. Knoxville: University of Tennessee Press.

Dreessen, Waldemar C., J. M. Dallavalle, Thomas I. Edwards, R. R. Sayers, H. F. Easom, and M. F. Trice. 1940. "Penumoconiosis among Mica and Pegmatite Workers." *Public Health Bulletin* No. 250. Washington, D.C.: Government Printing Office.

Dublin, Thomas. 1979. *Women at Work: The Transformation of Work and Community in Lowell, Massachusetts, 1826–1860*. New York: Columbia University Press.

Dunaway, Wilma A. 1996. *The First American Frontier: Transition to Capitalism in Southern Appalachia, 1700–1860*. Chapel Hill: University of North Carolina Press.

Duncan, Cynthia. 1999. *Worlds Apart: Why Poverty Persists in Rural America*. New Haven, Conn.: Yale University Press.

Dunn, Durwood. 1988. *Cades Cove: The Life and Death of a Southern Appalachian Community, 1818–1937*. Knoxville: University of Tennessee Press.

Dykeman, Wilma. 1955. *The French Broad*. Knoxville: University of Tennessee Press.

Eagan, Shirley C. 1990. "'Women's Work, Never Done': West Virginia Farm Women, 1880s–1920s." *West Virginia History* 46:21–36.

Eaton, Allen. 1973. *Handicrafts of the Southern Highlands.* 1937. Reprint, New York: Russell Sage Foundation.

Fagan, Brian M. 1995. *Ancient North America: The Archaeology of a Continent.* 2d ed. London: Thames and Hudson.

Federal Reporter (2d ser.). 1952. National Labor Relations Board, no. 6303:988–87.

Fernandez-Kelly, M. Patricia. 1983. *For We Are Sold, I and My People: Women and Industry in Mexico's Frontier.* Albany: State University of New York Press.

Fernandez-Kelly, M. Patricia, and Anna M. Garcia. 1989. "Informalization at the Core: Hispanic Women, Homework, and the Advanced Capitalist State." In *The Informal Economy: Studies in Advanced and Less Developed Countries.* Ed. Alejandro Portes, Manuel Castells, and Lauren A. Benton. 247–64. Baltimore: Johns Hopkins University Press.

Fernandez-Kelly, M. Patricia, and Saskia Sassen. 1995. "Recasting Women in the Global Economy: Internationalization and Changing Definitions of Gender." In *Women in the Latin American Development Process.* Ed. Christine E. Bose and Edna Acosta-Belen. 99–124. Philadelphia: Temple University Press.

Fine, Elizabeth. 1998. "Review Essay: *A Space on the Side of the Road: Cultural Poetics in an "Other" America." Journal of Appalachian Studies* 4:153–59.

Fine, Michelle. 1994. "Working the Hyphens: Reinventing Self and Other in Qualitative Research." In *Handbook of Qualitative Research.* Ed. Norman K. Denzin and Yvonne S. Lincoln. 70–82. Thousand Oaks, Calif.: Sage Publications.

Finger, John. 1984. *The Eastern Band of the Cherokees, 1819–1900.* Knoxville: University of Tennessee Press.

———. 1995. "Cherokee Accommodation and Persistence in the Southern Appalachians." In *Appalachia in the Making: The Mountain South in the Nineteenth Century.* Ed. Mary Beth Pudup, Dwight B. Billings, and Altina Waller. 25–49. Chapel Hill: University of North Carolina Press.

Fisher, David H. 1989. *Albion's Seed: Four British Folkways in America.* New York. Oxford University Press.

Fisher, Ron. 1998. *National Geographic Park Profiles: Blue Ridge Range—The Gentle Mountains.* Washington, D.C.: National Geographic Society Book Division.

Fisher, Stephen L. 1977. "Folk Culture or Folk Tale: Prevailing Assumptions about the Appalachian Personality." In *An Appalachian Symposium.* Ed. Jerry Williamson. 14–25. Boone, N.C.: Appalachian Consortium Press.

———. 1983. "Victim-Blaming in Appalachia: Cultural Theories and the Southern Mountains." In *Appalachia: Social Context Past and Present.* Ed. Bruce Ergood and Bruce Kuhre. 185–94. Dubuque, Iowa: Kendall/Hunt.

———, ed. 1993. *Fighting Back in Appalachia: Traditions of Resistance and Change.* Philadelphia: Temple University Press.

Flanning, Douglas. 1992. *Creating the Modern South: Millhands and Managers in Dalton, Georgia, 1884–1984.* Chapel Hill: University of North Carolina Press.

Folbre, Nancy. 1991. "The Unproductive Housewife: Her Evolution in Nineteenth-Century Economic Thought." *Signs* 16:463–84.

Ford, Thomas R. 1962. *The Southern Appalachian Region: A Survey.* Lexington: University of Kentucky Press.

Foucault, Michel. 1979. *Discipline and Punish: The Birth of the Prison.* Trans. Alan Sheridan. New York: Vintage.

Fout, John C., and Maura S. Tantillo, eds. 1993. *American Sexual Politics: Sex, Gender, and Race since the Civil War.* Chicago: University of Chicago Press.

Fox, John, Jr. 1901. *Bluegrass and Rhododendron: Outdoors in Old Kentucky.* New York: Charles Scribner's Sons.

Frankel, Linda. 1984. "Southern Textile Women: Generations of Survival and Struggle." In *My Troubles Are Going to Have Trouble with Me: Everyday Trials and Triumphs of Women Workers.* Ed. Karen Brodkin Sacks and Dorothy Remy. 39–60. New Brunswick, N.J.: Rutgers University Press.

Frankenberg, Ruth. 1995. "Whiteness and Americanness: Examining Constructions of Race, Culture, and Nation in White Women's Life Narratives." In *Race.* Ed. Steven Gregory and Roger Sanjek. 62–77. New Brunswick, N.J.: Rutgers University Press.

Friedenberg, Judith, ed. 1995. *The Anthropology of Low-Income Enclaves in New York City.* New York: New York Academy of Sciences.

Gaventa, John. 1980. *Power and Powerlessness: Quiescence and Rebellion in an Appalachian Valley.* Urbana: University of Illinois Press.

Gaventa, John, Barbara Ellen Smith, and Alex Willingham, eds. 1990. *Communities in Economic Crisis: Appalachia and the South.* Philadelphia: Temple University Press.

Giardina, Denise. 1987. *Storming Heaven.* New York: Ballantine Books.

Ginsburg, Faye D., and Rayna Rapp, eds. 1995. *Conceiving the New World Order: The Global Politics of Reproduction.* Berkeley: University of California Press.

Glen, John M. 1995. "The War on Poverty in Appalachia: Oral History from the 'Top Down' and the 'Bottom Up.'" *Oral History Review* 22:67–93.

Gordon, David M. 1988. "The Global Economy: New Edifice or Crumbling Foundations?" *New Left Review* 172:24–64.

Goshen, Charles E. 1970. "Characterological Deterrents to Economic Progress in People of Appalachia." *Southern Medical Journal* 63:1053–61.

Gramsci, Antonio. 1971. *Selections from the Prison Notebooks.* Ed. and trans. Quinten Hoare and Geoffrey Nowell Smith. London: Wishart.

Greene, Janet W. 1990. "Strategies for Survival: Women's Work in the Southern West Virginia Coal Camps." *West Virginia History* 46:37–54.

Griffin, James B. 1978. "The Midlands and Northeastern United States." In *Ancient Native Americans.* Ed. Jesse D. Jennings. 221–80. San Francisco: W. H. Freeman.

Groneman, Carol, and Mary Beth Norton. 1987. "Introduction." In *"To Toil the Livelong Day": America's Women at Work, 1780–1980.* Ed. Carol Groneman and Mary Beth Norton. 3–20. Ithaca, N.Y.: Cornell University Press.

Gwinn, G. Richards. 1943. "Strategic Mica." Information Circular 7258, Bureau of Mines, Washington, D.C.

Hall, Jaquelyn Dowd. 1986. "Disorderly Women: Gender and Labor Militancy in the Appalachian South." *Journal of American History* 73:346–82.

Hall, Jacquelyn Dowd, James Leloudis, Robert Korstad, Mary Murphy, Lu Ann Jones, and

Christopher B. Daly. 1987. *Like a Family: The Making of a Southern Cotton Mill World.* Chapel Hill: University of North Carolina Press.

Halperin, Rhoda H. 1990. *The Livelihood of Kin: Making Ends Meet "The Kentucky Way."* Austin: University of Texas Press.

Harney, Will Wallace. 1870. "A Strange Land and a Peculiar People." *Lippincott's Magazine,* October, pp. 429–38.

Harrington, Michael. 1962. *The Other America.* New York: Macmillan.

Harrison, Faye V. 1995. "The Persistent Power of 'Race' in the Cultural and Political Economy of Racism." *Annual Review of Anthropology* 24:47–74.

Hartman, Vladimir E. 1957. "A Cultural Study of a Mountain Community in Western North Carolina." Ph.D. diss., University of North Carolina at Chapel Hill.

Harvey, David. 1989. *The Condition of Postmodernity: An Enquiry into the Origins of Cultural Change.* Cambridge, Mass.: Basil Blackwell.

———. 1996. *Justice, Nature, and the Geography of Difference.* Malden, Mass.: Basil Blackwell.

———. 2000. *Spaces of Hope.* Berkeley: University of California Press.

Hatch, R. A., R. A. Humphrey, W. Eitel, and J. E. Comeforo. 1957. *Synthetic Mica Investigations IX: Review of Progress from 1947–1955.* Report of Investigations 5337, Bureau of Mines. Washington, D.C.: Government Printing Office.

Hatley, Thomas. 1991. "Cherokee Women Hold Their Ground." In *Appalachian Frontiers: Settlement, Society and Development in the Preindustrial Era.* Ed. Robert D. Mitchell. 37–51. Lexington: University Press of Kentucky.

Helly, Dorothy O., and Susan M. Reverby, eds. 1992. *Gendered Domains: Rethinking Public and Private in Women's History.* Ithaca, N.Y.: Cornell University Press.

Hicks, George L. 1992. *Appalachian Valley.* 1976. Reprint, Prospect Heights, Ill.: Waveland Press.

Hill, Sarah H. 1997. *Weaving New Worlds: Southeastern Cherokee Women and Their Basketry.* Chapel Hill: University of North Carolina Press.

Hinsdale, Mary Ann, Helen Lewis, and S. Maxine Waller. 1995. *It Comes from the People: Community Development and Local Theology.* Philadelphia: Temple University Press.

Horton, Claire F. 1984. "Women Have Headaches, Men Have Backaches: Patterns of Illness in an Appalachian Community." *Social Science and Medicine* 19:647–54.

Horwitz, Tony. 1999. "Letter from Nantahala: Run, Rudolph, Run: How the Fugitive Became a Folk Hero." *New Yorker,* March 15, pp. 46–52.

Hossfeld, Karen. 1990. "'Their Logic against Them': Contradictions in Sex, Race, and Class in Silicon Valley." In *Women Workers and Global Restructuring.* Ed. Kathryn Ward. 149–78. Ithaca, N.Y.: ILR Press, Cornell University.

Houk, Lawrence G. 1942. "Marketing Strategic Mica." Information Circular 7219, Bureau of Mines, Washington, D.C.: Government Printing Office.

Hughes, Arizona, as told to Thomas C. Chapman. 1976. *Aunt Zona's Web.* Banner Elk, N.C.: Puddingstone Press.

Hull, Anne. 1997. "Coming Down from Oil Rig Hollow." *St. Petersburg Times,* October 12, 1997, pp. 1A, 8A, 9A, 10A.

Humphrey, Richard A. 1981. "The Civil War and Church Schisms in Southern Appalachia."

Paper presented at the Appalachian Studies Conference, March 20–22, Black Mountain, N.C.

Indian Institute of Foreign Trade. 1977. *Market Survey on Problems and Prospects for Mica Manufactures in Japan, USA, UK, and West Germany.* New Delhi: Indian Institute of Foreign Trade.

Inscoe, John C. 1984. "Mountain Masters: Slaveholding in Western North Carolina." *North Carolina Historical Review* 61:143–73.

———.1989. *Mountain Masters, Slavery, and the Sectional Crisis in Western North Carolina.* Knoxville: University of Tennessee Press.

———. 1995. "Race and Racism in Nineteenth-Century Appalachia: Myths, Realities, and Ambiguities." In *Appalachia in the Making: The Mountain South in the Nineteenth Century.* Ed. Mary Beth Pudup, Dwight B. Billings, and Altina Waller. 103–31. Chapel Hill: University of North Carolina Press.

———, ed. 2001. *Appalachians and Race: The Mountain South from Slavery to Segregation.* Lexington: University Press of Kentucky.

Isserman, Andrew M. 1997. "Appalachia Then and Now: Update of 'The Realities of Deprivation' Reported to the President in 1964." *Journal of Appalachian Studies* 3:43–69.

Jaeckel, Louis E. 1955. "'Black Gold'—Mica Pops Up Again in Mountainous N.C." *Charlotte Observer*, January 16.

Jahns, Richard H., and Forrest W. Lancaster. 1950. "Physical Characteristics of Commercial Sheet Muscovite in the Southeastern United States." Geological Survey Professional Paper 225. Washington, D.C.: Government Printing Office.

———. 1952. "Mica Deposits of the Southeastern Piedmont, Part 1, General Features." Geological Survey Professional Paper 248-A. Washington, D.C.: Government Printing Office.

Jaimes, M. Annette. 1994. "American Racism: The Impact on American-Indian Identity and Survival." In *Race.* Ed. Steven Gregory and Roger Sanjek. 41–61. New Brunswick, N.J.: Rutgers University Press.

Janiewski, Dolores. 1985. *Sisterhood Denied: Race, Gender, and Class in a New South Community.* Philadelphia: Temple University Press.

Jensen, Joan. 1980. "Cloth, Butter, and Boarders: Women's Production for Market." *Review of Radical Political Economics* 12:14–24.

Jones, Beverly W. 1995. "Race, Sex, and Class: Black Female Tobacco Workers in Durham, North Carolina, 1920–1940, and the Development of Female Consciousness." In *U.S. Women in Struggle: A Feminist Studies Anthology.* Ed. Claire Moses and Heidi Hartmann. 134–44. Urbana: University of Illinois Press.

Jones, Jacqueline. 1986. *Labor of Love, Labor of Sorrow: Black Women, Work and the Family, from Slavery to the Present.* New York: Random House.

Kearney, Michael. 1995. "The Local and the Global: The Anthropology of Globalization and Transnationalism." *Annual Review of Anthropology* 24:547–65.

Kephart, Horace. 1922. *Our Southern Highlanders: A Narrative of Adventure in the Southern Appalachians and a Study of Life among the Mountaineers.* 2d ed. New York: Macmillan.

Kerr, W. C. 1867. *Report of the Progress of the Geological Survey of North Carolina, 1866.* Raleigh, N.C.: William E. Pell.

————. 1875. *Report of the Geological Survey of North Carolina*, vol. 1. Raleigh, N.C.: Josiah Turner.

————. 1880. "The Mica Veins of North Carolina." *Transactions of the American Institute of Mining Engineers* 3:457–62.

Kessler-Harris, Alice. 1982. *Out to Work: A History of Wage-Earning Women in the United States*. New York: Oxford University Press.

Kiffmeyer, Thomas J. 1998. "From Self-Help to Sedition: The Appalachian Volunteers in Eastern Kentucky, 1964–1970." *Journal of Southern History* 64:65–94.

Kingsolver, Ann. 1992. "Tobacco, Toyota, and Subaltern Development Discourses: Constructing Livelihoods and Community in Rural Kentucky." In *Anthropology and the Global Factory: Studies of the New Industrialization in the Late Twentieth Century*. Ed. Frances A. Rothstein and Michael L. Blim. 191–205. New York: Bergin and Garvey.

————. 1998. "Introduction." In *It Takes More Than Class: Studying Power in U.S. Workplaces*. Ed. Ann E. Kingsolver. 1–20. Albany: State University of New York Press.

Kondo, Dorinne K. 1990. *Crafting Selves: Power, Gender, and Discourses of Identity in a Japanese Workplace*. Chicago: University of Chicago Press.

"Laborers' Views." 1989 [1870]. *Newsletter of the High Mountains* 1, no. 4.

Labour Bureau. 1972. *Report on Survey of Labour Conditions in Mica Factories in India, 1969*. New Delhi: Department of Labour and Employment.

Lamphere, Louise. 1985. "Bringing the Family to Work: Women's Culture on the Shop Floor." *Feminist Studies* 11:519–40.

————. 1987. *From Working Daughters to Working Mothers: Immigrant Women in a New England Industrial Community*. Ithaca, N.Y.: Cornell University Press.

Leacock, Eleanor B., and Helen I. Safa, eds. 1986. *Women's Work: Development and the Division of Labor by Sex*. South Hadley, Mass.: Bergin and Garvey.

Leinbach, William S. 1952. "Mica Mining Booms In Carolina." *Raleigh News and Observer*, May 4, 1952.

Leith, C. K. 1931. *World Minerals and World Politics*. New York: Whittlesey House/McGraw-Hill.

Lesure, Frank G. 1968. "Mica Deposits of the Blue Ridge in North Carolina." Geological Survey Professional Paper 577. Washington, D.C.: Government Printing Office.

Lewis, Helen M. 1976. "Fatalism or the Coal Industry." In *Appalachia: Social Context Past and Present*. Ed. Bruce Ergood and Bruce Kuhre. 180–89. Dubuque, Iowa: Kendall/Hunt.

Lewis, Helen M., Linda Johnson, and Donald Askins, eds. 1978. *Colonialism in Modern America: The Appalachian Case*. Boone, N.C.: Appalachian Consortium Press.

Lewis, Ronald L. 1987. *Black Coal Miners in America: Race, Class, and Community Conflict, 1780–1980*. Lexington: University Press of Kentucky.

————, ed. 1994. *Scotts Run*. Special issue of *West Virginia History* 53:1–117.

Lewis, Ronald L., and Dwight B. Billings. 1997. "Appalachian Culture and Economic Development: A Retrospective View of the Theory and Literature." *Journal of Appalachian Studies* 3:3–42.

Lock, Margaret, and Patricia Kaufert, eds. 1998. *Pragmatic Women and Body Politics*. New York: Cambridge University Press.

Looff, David H. 1971. *Yesterday's Children: The Challenge of Mental Health*. Lexington: University Press of Kentucky.

Lyon, George Ella. 1992. "Another Vicious Cycle." *ACE Magazine,* July 1992, p. 10.

Lucas, Marion B. 1997. "African Americans on the Kentucky Frontier." *Register of the Kentucky Historical Society* 95:121–34.

Maggard, Sally W. 1986. "Class and Gender: New Theoretical Priorities in Appalachian Studies." In *The Impact of Institutions in Appalachia: Proceedings of the Eighth Annual Appalachian Studies Conference.* Ed. Jim Lloyd and Anne G. Campbell. 100–113. Boone, N.C.: Appalachian Consortium Press.

————. 1994. "Will the Real Daisy Mae Please Stand Up?: A Methodological Essay on Gender Analysis in Appalachian Research." *Appalachian Journal* 21:136–50.

————. 1998. "'We're Fighting Millionaires!': The Clash of Gender and Class in Appalachian Women's Union Organizing." In *No Middle Ground: Women and Radical Protest.* Ed. Kathleen M. Blee. 289–306. New York: New York University Press.

Mann, Ralph. 1992. "Mountains, Land, and Kin Networks: Burkes Garden, Virginia, in the 1840s and 1850s." *Journal of Southern History* 48:411–34.

————. 1993. "Guerilla Warfare and Gender Roles: Sandy Basin, Virginia, as a Test Case." In *Diversity in Appalachia: Images and Realities.* Ed. Tyler Blethen. Special issue of *Journal of the Appalachian Studies Association* 5:59–66.

Manning-Miller, Don. 1993. "Racism and Organizing in Appalachia." In *Fighting Back in Appalachia: Traditions of Resistance and Change.* Ed. Stephen L. Fisher. 57–68. Philadelphia: Temple University Press.

Marx, Karl. 1972. "The Eighteenth Brumaire of Louis Bonaparte." In *The Marx-Engels Reader.* Ed. Robert C. Tucker. New York: W. W. Norton.

————. 1975. *Capital: A Critique of Political Economy,* vol. 1. New York: International Publishers.

Mason, Bobbie Ann. 1993. "Recycling Kentucky." *New Yorker,* November 1, 1993, pp. 50–62.

Mathews, Elmora. 1965. *Neighbor and Kin.* Nashville: Vanderbilt University Press.

McCauley, Deborah V. 1995. *Appalachian Mountain Religion: A History.* Urbana: University of Illinois Press.

McCurry, Stephanie. 1992. "The Politics of Yeoman Households in South Carolina." In *Divided Houses: Gender and the Civil War.* Ed. Catherine Clinton and Nina Silber. 22–38. New York: Oxford University Press.

McDonald, Forrest, and Grady McWhiney. 1975. "The Antebellum Southern Herdsman: A Reinterpretation." *Journal of Southern History* 41:147–66.

McKenzie, Robert T. 1994. "Wealth and Income: The Preindustrial Structure of East Tennessee in 1860." *Appalachian Journal* 21:260–78.

McKinney, Gordon B. 1988. "Subsistence Economy and Community in Western North Carolina, 1860–1865." Paper presented at the Annual Meeting of the Organization of American Historians, Reno, Nevada.

————. 1992. "Women's Role in Civil War Western North Carolina." *North Carolina Historical Review* 69:37–56.

————. 1995. "Economy and Community in Western North Carolina." In *Appalachia in the Making: The Mountain South in the Nineteenth Century.* Ed. Mary Beth Pudup, Dwight B. Billings, and Altina Waller. 163–84. Chapel Hill: University of North Carolina Press.

"Mica Miners Work Double Shifts in North Carolina." 1939. *Raleigh News and Observer,* November 9.

Mihailov, P., and N. Berova. 1968. "Professional Injuries during Production and Work with Asbestos and Mica." *Higiena I Zdraveopazvane* 11:145–50.

Milkman, Ruth, ed. 1985. *Women, Work, and Protest: A Century of U.S. Women's Labor History.* Boston: Routledge and Kegan Paul.

Mitchell, Robert D., ed. 1991. *Appalachian Frontiers: Settlement, Society, and Development in the Preindustrial Era.* Lexington: University Press of Kentucky.

Moody, Kim. 1995. "NAFTA and the Corporate Redesign of North America." *Latin American Perspectives* 84:95–116.

Moore, Marat. 1990. "Ten Months That Shook the Coalfields: Women's Stories from the Pittston Strike." *Now and Then* 7:6–11, 32–35.

————. 1996. *Women in the Mines: Stories of Life and Work.* New York: Twayne.

Morgan, W. Keith, and Anthony Seaton. 1984. *Occupational Lung Diseases.* Philadelphia: W. B. Saunders.

Morley, Margaret W. 1913. *The Carolina Mountains.* Boston: Houghton Mifflin.

Mountain Resource Center. 1998. "County Development Information." Economic Development Administration, University Center, Western Carolina University, Cullowhee, N.C.

Mullings, Leith. 1997. *On Our Own Terms: Race, Class, and Gender in the Lives of African American Women.* New York: Routledge.

Murdock, T. G. 1942. "Production of Mica in North Carolina." Information Circular 2, Division of Mineral Resources. Raleigh, N.C.: Department of Conservation and Development.

Murthy, M. V. N. 1964. *Mica Fields of India.* International Geological Congress, Twenty-second Session, India. New Delhi: International Geological Congress.

Nash, June, and Maria Patricia Fernandez-Kelly, eds. 1983. *Women, Men and the International Division of Labor.* Albany: State University of New York Press.

National Labor Relations Board. 1950. Case No. 34-CA-168. *NLRB* 92 (118): 766–90.

National Recovery Administration. 1934. "Code of Fair Competition for the Mica Industry." Washington, D.C.: Government Printing Office.

Norman, Gurney. 1993. "*The Kentucky Cycle* Still Perplexes." *Lexington Herald Leader,* June 6, p. D6.

North Carolina Child Advocacy Institute. 1998. "NC Data Guide to Child Well-Being." Raleigh, N.C.

North Carolina Department of Commerce. 1998. "County and Regional Data Scans." <http://www.commerce.state.nc.us>.

North Carolina Office of State Planning. 1998. "State Demographics: 1990 Census Counts, Revised Estimates for 1991–1996." <http://www.ospl.state.nc.us/demog/>.

North Carolina State Data Center. 1986. *Profile: North Carolina Counties.* 7th ed. Raleigh, N.C.: Office of State Budget and Management.

Oberhauser, Ann. 1996. "Gender Analysis and Economic Development in West Virginia." *West Virginia Public Affairs Reporter* 13:2–13.

Padgett, James A., ed. 1943. "Reconstruction Letters from North Carolina," pt. 10: "Letters to Benjamin Franklin Butler." *North Carolina Historical Review* 20:157–75.

Patterson, Thomas C. 1998. "Globalization and the End of the Nation State?" Paper presented at the Annual Meeting of the American Anthropological Association, December 2–6, Philadelphia.

Pearsall, Marion. 1959. *Little Smoky Ridge.* Tuscaloosa: University of Alabama Press.

Perdue, Theda. 1979. *Slavery and the Evolution of Cherokee Society.* Knoxville: University of Tennessee Press.

———. 1985. "Southeastern Indians and the Cult of True Womanhood." In *The Web of Southern Social Relations: Women, Family, and Education.* Ed. Walter J. Frazer Jr., R. Saunders, and Jon R. Wakelyn. 35–52. Athens: University of Georgia Press.

———. 1990. "From Public Roles to Private Lives: Cherokee Women in the Eighteenth Century." Paper presented at Private Lives/Public Roles: A Symposium on North Carolina Women's History, Raleigh, N.C.

———. 1998. *Cherokee Women: Gender and Culture Change, 1700–1835.* Lincoln: University of Nebraska Press.

Pimentel, J. Cortez, and A. Peixoto Menezes. 1978. "Pulmonary and Hepatic Granulomatous Disorders Due to the Inhalation of Cement and Mica Dusts." *Thorax* 33:219–27.

Portes, Alejandro, and Jozsef Borocz. 1988. "The Informal Sector under Capitalism and State Socialism: A Preliminary Comparison." *Social Justice* 15:17–28.

Portes, Alejandro, and Manuel Castells. 1989. "World Underneath: The Origins, Dynamics and Effects of the Informal Economy." In *The Informal Economy: Studies in Advanced and Less Developed Countries.* Ed. Alejandro Portes, Manuel Castells, and Lauren A. Benton. 11–37. Baltimore: Johns Hopkins University Press.

Pudup, Mary Beth. 1989. "The Boundaries of Class in Preindustrial Appalachia." *Journal of Historical Geography* 15:139–62.

———. 1991. "Social Class and Economic Development in Southeast Kentucky, 1820–1880." In *Appalachian Frontiers: Settlement, Society, and Development in the Preindustrial Era.* Ed. Robert D. Mitchell. 235–60. Lexington: University Press of Kentucky.

Pudup, Mary Beth, Dwight B. Billings, and Altina Waller, eds. 1995. *Appalachia in the Making: The Mountain South in the Nineteenth Century.* Chapel Hill: University of North Carolina Press.

Puglisi, Michael J., ed. 1997. *Diversity and Accommodation: Essays on the Cultural Composition of the Virginia Frontier.* Knoxville: University of Tennessee Press.

Rajgarhia, Chand Mull. 1951. *Mining, Processing, and Uses of Indian Mica.* New York: McGraw-Hill.

Reeves, Rhonda. 1998. "Appalachian Legacy: Controversial Photographer Shelby Lee Adams *Has* Gone Home Again." *ACE Magazine,* July 8–21, pp. 10–18.

Regional Economic Information System. 1990. "Regional Economic Profile for States and Counties." Bureau of Economic Analysis. <http://www.bea.doc.gov/>.

Reid, Herbert G. 1980–81. "Appalachian Policy, the Corporate State, and American Values: A Critical Perspective." *Policy Studies Journal* 9:622–33.

———. 1996. "Global Adjustments, Throwaway Regions, Appalachian Studies: Regulating *The Kentucky Cycle* on the Postmodern Frontier." *Journal of Appalachian Studies* 2:235–62.

Reid, Joseph D. 1976. "Antebellum Southern Rental Contracts." *Explorations in Economic History* 13:69–83.

Robnett, Belinda. 1996. "African-American Women in the Civil Rights Movement, 1954–1965: Gender, Leadership, and Micromobilization." *American Journal of Sociology* 101:1661–93.

———. 1997. *How Long? How Long?: African American Women in the Struggle for Civil Rights.* New York: Oxford University Press.

Roediger, David. 1991. *The Wages of Whiteness.* London: Verso.

Roseberry, William. 1989. *Anthropologies and Histories: Essays in Culture, History, and Political Economy.* New Brunswick, N.J.: Rutgers University Press.

Rosenberg, Ellen M. 1989. *The Southern Baptists: A Subculture in Transition.* Knoxville: University of Tennessee Press.

Rowbotham, Sheila, and Swasti Mitter, eds. 1994. *Dignity and Daily Bread: New Forms of Economic Organizing among Poor Women in the Third World and the First.* New York: Routledge.

Roy, Rustum. 1952. *Synthetic Mica: A Critical Examination of the Literature.* State College: Pennsylvania State College.

Rural Policy Research Institute. 1999. "Rural America and Welfare Reform: An Overview Assessment." <http://www.rupri.org/pubs.archive/old/welfare>. February 10.

Sacks, Karen Brodkin. 1988. *Caring by the Hour: Women, Work, and Organizing at Duke Medical Center.* Urbana: University of Illinois Press.

———. 1989. "Toward a Unified Theory of Class, Race, and Gender." *American Ethnologist* 16:534–50.

Sacks, Karen, and Dorothy Remy, eds. 1984. *My Troubles Are Going to Have Trouble with Me: Everyday Trials and Triumphs of Women Workers.* New Brunswick, N.J.: Rutgers University Press.

Sahu, A. P., K. P. Singh, L. J. Shukla, and Ravi Shanker. 1985. "Choline and Mica Dust Induced Pulmonary Lesions in Rats." *Industrial Health* 23:135–44.

Salstrom, Paul. 1991. "The Agricultural Origins of Economic Dependency, 1840–1880." In *Appalachian Frontiers: Settlement, Society, and Development in the Preindustrial Era.* Ed. Robert D. Mitchell. 261–83. Lexington: University Press of Kentucky.

Sanjek, Roger, ed., 1990. *Fieldnotes: The Makings of Anthropology.* Ithaca, N.Y.: Cornell University Press.

Schenkkan, Robert. 1993. *The Kentucky Cycle.* New York: Penguin.

Schmink, Marianne. 1984. "Household Economic Strategies: Review and Research Agenda." *Latin American Research Review* 19:87–101.

Schneider, Jane, and Rayna Rapp, eds. 1995. *Articulating Hidden Histories: Exploring the Influence of Eric R. Wolf.* Berkeley: University of California Press.

Scott, James. 1985. *Weapons of the Weak: Everyday Forms of Peasant Resistance.* New Haven, Conn.: Yale University Press.

———. 1990. *Domination and the Arts of Resistance.* New Haven, Conn.: Yale University Press.

Scott, Joan W. 1986. "Gender: A Useful Category of Analysis." *American Historical Review* 91:1053–75.

Scott, Shaunna L. 1995. *Two Sides to Everything: The Cultural Construction of Class Consciousness in Harlan County, Kentucky.* Albany: State University of New York Press.

———. 1996. "Gender among Appalachian Kentucky Farm Families: The Kentucky Farm Family Oral History Project and Beyond." *Journal of Appalachian Studies* 2:103–13.

Seitz, Virginia R. 1995. *Women, Development, and Communities for Empowerment in Appalachia.* Albany: State University of New York Press.

Sen, Gita. 1980. "The Sexual Division of Labor and the Working-Class Family: Towards a New Conceptual Synthesis of Class Relations and the Subordination of Women." *Review of Radical Political Economics* 12:76–86.

Setzer, Curtis. 1985. *Fire in the Hole: Miners and Managers in the American Coal Industry.* Lexington: University Press of Kentucky.

Shanker, Ravi, Anand P. Sahu, Ram K. S. Dogra, and Sibte H. Zaidi. 1975. "Effect of Intratracheal Injection of Mica Dust on the Lymph Nodes of Guinea Pigs." *Toxicology* 5:193–99.

Shapiro, Henry D. 1978. *Appalachia on Our Mind: The Southern Mountains and Mountaineers in American Consciousness, 1870–1920.* Chapel Hill: University of North Carolina Press.

Shapiro-Perl, Nina. 1984. "Resistance Strategies: The Routine Struggle for Bread and Roses." In *My Troubles Are Going to Have Trouble with Me: Everyday Trials and Triumphs of Women Workers.* Ed. Karen Sacks and Dorothy Remy. 193–208. New Brunswick, N.J.: Rutgers University Press.

Shelby, Anne. 1999. "The 'R' Word." In *Confronting Appalachian Stereotypes: Back Talk from an American Region.* Ed. Dwight B. Billings, Gurney Norman, and Katherine Ledford. 153–60. Lexington: University Press of Kentucky.

Sheppard, Muriel Earley. 1935. *Cabins in the Laurel.* Chapel Hill: University of North Carolina Press.

Shirley, Lawrence E., and Eldon P. Allen. 1976. "The Mineral Industry of North Carolina." *Bureau of Mines Minerals Yearbook* (Preprint) 2:1–17.

Sischy, Ingrid. 1999. "The Studio System." *New York Times Magazine,* April 4, 1999, pp. 39, 48.

Skow, Milford L. 1962. "Mica: A Materials Survey." Information Circular 8125, Bureau of Mines. Washington, D.C.: Government Printing Office.

Skulberg, Knut R., Bjorn Gylseth, Bidar Skaug, and Rolf Hanoa. 1985. "Mica Pneumoconiosis: A Literature Review." *Scandinavian Journal of Work and Environmental Health* 11:65–74.

Smith, Barbara Ellen. 1987. *Digging Our Own Graves: Coal Miners and the Struggle over Black Lung Disease.* Philadelphia: Temple University Press.

———. 1998. "Walk-ons in the Third Act: The Role of Women in Appalachian Historiography." *Journal of Appalachian Studies* 4:5–28.

Sparr, Pamela, ed. 1994. *Mortgaging Women's Lives: Feminist Critiques of Structural Adjustment.* Atlantic Highlands, N.J.: Zed Books.

Spence, Hugh S. 1912. *Mica: Its Occurrence, Exploitation, and Uses.* Ottawa: Canada Department of Mines, Government Printing Bureau.

Spivak, Gayatri C. 1985. "Subaltern Studies: Deconstructing Historiography." In *Subaltern Studies IV.* Ed. Ranajit Guha. 330–63. New York: Oxford University Press.

Sprague, Stuart. 1993. "From Slavery to Freedom: African-Americans in Eastern Kentucky, 1864–1884." In *Diversity in Appalachia: Images and Realities.* Ed. Tyler Blethen. Special issue of *Journal of the Appalachian Studies Association* 5:67–74.

Stack, Carol B. 1974. *All Our Kin.* New York: Harper and Row.

Stephenson, Florence. 1912. *Child Life of the Southern Mountaineers.* New York: A. E. Dittrich for the Woman's Board of Home Missions of the Presbyterian Church in the U.S.A.

Stephenson, John B. 1968. *Shiloh: A Mountain Community.* Lexington: University Press of Kentucky.

Sterrett, Douglas B. 1923. "Mica Deposits of the United States." Bulletin 740, U.S. Geological Survey. Washington, D.C.: Government Printing Office.

Stewart, Kathleen. 1990. "Backtalking the Wilderness: 'Appalachian' Engenderings." In *Uncertain Terms: Negotiating Gender in American Culture.* Ed. Faye Ginsburg and Anna Tsing. 43–56. Boston: Beacon Press.

———. 1996. *A Space on the Side of the Road: Cultural Poetics in an "Other" America.* Princeton, N.J.: Princeton University Press.

Stuckey, Jasper L. 1965. *North Carolina: Its Geology and Mineral Resources.* Raleigh, N.C.: Department of Conservation and Development.

———. 1970. "Mineral Industry of North Carolina from 1960 through 1967." Economic Paper 68, Division of Mineral Resources. Raleigh, N.C.: Department of Conservation and Development.

Susser, Ida. 1996. "The Construction of Poverty and Homelessness in U.S. Cities." *Annual Review of Anthropology* 25:411–35.

———. 1997. "The Flexible Woman: Regendering Labor in the Informational Society." *Critique of Anthropology* 17:389–402.

Swasy, Alecia. 1990. "Mothers Bear Burden of Poverty as the Men Drift from Appalachia." *Wall Street Journal,* May 17, 1990, pp. A1, A11.

Tat, M., and C. Simonescu. 1972. "Functional Respiratory Changes by the Influence of Concentrations of Cement, Mica, Marble, Asbestos, and Coal Dust." *Archives des Maladies Professionelles, de Medecine du Travail* 33:553–58.

Tedesco, Marie. 1993. "Freedman and Slave Owner: The Strange Case of Adam Waterford." Paper presented at the Annual Meeting of the Appalachian Studies Association, Johnson City, Tenn.

"Three WNC Counties Hard Hit as Demand for Mica Stops." 1962. *Asheville Citizen Times,* August 16.

Tice, Karen. 1998. "School-Work and Mother-Work: The Interplay of Maternalism and Cultural Politics in the Educational Narratives of Kentucky Settlement Workers, 1910–1930." *Appalachian Journal* 4:191–224

Tice, Karen, and Dwight B. Billings. 1991. "Appalachian Culture and Resistance." *Journal of Progressive Human Services* 2:1–18.

Tickamyer, Ann R., and Cecil Tickamyer. 1987. "Poverty in Appalachia." Appalachian Data Bank Report No. 5, Appalachian Center. Lexington: University of Kentucky.

Tilly, Louise A., and Scott, Joan W. 1978. *Women, Work, and Family.* New York: Holt, Rinehart, and Winston.

Trotter, Joe William, Jr. 1990. *Coal, Class, and Color: Blacks in Southern West Virginia, 1915–1932.* Urbana: University of Illinois Press.

————. "Black Miners in West Virginia: Class and Community Responses to Workplace Discrimination." In *The United Mine Workers of America: A Model of Industrial Solidarity.* Ed. John H. M. Laslett. 269–96. University Park: Pennsylvania State University Press.

Trouillot, Michel-Rolph. 1995. *Silencing the Past: Power and the Production of History.* Boston: Beacon.

Tryon, Rolla M. 1917. *Household Manufactures in the United States, 1640–1860.* Chicago: University of Chicago Press.

Tullos, Allen. 1989. "Cultural Politics and Political Culture in Appalachia." *Radical History Review* 45:181–86.

Turbin, Carole. 1987. "Beyond Conventional Wisdom: Women's Wage Work, Household Economic Contribution, and Labor Activism in a Mid-Nineteenth Century Working-Class Community." In *"To Toil the Livelong Day": America's Women at Work, 1780–1980.* Ed. Carol Groneman and Mary Beth Norton. 47–67. Ithaca, N.Y.: Cornell University Press.

Turner, William H. 1985. "The Demography of Black Appalachia, Past and Present." In *Blacks in Appalachia.* Ed. William H. Turner and Edward J. Cabbell. 237–61. Lexington: University Press of Kentucky.

Turner, William H., and Edward J. Cabbell, eds. 1985. *Blacks in Appalachia.* Lexington: University Press of Kentucky.

U.S. Bureau of Mines. 1880–1920. *Mineral Resources of the United States.* Annual publication of the U.S. Geological Survey. Washington, D.C.: Government Printing Office.

————. 1934–86. *Minerals Yearbook.* Annual publication of the U.S. Geological Survey. Washington, D.C.: Government Printing Office.

————. 1956–85. *Mineral Facts and Problems.* Annual publication of the U.S. Geological Survey. Washington, D.C.: Government Printing Office.

U.S. Bureau of the Census. 1860. *Manuscript Census,* schedule 4: *Productions of Agriculture.* Department of the Interior. Washington, D.C.: Government Printing Office.

————. 1880. *Manuscript Census,* schedule 1: *Population.* Department of the Interior. Washington, D.C.: Government Printing Office.

————. 1883a. *Tenth Census of the United States, 1880,* vol. 1: *Population.* Department of the Interior. Washington, D.C.: Government Printing Office.

————. 1883b. *Tenth Census of the United States, 1880,* vol. 3: *Agriculture.* Department of the Interior. Washington, D.C.: Government Printing Office.

————. 1990a. *1990 Census of Population and Housing: Population and Housing Characteristics for Congressional Districts of the 103rd Congress, North Carolina.* Department of Commerce. Washington, D.C.: Government Printing Office.

————. 1990b. *1990 U.S. Census Data.* <http://venus.census.gov/cdrom/>.

————. 1990c. *1990 Census of Population: Social and Economic Characteristics, North Carolina.* Department of Commerce. Washington, D.C.: Government Printing Office.

————. 1992a. *1992 Economic Census: Area Profile.* <http://www.census.gov/epcd/www/92profiles/>.

————. 1992b. *1992 Census of Agriculture,* vol. 1: *Geographic Area Series, Part 33: North Carolina State and County Data.* Department of Commerce. Washington, D.C.: Government Printing Office.

———. 1997. *Census of Agriculture: Highlights of Agriculture, 1992 and 1997.* <http://www.nass.usda.gov/census/census92/>.

———. 1998. "Updated Hispanic Population List." Population Estimates Program. <http://www.census.gov/population/estimates/county/crh/>.

U.S. Department of Agriculture. 1999. National Agricultural Statistics Service. <http://www.nass.usda.gov/census/census99>.

U.S. Geological Survey. 1994–99. *Minerals Yearbook.* Annual publication. <http://minerals.usgs.gov.minerals/pubs/commodity/mica>.

———. 2001. *Mineral Commodity Summaries.* <http://minerals.usgs.gov/minerals/pubs/commodity/mica>.

U.S. Tariff Commission. 1938. *Mica: A Survey of the Production of Mica in the Principal Producing Countries, Its Preparation, Fabrication, Uses, and Distribution, with Special References to International Trade and Tariff Considerations.* Report 130. Washington, D.C.: Government Printing Office.

———. 1947. *Mica: Prepared in Response to Requests from the Committee on Finance of the United States Senate and the Committee on Ways and Means of the House of Representatives.* War Changes in Industry Series Report No. 21. Washington, D.C.: Government Printing Office.

Urban, H. M. 1932. "Mica-Mining Methods, Costs and Recoveries." Information Circular 6616, Bureau of Mines, Department of Commerce. Washington, D.C.: Government Printing Office.

Vance, Rupert. 1965. "An Introductory Note." In *Yesterday's People,* by Jack Weller. v–ix. Lexington: University Press of Kentucky.

Van Noppen, Ina W., and John J. Van Noppen. 1973. *Western North Carolina since the Civil War.* Boone, N.C.: Appalachian Consortium Press.

Van Shaik, Eileen. 1989. "Paradigms Underlying the Study of Nerves as a Popular Illness in Eastern Kentucky." *Medical Anthropology Quarterly* 11:15–28.

Verghese, Abraham. 1994. *My Own Country: A Doctor's Story of a Town and Its People in the Age of AIDS.* New York: Simon and Schuster.

Waller, Altina. 1988. *Feud: Hatfields, McCoys, and Social Change in Appalachia, 1860–1900.* Chapel Hill: University of North Carolina Press.

"War Board Wants State to Double Mica Output." 1942. *Raleigh News and Observer,* February 27.

Weiler, Stephan. 1997. "The Economics of the Struggling Structurally Unemployed." *Journal of Appalachian Studies* 3:71–97.

Weller, Jack. 1965. *Yesterday's People: Life in Contemporary Appalachia.* Lexington: University Press of Kentucky.

Wellman, Manley Wade. 1973. *The Kingdom of Madison: A Southern Mountain Fastness and Its People.* Chapel Hill: University of North Carolina Press.

Whisnant, David. 1980. *Modernizing the Mountaineer: People, Power, and Planning in Appalachia.* Boone, N.C.: Appalachian Consortium Press.

———. 1983. *All That Is Native and Fine: The Politics of Culture in an American Region.* Chapel Hill: University of North Carolina Press.

White, Caroline. 1989 "Why Do Workers Bother?: Paradoxes of Resistance in Two English Factories." *Critique of Anthropology* 7:51–68.

White, Connie. 1994. "Fighting Back in Appalachia: Reports from the Front." *Journal of the Appalachian Studies Association* 6:5–14.

Whites, Lee Ann. 1992. "The Civil War as a Crisis in Gender." In *Divided Houses: Gender and the Civil War*. Ed. Catherine Clinton and Nina Silber. 3–21. New York: Oxford University Press.

Williams, Brackette. 1989. "A Class Act: Anthropology and the Race to Nation across Ethnic Terrain." *Annual Review of Anthropology* 18:401–44.

Williams, Cratis D. 1961. "The Southern Mountaineer in Fact and Fiction. Ph.D. diss., New York University.

Williams, Raymond. 1977. *Marxism and Literature*. London: Oxford University Press.

———. 1989. *Resources of Hope: Culture, Democracy, Socialism*. Ed. Robin Gable. London: Verso.

Wilson, Darlene. 1995. "The Felicitous Convergence of Mythmaking and Capital Accumulation: John Fox Jr. and the Formation of An(Other) Almost-White Underclass." *Journal of Appalachian Studies* 1:5–44.

———. 1998. "Multicultural Mayhem and Murder in Virginia's Backcountry: The Case of Pierre-Francois Tubeuf, 1792–1795." *Journal of Appalachian Studies* 4:57–86.

Wilson, Darlene, and Patricia D. Beaver. 1999. "Transgressions in Race and Place: The Ubiquitous Native Grandmother in America's Cultural Memory." In *Neither Separate nor Equal: Women, Race, and Class in the South*. Ed. Barbara E. Smith. 34–56. Philadelphia: Temple University Press.

Wingerd, Mary L. 1996. "Rethinking Paternalism: Power and Parochialism in a Southern Mill Village." *Journal of American History* 83:872–902.

Wolf, Eric. 1982. *Europe and the People without History*. Berkeley: University of California Press.

———. 1990. "Distinguished Lecture: Facing Power—Old Insights, New Questions." *American Anthropologist* 92:586–96.

———. 1999. *Envisioning Power: Ideologies of Dominance and Crisis*. Berkeley: University of California Press.

Wray, William, Jr. 1931. *The Clinchfield Railroad: The Story of a Trade Route across the Blue Ridge Mountains*. Chapel Hill: University of North Carolina Press.

Yanigasako, Sylvia, and Carol Delaney. 1995. "Naturalizing Power." In *Naturalizing Power: Essays in Feminist Cultural Analysis*. Ed. Sylvia Yanigasako and Carol Delaney. 1–22. New York: Routledge.

Yarrow, Michael. 1990. "Voices from the Coalfields: How Miners' Families Understand the Crisis of Coal." In *Communities in Economic Crisis: Appalachia and the South*. Ed. John Gaventa, Barbara E. Smith, and Alex Willingham. 38–52. Philadelphia: Temple University Press.

Zahavi, Gerald. 1988. *Workers, Managers, and Welfare Capitalism: The Shoeworkers and Tanners of Endicott Johnson, 1890–1930*. Urbana: University of Illinois Press.

Zavella, Patricia. 1987. *Women's Work and Chicano Families: Factory Workers of the Santa Clara Valley*. Ithaca, N.Y.: Cornell University Press.

Zimmerman, Julie N., and Lorraine Garkovich. 1999. "The Challenge of Welfare Reform: Earnings and the Cost of Living in Rural Kentucky." *Southern Rural Sociology* 14:41–66.

Index

Fields, Lonnie, 94, 97
Finger, John, 5
Fisher, Carl, 32, 69, 77–78, 91, 114
Fisher, Jack, 32, 69
Fisher, Ron, 6
Flanning, Douglas, 102
Forbes, Nola, 94
Forbes, Ben, 94

Gardner, Al, 71, 106, 141n.6
Gardner, Arval, 31, 112–13, 114, 123
Gardner, Jay, 71, 123
Gardner, Jimmy, 71, 76
Gardner, Vicki, 71
Gaventa, John, 99–100, 104
gender, 4, 8, 9, 10, 24–25, 98; and labor, 21–
    22, 30, 33, 65, 67, 80, 105–24. *See also* labor:
    men's; labor: women's
General Services Administration (GSA), 54–
    55, 57, 59
Gramsci, Antonio, 10, 100–101
Great Depression, 103
GSA. *See* General Services Administration

Harrington, Michael, 22
Harris, Mary (Mother Jones), 97
Hatley, Thomas, 5
Hayes, Parnell, 96, 98, 120
Heap, John R., 42, 44, 58
hegemony, 101, 143n.1
Henson, Pearl, 66–67
Hill, Sarah, 5
Hollifield, Dorothy, 110
Horwitz, Tony, 6

India, 44–45, 58, 59, 74
Inscoe, John, 5

Johnson, Billy, 72–73, 77
Johnson, Ruby, 48, 49
Jonesboro, N.C., 17, 20

Kerr, W. C., 44
kinship, 15, 16, 25, 79, 145n.20; in churches,
    120, 142n.15; in the mica factory, 10, 29, 34,
    64–74, 104–5, 113, 115–18, 124
Korean War, 54, 74

labor, 9, 20–21, 39–40, 45, 56, 79, 131n.24;
    child, 8, 135n.5, 138n.28; and local cultures,
    79–98, 115–18, 121–24; men's, 30, 40, 47,
    49, 68, 73–76, 101; organized, 101–5, 113;

waged, 18–20, 70, 80, 107, 124; women's,
    3–4, 8, 10, 14, 17, 34–40, 47–50, 62–78, 101,
    106, 120, 130nn.13–14; slave, 6
Liston's Branch, 80, 81, 82, 84, 120
Liston's Branch Baptist Church, 87–88
local color, 7–9
Long, Etta, 94–95, 97, 122–23
Long Hill Baptist Church, 33, 92–98, 122–
    123, 142nn.14–16

McKinney, Gordon B., 5
McRae, Jess, 49
mica, 3, 25–26, 30–31, 35–38, 41–42, 102,
    127n.2, 139n.36; production of, 46–60, 62–
    63, 74–78, 137nn.14–19, 143n.5; uses of, 43–
    45, 53–54, 58–59, 74, 138nn.22, 30
mica factories, 25, 37, 45–50, 61–63; labor
    relations in, 63–78; safety in, 108–12,
    144nn.13–16, 145n.17
mica houses. *See* mica factories
mica industry, 4, 10, 22, 25–27, 38–60, 74, 89,
    120, 135n.1
mica mining, 37–38, 41–46, 52–59, 74, 85,
    103–4, 136n.12, 137n.13
Monroe, Julia, 49
Monroe, N.C., 62, 86, 103
Moody, Alma, 71, 117
Moody, Dale, 122
Mother Jones. *See* Harris, Mary
Moth Hill Mica Company, 10, 23, 26–36, 125,
    144nn.12–16, 145nn.18–19; and dissent, 4,
    107–18, 123; and labor practices, 46–50, 59,
    61–78, 102–6; and local cultures, 4, 80–98,
    121
Mountain Mining Company, 42

narratives, 4, 10, 14, 24, 26, 98
National Labor Relations Board (NLRB), 104
National Recovery Act, 103
National Recovery Administration (NRA), 48
NLRB. *See* National Labor Relations Board
North Carolina: farming in, 6, 15–17, 18;
    labor practices in, 19, 13–22, 84, 101, 104,
    111, 125; mica production in, 4, 26, 36–61,
    119; social landscape of, 13–22; stereotypes
    of, 1, 8, 23
North Carolina Land Company, 41
NRA. *See* National Recovery Administration

Occupational Safety and Health Adminis-
    tration, 49
oral histories, 25–27

MARY K. ANGLIN, PH.D., M.P.H., is an associate professor
in the Department of Anthropology at the University of Kentucky.
Her research focuses on analyses of local cultures in North
America and prospects for social justice.

The University of Illinois Press
is a founding member of the
Association of American University Presses.

Composed in 10.5/13 Minion
by Jim Proefrock
at the University of Illinois Press
Manufactured by Thomson-Shore, Inc.

University of Illinois Press
1325 South Oak Street
Champaign, IL 61820-6903
www.press.uillinois.edu